History
as
Apocalypse

SUNY Series in Religion
Edited by Robert C. Neville

History
as
Apocalypse

Thomas J. J. Altizer

State University of New York Press • Albany

The following publishers have generously given permission to use extended quotations from copyrighted works: from *Finnegan's Wake* by James Joyce: Copyright 1939
by James Joyce and renewed 1967 by George Joyce and Lucia Joyce. Reprinted
be permission of Viking Penguin Inc. From *Novitas Mundi*: Perception of the History
of Being by D. G. Leahy. Copyright 1980 by New York University. Reprinted by
permission of New York University Press.

Published by
State University of New York Press, Albany

© 1985 State University of New York

For information, address State University of New York Press,
State University Plaza, Albany, New York 12246

Library of Congress Cataloging in Publication Data

Altizer, Thomas J. J.
     History as apocalypse.

     (SUNY series in religious studies)
     1. History (Theology) 2. Revolution (Theology)
3. EPIC literature—History and criticism.
II. Series.
BR115.H5A428 1985   231.7'6   84-16289
ISBN 0-88706-013-7
ISBN 0-88706-014-5 (pbk.)

10 9 8 7 6 5 4 3 2 1

For John Jackson and Katharine Blake Altizer

Contents

Preface

A pocalypse is at the center of attention today, and of world attention, a situation which is unique in history, but which is nevertheless a reenactment of the great fissures or turning points of our
Christian and Western history. Christianity begins with apocalypse,
with the proclamation and enactment of the advent of a new eon or
new world which can only be the end of an old eon and old creation.
Even if this original apocalyptic ground was eroded and reversed by
the evolution of the Christian Church, it returned again and again
at crucial moments in Western history, moments which were commonly experienced by their participants as being revolutionary
breakthroughs to new worlds. For revolution and apocalypse have been
twins in Western history; each when when it fully appears has been
accompanied by the other, and so much so that it is impossible to
dissociate apocalyptic and revolutionary thinking and vision. Such
vision and thinking have revolved about the ending of an old world
and the beginning of a new, and nowhere have they been more fully
present than in the Christian epic tradition, a tradition that to this
day has not yet been understood as an organic and historical whole.
But neither Christian epic nor any other apocalyptic and revolutionary
phenomenon can be understood as an organic whole so long as it is
approached through a single discipline or mode of understanding.
Therefore this study conjoins historical, literary, and theological
perspectives in an attempt to draw forth or evoke the totality of epic
vision and enactment.

1

Some thirty-five years of work lie behind and beneath these pages, beginning with a master's thesis on nature and grace in the theology of St. Augustine, a premature attempt to attack and resolve the deepest theological division between Protestantism and Catholicism. This was followed by a movement into the then precarious and all too tiny discipline of the History of Religions, where my doctoral work was focused upon Mahayana Buddhist philosophy and classical Greek religion. Such oddities were possible in the innocent days of religious studies, and this odd conjunction did allow me to come to grips with a previously failed attempt to become a Greek scholar. But more importantly it provided an initial arena for exploring a persuasion that I then adopted and have never abandoned: the conviction that Christian theology can be reborn only by way of an immersion in Buddhism. Perhaps no principle offers a deeper way into our lost epic and theological tradition than does the Mahayana Buddhist dialectical identification of Nirvana and Samsara. Simply to translate this principle into Christian terms is to sense its possibilities, for then we apprehend the possibility of the dialectical identification or marriage of Christ and Satan, of sin and grace, of Heaven and Hell. It is not insignificant that the Western mind and imagination has been so powerfully attracted to Buddhism in the twentieth century, and particularly so in the late twentieth century, a truly apocalyptic time.

Buddhism and Christianity once shared, although it was first present in Buddhism, a movement of faith or meditation into the very center of thinking and understanding. This movement was shattered in Christianity in the late Middle Ages, and particularly so in nominalism, a shattering that was finally consummated in the Reformation and Counter-Reformation, and was reversed only in forms that appeared to be antithetically related to Christianity. One of these forms is the Christian epic, which already in Dante is anti-ecclesiastical, and finally in Joyce is seemingly anti-Christian. Indeed, there is a historical progression in Christian epic ever in the direction of heretical or subversive faith and understanding; and this evolution is essentially related to its revolutionary ground. There is no apparent parallel to this in

Buddhism, perhaps because subversion or negation was always essentially integrated into the Buddhist way. Nevertheless, Buddhism does present itself as being subversive or negative to the Western and Christian mind, and it is precisely as such that it is most attractive and real to us. So it is that it is a postmodern nihilism that is most open to Buddhism, a nihilism that pervades our world, and a nihilism that must inevitably be the arena of a study such as *History as Apocalypse.*

Within this arena, traditional and even scholarly modes of analysis and understanding must erode and break down, and break down upon impact with the very terrain that here is present. Foremost among the erosions effected by nihilism are both logical and scholarly authority, that very authority which is a primary target of modern epic, and which is now being transformed in our very midst. Just as we are now bereft of master scholars, so likewise are we bereft of master logicians, at least outside the confines of highly technical fields. And just as American philosophy has virtually ceased to exist outside of the classroom, American theology has seemingly perished except in a sectarian and ecclesiastical form, and American literary criticism has almost wholly retreated in face of the challenge of the mass media. In this situation, to write in the tradition of our fathers would be to write as though the present world simply did not exist, or as though it were possible simply to ignore nihilism. But nihilism is an essential ground of our epic tradition, perhaps of all epic as such, for epic can enact itself only by way of a voyage through darkness and chaos, a chaos and darkness that is cosmos and light in pure nihilism.

Nonetheless whatever strengths are present in this study derive largely from the impact of great scholars who are now almost wholly dead or retired. Simply to read their work is to become aware of the intellectual poverty in which we now live, but it is also to become aware that such power can no longer be imitated, at least not by this writer. No attempt is made here to write in their spirit, but the attempt is made to carry their work into new directions, and thus to open new vistas. Though each section of this book is the consequence of years of study, documentation is absent, both to avoid the appearance of a false authority, and to seek a postmodern style (scholarly documentation is historically confined to the modern age). However, there is no exegesis here that will appear either as strange or unfounded to critical students of our epic texts; what is new here is rather the attempt to conjoin and unite these epics. There are occasions herein when I have found the very words of a master scholar to be so overwhelming that I have simply paraphrased them rather than be willing to dilute their power. Here, I can only record those scholars whom I have consciously so employed: Erich Auerbach, Marc Bloch, Rudolf Bultmann, Alfred Cobban, E. R. Dodds, Richard Ellmann, Etienne Gilson, Adolf Harnack, Christopher Hill, Alexander Koyré, Walter F. Otto, Henri Pirenne, R. W. Southern, Lawrence Stone, and George Williams. The quotations from *Paradise Lost* are from the edition of Alastair Fowler; the citations from *De Doctrina Christiana* are from the Sumner translation; the Blake quotations are from the 1965 Doubleday edition of Blake, edited by my colleague, David V. Erdman; the quotations from *Stephen Hero* are from the New Directions edition edited by Theodore Spencer; the quotations from *A Portrait of the Artist as a Young Man* are from the Viking *Portable Joyce*; the quotations from *Ulysses* are from the Random House Modern Library edition; and the quotations from *Finnegans Wake* are from the Penguin Books edition of 1976. I must also confess that there are phrases here from my book on Blake (*The New Apocalypse*, Michigan State University Press, 1967).

Three of my friends and colleagues have brilliantly and critically responded to the manuscript as a whole: Robert C. Neville, Mark C. Taylor, and Edith Wyschogrod. Valuable critical responses to sections of the manuscript have been freely given by Robert Boyle, S.J., Germaine Breé, Norman O. Brown, Debbie Chaffin, Arthur A. Cohen, Kathy Dahlman, Veroniqué Foti, Robert Goldenberg, Don Gifford, Norman K. Gottwald, John Grant, Jonathan Hay, Meredith C. Hoppin, John Howett, Christine Kondoleon, Justus George Lawler, D. G. Leahy, Wendy O'Flaherty, Clara C. Park, John F. Reichert, Gladys Rothbell, Gregor Sebba, Robert P. Scharlemann, Bernard Semmel, Walter A. Strauss, Dan Via, Eric Voegelin, Dick White, John and Pat Wilcox, Amost N. Wilder and Charles E. Winquist. Eileen Sahady has performed many of the duties of an editor in typing the manuscript. And I owe a particular debt to the copy-editor, Kathryn Schmidt, and to the production editor, Peggy Gifford, to say nothing of the deep gratitude I owe William Eastman, the publisher of the State University of New York Press.

Prologue

No greater danger lies before us today than that of the loss of our deeper or primal identity, an identity that has always been the center of mythical and ritual traditions throughout the world, just as it has been the center of our imaginative and intellectual creations. All such identity now threatens either simply to pass away or to become bound to an inactive and passive immobility. Both our interior and our exterior identities have become not only questionable but dislodged, and dislodged not simply from their given or apparent modes and manifestations, but also from their origins. We are in exile from our origin, our deep or far beginning, and so much so that we have long since lost the power of naming and envisioning a truly human beginning, even if that loss has seemingly given us the power of envisioning and naming our end. Nothing either more threatens or more embodies the loss of our beginning than the ever increasing loss of our historical consciousness. That loss may not be final or irretrievable, but it is overwhelming nonetheless, and most particularly so insofar as our sense of historical beginning is dissolved and erased. If the naming of ultimate origin is the most primal ground of mythical language, an origin which by necessity is primordial and prehistoric, then a consciousness of concrete or actual beginning might be said to be a primal ground of historical language and consciousness. This ground can be real or realized only with the advent of a uniquely human consciousness, which is to say a consciousness that is either liberated or distanced from both the sacred and the natural realms.

But this is precisely the consciousness and identity that is ever increasingly becoming distant and unreal to us, and that very loss not only embodies our exile from an actual historical beginning, but also and even thereby promises to transform the identity of that exile itself: so that an exile from actual beginning will pass into the genesis of an eternal return. Beginning itself is becoming a surd in our consciousness, a cipher without a code, the only code ready to hand being one which reverses our given identity of beginning by apprehending it as the beginning of the end. Just as the primordial myth of eternal return has been reborn in late modernity, and reborn in many of the deepest centers of thinking and consiousness, so all sense of a uniquely human as opposed to a natural or cosmic beginning is withering away, and this despite the fact that our new cosmologies have seemingly cast aside forever the very possibility of a cyclical universe. While the paradigm of evolution wholly dominates our cosmological and biological thinking, and does so even when evolution is conceived as being wholly contingent and fortuitous, the very possibility of a human as opposed to a material evolution is now banished from our historical and cultural thinking, and it is banished in the name of both truth and moral principle.

Yet with the loss of the paradigm of social and cultural evolution, or the loss of a nonnatural or noncyclical evolution, has come the inevitable loss of a specifically or uniquely human identity, and most particularly so insofar as that identity is seen and known to be everywhere the same. Then the beginning of humanity can be at most the beginning of a new natural species, and within that species there are no truly significant divisions or distinctions either temporally or spatially, for consciousness itself then has no more significance than any other natural organ. Uniqueness, as opposed to natural particularity, then vanishes in all its forms, and human meanings and identities can then never transcend the boundaries of the natural cycle. Consciousness can then be itself only by being everywhere the same. Therewith vanishes any possibility of the integrally and essentially different or new, and thus perishes all actual beginning, and all that is truly and actually new. Nietzsche knew this form of eternal recurrence as nihilism, and we have subsequently found no better name for it, even if it has now passed into the very center of our thinking and consciousness. For nihilism has become not only the consequence but also the ground of our thinking, and thus there becomes no possibility whatsoever of transcending nihilism, unless nihilism is thought through to its own contradiction and reversal.

No problem is more overwhelming in our situation than that of the relation between Alpha and Omega, beginning and end, and most forefully so insofar as their respective and contrary identities now appear to be passing into each other, thereby dissolving and erasing the integral and individual identities of both beginning and end. Although the advent or the beginning of consciousness once was manifest as a true and even absolute beginning, or a beginning that could never be repeated or renewed, it cannot continue to be manifest as a true beginning if its irreversibility comes into question. That questioning is not simply occurring, it is becoming overwhelming, and most overwhelmingly so in a new society and a new consciousness in which an integrally individual presence and activity or movement is either invisible or unregistered, or unregistered and unheard in the organs and instruments of a new knowledge and communication. Above all it is the interior center of consciousness that is now most profoundly in question, a center which once was manifest and real as self-consciousness. That self-consciousness gradually and ever more decisively realized and embodied itself as a primal ground of our Western society and consciousness. And just as a uniquely Western culture and society now promises to come to an end, if it has not done so already, so self-consciousness itself, and all integral and individual interiority, appears either to be ending or to have ended. With that ending the beginning of everything which the West has known as consciousness will truly have been reversed and annulled.

It is the Western literary tradition, and more particularly the Western epic tradition, that most fully embodies and makes manifest the historical evolution and realization of self-consciousness. Here, one discovers a historical origin or beginning of the individuality and interiority of consciousness, an interiority and individuality of consciousness that passes into self-consciousness with the advent of Christianity and then into an integral, necessary, and final movement and destiny of self-consciousness with the birth, evolution, and resolution or consummation of the Christian epic tradition. Our individual and interior consciousness begins with Homer; at least, there is no available evidence of its prior appearance. So likewise an interior and individual consciousness ends with Joyce, or so it would seem in our perspective, and certainly nothing in our world offers any possibility of going "beyond" *Finnegans Wake*. Consequently, *The Iliad* and *Finnegans Wake* mark the historical boundaries of our consciousness and self-consciousness, thereby giving our consciousness an integral and individual identity that otherwise would be absent. But it is also true that there is a historical movement and development between these boundaries, an integral and organic development wherein a unique form of consciousness that begins with or dawns in Homer has its ending in Joyce, and an ending which is its own ending, and ending which is a fulfillment and resolution of its own individual and unique beginning.

Unfortunately, there has not yet come into existence either a critical or a historical understanding of our epic tradition or traditions. There are many reasons for this absence, not least being the enormous distance between our epics, a distance that is deepened by our scholarly specialties, specialties that are the product of uniquely modern divisions between the esthetic and literary, the social and political, and the religious and philosophical realms. For the simple truth is that the fullest and most powerful forms and expressions of epic transcend all such distinctions and divisions, as can most easily be seen in Dante's *Commedia*. Nothing so dissolves and erases the original identity of epic than does a purely esthetic or literary reading of epic poetry. In such interpetations the epic poem is apprehended as a formal and lifeless object or text, which is possible only when it is wholly wrenched away from its own historical and human world. That historical and human world is inevitably and necessarily a revolutionary world, for our great epics, our primal and paradigmatic epics, are works of art and vision that both embody and express revolutionary breakthroughs in consciousness and society, and breakthroughs which occur and are realized in all of the dimensions and domains of human life and existence.

If we employ the paradigm of the origin, the evolution, and the ending of the individuality and interiority of consciousness, we will find a way into the historical and organic identity of our epic tradition, and one that will offer the possibility of understanding that tradition as an organic whole. Although an enormous body of thinking and scholarship has continually been moving toward some such resolution, there remain deep gaps or gulfs in our understanding, such as those which now appear to exist between the Christian and the Classical and the Christian and Hebraic or Old Testament worlds. We still have not been able to establish continuity between the Old Testament or the Hebrew Bible and Christian epic poetry, and this despite the fact that this continuity is so manifestly important and primal for Dante, Milton, and Blake, and perhaps for Joyce as well. So likewise, and despite the Homeric form of *Ulysses* and the Virgilian form of the *Commedia*, we cannot yet correlate Christian and Classical epic, even if we do know that Christian epic from its beginning to its ending integrally arises from and is grounded in a Classical language and form. Perhaps we shall never be able to close this gap until we grasp and understand an ultimate harmony or coinherence between Athens and Jerusalem, but no such continuity has yet arisen in either our critical thinking or our historical understanding.

While we know virtually nothing about the individual figure of Homer, we do know that the Homeric epics were the primal expressions of as great a revolution as has ever occurred in history, and one affecting a transformation of consciousness and society as a whole. Perhaps *The Iliad* and *The Odyssey* are like *The Aeneid* in being a reflection of a social and political revolution that has already occurred, for *The Aeneid* is the fullest embodiment which we possess of the Roman Empire, just as it also gives us our most intimate portrait of the new Hellenistic world. Nevertheless, all three of these epics are more distant from us than are our Christian epics, and this distance can readily be seen by comparing our critical interpretations of Homer and Virgil with our critical readings of Dante, Milton, and Blake. For the Classical world has long since decisively come to an end as an historical world, whereas the Christian world lingers even into our own day, and its last epic was written within the lifetime of many of those who study epic today. It is also significant that we know so much about Dante, Milton, and Joyce. More than any other artist, the epic poet is himself fully embodied in his work; and a major if not the major reason for the difficulty of Blake's epics is that Blake himself is so little known to us, and he alone among our epic poets since Homer was not immediately and publicly accepted as a great epic artist.

There is something very puzzling about the extraordinary fact that even such radically original artists as Dante, Milton, and Joyce were so immediately accepted as great and revolutionary poets in their own historical worlds. Obviously, full epic poetry embodies an anthority that is immediate and irresistible, but it is also a universal authority, and not only in its own world but in every world it enters. Moreover, each of us has been deeply and interiorly shaped by our epic poets, and shaped and molded as we have been by no other body of artists and thinkers. Nowhere else may we find an origin that is more integrally and intimately our own, and nowhere else is our heritage and history more fully embodied and expressed. If Homer was the Bible of the Greeks, our epic poetry is the Bible of us all. For in modernity our Western epic becomes a universal epic, an epic enacting the origin and destiny of a universal humanity. But just as the Ireland of Joyce's epic creations is the world and cosmos as a whole, the world of every great epic is a universal world, clearly and manifestly universal in its impact and affect. Indeed, it is the overwhelming impact of the true epic that is the most pragmatic and irrefutable test of the genuinely epic status of an epic poem or work.

Epic poetry is everything that the great body of our literary critics and scholars assure us that poetry is not. First of all, it is Scripture.

It was so regarded by its own creators, for each of our Christian epic poets consciously and deliberately not only grounded their epics in the Bible, but enacted their epics as embodiments of Bible or revelation. At the very least, Christian epic poetry comprises a Christian Talmud, and particularly so in the perspective of the rabbinic identification of Talmud and Torah. Secondly, every epic poem is a revolutionary political work. Indeed, the true epic is the most revolutionary, and the most comprehensively revolutionary, political document or text that has arisen or been given us from its own revolutionary world. Already it is becoming apparent that the prophetic and epic poetry of Blake is more politically revolutionary than the texts of Marx, and is so precisely because of its universal horizon. The *Commedia* and *Paradise Lost* have long since been established as politically no less than religiously revolutionary poems, and it can confidently be expected that soon *Ulysses* and *Finnegans Wake* will unveil their politically revolutionary ground. For we already know that no other documents or texts from our world so fully and so decisively not only call for but actually embody the final ending of all distinctions and divisions between human beings.

Thirdly, epic poetry, or, more particularly, Christian epic poetry, is psychological poetry, and psychological poetry which is autobiographical and universal at once. With the possible and all too doubtful exception of *Paradise Lost*, it is the epic poet himself who is the primary actor in the Christian epic. This gives epic poetry an interior immediacy and compelling reality transcending even the greatest dramatic poetry. So it is that the cosmic voyage in Christian epic poetry is an interior voyage, a voyage actually realized and enacted by the epic poet, who thereby initiates his audience into a new interior world. This is also one of the fundamental points at which Christian epic poetry differs from Classical epic poetry, and if only for this reason Classical epic poetry can never be for us either an intimate or an interior world. It is the Christian epic poet in his own person who initiates us into his world, thereby his world can be for us our world as well, and thereby and precisely thereby that world transcends all fantasy and illusion. And nothing so startles us about epic poetry as when we recognize that it is not illusory. For a real reading of the epic re-creates its voyage within ourselves, and deeply within ourselves, so deeply that having made this voyage we will never be the same again.

Finally, epic poetry is philosophical poetry, and philosophical in the fullest sense. This statement seems odd because philosophy in our world has largely become almost wholly an academic and pedagogical enterprise, having virtually no consequence or impact beyond its own all too narrow world. And where this is not true, as in the Soviet Union or the Roman Catholic Church before Vatican II, philosophy is a dogmatic and ideological instrument of political order and control. What has not existed in the twentieth century, or, at least, not in the latter half of our century, is philosophical thinking that is both original and comprehensive or universal, a thinking directed to understanding the deepest grounds and horizons of its own world. Such thinking was present in all the great philosophers of the past, which is why our great philosophers were creators of new conceptual worlds that comprehended all the identities within them. Although epic poets are not philosophers in this sense, they are nevertheless philosophical, and deeply philosophical, in that the worlds which they embody and enact are integrally coherent and unitary worlds, and therefore worlds which can be conceptually understood and known. When this is not true, as in the epics of Blake and Joyce, that is becuse these epics embody a new cosmos which is chaos and cosmos at once, and such a world or cosmos must by necessity break down and reverse all given or manifest sources and forms of order. But an epic reversal and shattering of that order is just as fully a conceptual as it is an imaginative act, for it unthinks order itself, or all established order, and thereafter and therein an integral and unitary order and structure can never truly or actually be thought again. Thus it was Milton and not Luther or Descartes who first fully ended Classical thinking, just as it was Blake and not Nietzsche who first realized and enacted the death of God.

As everyone once knew, epic poetry is to literate society what

mythology is to preliterate society, and this is saying a very great deal
indeed. Mythology itself has been most integrally alive in Western
culture and society through epic poetry, and it is above all in epic poetry
that new mythologies have entered our world. While Christianity did
not truly or decisively enter the language of poetry for well over a
thousand years, thereby differing from all other major religious traditions, when it did become embodied in the *Commedia*, it revolutionized
the Western poetic tradition as a whole. And if only through Virgil,
the Classical poet is present in Dante, and the Classical world speaks
in the *Commedia*, and even in the *Paradiso*. For the first time Athens
and Jerusalem are integrally harmonized in the *Commedia*, and if this
was made possible by Augustine and Aquinas, no world as comprehensive as the *Commedia* ever appears in a theological work. But the *Commedia* did make possible *Paradise Lost*, and *Paradise Lost* is the last great
imaginative work that both integrates the Classical and the Biblical
worlds and envisions a unitary and harmonious cosmos. Of course,
a harmonious cosmos can now only be a prefallen world, just as a
language that is Biblical and Classical at once can now only be a fallen
or Satanic language. No work so deeply embodies and enacts that
absolute polarity which is at the heart of the birth of modernity as
does *Paradise Lost*, thus necessitating new epiphanies of a cosmic Satan
and a cosmic Son of God. At the birth of modernity, and of a revolutionary modernity, those deep and primal powers could dwell and exist
in a precarious harmony. But that harmony broke asunder, thus ending
the integral order and structure not only of Western epic but of the
Western mind and imagination. That cataclysmic shattering epically
occurs and is enacted in Blake's prophetic epics, epics which reverse
our past so as to promise a new and universal future, a future which
is Apocalypse. That Apocalypse is finally enacted in *Ulysses* and *Finnegans Wake*, and therein and thereby a universal past becomes present
as our apocalyptic future.

While such a brief summary says very little about our epic tradition, it perhaps suggests the possibility that that tradition is an organic
tradition, and that it has organically developed or evolved from a real

and actual beginning to an actual and apocalyptic ending. The organic evolution of Western epic is not only the record of the deeper history of a uniquely Western humanity: it is also a vision of an interior, cosmic, and eternal voyage of a universal humanity. With the very evolution and execution of that voyage, earlier worlds and earlier voyages have come to an end, an ending which is irrevocable in the full actuality of historical time. But later epics do not cancel and annul earlier epics; rather they resolve and fulfill them, and fulfill them by carrying their own movement and direction into new and ever more finally and apocalyptically universal worlds. We shall never interiorly know Homer and Virgil save through Dante and Milton, but so likewise we can now truly know Milton and Dante only through Blake and Joyce. And if it is precisely by reading Dante through Joyce and Milton through Blake that we can know and interiorly enact the actual presences of Milton and Dante, then those presences truly become real presences, and our own history then truly and actually becomes realized as our own.

Chapter One

The Birth of Vision

B eginning is anonymous, hence by necessity it is the province of myth and rite, the domain of the mask in all its innumerable forms, and the primal if elusive motif of epic traditions throughout the world. While we know that the origins of humanity occurred some two or three million years ago, we have no internal or interior evidence of that advent until about 20,000 B.C.E., for it is not until then that there is available to us actual traces left by *Homo sapiens*, tracings which are the apparent origin of art, or, at least, the earliest full art now known to us. The chronological site of the beginning of painting is what has come to be identified as the Middle Paleolithic period, and more particularly the Mousterian and Aurignacian periods in Southwestern Europe, where some thirty to forty thousand years ago people in the caves of Dordogne and northern Spain began drawing irregular lines with the fingers of one hand on damp clay walls. These drawings passed into full painting in the Solutrian and Magdalenian periods, and by 12,000 B.C.E. a painting had been created which has never since been surpassed in its sheer esthetic power. But the human face is wholly absent in the rock art of these hunters, and, indeed, will not truly appear in art until well after the agricultural and urban revolutions.

An all too vacuous reflection of the human face is found in Paleolithic and Neolithic figurines of the Great Goddess. But these images almost invariably succeed in presenting a faceless figure or icon, one in which the face is either barely suggested, or absent, or empty, as though the very presence of primordial deity foreclosed the possibility of the presence of the human face. The advent of the individual human face in art does not occur until the third millennium B.C.E.. This happens with the birth of the statue in Sumeria, and is most manifestly present in the statue, *Steward Ebil-il*, which is a realistically carved sacred image that was originally placed in a sanctuary and intended to perpetuate Ebil-il's adoration of his god. Nothing is more forceful here or elsewhere in Sumerian art than the subject's eyes, eyes which are consumed by the deity they behold, and eyes reflecting a long Mesopotamian tradition in which other-worldly forces are either alien or hostile. Here, the eyes are the very embodiment of the face, a face, even as all Sumerian faces which are given us, that is a face only by way of its reflection of its god, before whom face itself is faceless. Significantly enough, the eyes of Sumerian images of bulls are natural or neutral by comparison, for it is only the human eye or face that dawns in art with a self-lacerating identity.

While this identity is seemingly lost in Neo-Sumerian art, and is commonly absent in Egyptian art, it is present in a new interior form in Egyptian portraits of the Pharaohs, and the Egyptian monarch, unlike his Mesopotamian counterpart, was reverenced as incarnate deity. Above all it is in the head of a colossal statue of Amenhotep IV in his temple of Aten at Karnak that we may encounter the most disconcerting of all ancient faces, as the one whom Freud regarded as the father both of monotheism and of Israel stands above us with a countenance of almost mystical disequilibrium. A contemporary portrait of Amenhotep IV with his wife and daughters reveals him being negatively transfigured by the rays of the solar deity, Aten, rays which apparently have no destructive effect upon his family. Only in its portraits of kings and queens do we find negative epiphanies in Egyptian art. Elsewhere harmony and tranquility prevail, even in human portraiture. But it was only in the monarchs that deity was fully present in the ancient Egyptian world, and if that presence made possible a full harmony and equilibrium in the Egyptian cosmos — one which even tamed the terror of death and chaos — it was also a presence giving us the alien faces of the Pharaohs, for they are faces embodying the gaze of deity.

In the eighth century B.C.E. a revolutionary transformation occurred in the ancient world, perhaps the most profound revolution in history. It erupted simultaneously and apparently spontaneously in Greece, Israel, and India, and somewhat later in China and Iran. This was a comprehensive and radical breakthrough from the archaic world and consciousness to the birth of full and actual individual consciousness. While the modes and identities of this consciousness differed radically from each other in these disparate axial centers, each realized a primacy and finality of a truly new interior center of consciousness. Nowhere does evidence remain to us establishing any genuine continuity between the axial revolutions and the historical worlds out of which they arose; it is as though they were purely gratuitous events, revolutions without precedence, cause, or ground, revolutions which almost certainly occurred independently of each other and at virtually the same moment of time. Only in Greece does one name embody this initial or original revolution, and that name is Homer. For even if *The Iliad* and *The Odyssey* evolved out of bardic traditions and schools, they are nonetheless fully individual and organic poems, and so much so that it is only with the advent of these poems that we can speak historically of the poet as creator. A decisive sign of the presence of the poet as creator is the birth of the poem as an integrated and unified whole or world, a world and a work which for the first time in history evolves out of its own center or ground, a ground deriving from a new center of consciousness which stands out from its own horizon and world.

We do know that a universal transformation occurred in Greece in the eighth century. This transformation is manifest in the dawning consciousness of the deeper unity of the Greek city-states, a unity which concretely appears with the founding of the Olympic Games and the Delphic Oracle. The eighth century also saw the beginning of the two hundred years of colonial expansion from Greece, and the Greek colonies were centers of revolutionary advance and discovery, and also significant points where Greece absorbed Oriental influences while thereby becoming even more deeply itself. Ionia, a Greek colony in Asia Minor and thus the crossroads between two worlds, was both the birthplace of Greek philosophy and an original site of a new art reflecting the continuous interaction and interrelation between quite different civilizations. There, on the island of Samos, we can almost see the birth of Greek sculpture. We see it in the *Hera of Samos*, a marble sculpture of the sixth century, and a sculpture in which a column seemingly undergoes a metamorphosis into a woman. But this is a woman whose grace and dignity is itself a temple, a temple both sacred and profane, or fully divine and yet wholly human, as a new and vibrant humanity is drawn forth from an archaic Gate of Horn. Here, the Great Goddess passes into an individual woman, as the majesty of the Goddess is obviously present as ground, and even a hierarchic ground, but before our very eyes that ground is individually and humanly present. Indeed, it is present in the fullness of the moment before us, a fullness made possible only by the transformation of an archaic origin or source.

The great discovery of Greek art in the sixth century was of the statue as an integral and individual organism, an organism embodying and realizing its own world, a world which is at once a truly individual world and form, and yet a world making organically present in its own center of space a universal cosmos. By the time of the *Apollo of Piombino* (*circa* 500 B.C.E.), Greek sculpture is almost fully born, as the individual stands forth in his full presence, and Apollo is present to us as deity and humanity at once, a god still bearing discrete signs of his archaic origin, but standing before us with a full individual identity, as deity undergoes a metamorphosis into a full human form. Yet is is impossible to imagine this Apollo as an isolated deity. It is not only an individual figure who is present here, but a world or cosmos of dawning light, a light enveloping the figure before us but also a light which is all encompassing, a light embodying a new world. That world is here present as body. This is a new body which had never hitherto been present, an organic body which is an integral whole, a whole in which head and torso are one, and in which face is body and body is face. Thereby face knows a repose which had never previously been present in art, a repose anticipated by the Cycladic heads of the late third millennium. But those heads and their archaic counterparts are faceless, whereas the face of this Apollo is truly face, even if it is a face which is interior and exterior simultaneously, a face in which body and soul are one.

In the heads that remain to us of Greek sculpture the eyes are never directed at their beholder. No glance is here manifest which confronts or even engages its world. Indeed, the eyes do not appear as eyes for they do not stand out from their face, and thereby a face is present that releases a profound calm and peace. When portraiture is born in the fifth century, as can be seen in the *Head of Apollo* from Attica, the eyes of Apollo are looking at us, but we are not being seen, or not being seen as objects of vision. For these eyes are not the eyes of another, they are eyes which are present as our own. This face and these eyes release a new vision, a vision which simply and purely sees, for it sees in a dawn in which a primeval darkness is ending. With the ending of that darkness, even if it is only in the moment before us, we can open our eyes without awe or dread, and see without terror or fear. Then we are awake, as if resurrected from the dead, and can see a new world of light, a light in which darkness is absent, and a light releasing a vision in which the seer is the center of its world. In this moment the eyes of Apollo are our eyes. We ourselves see in his vision, and therefore we are not seen. His portrait is our portrait as well, for the birth of portraiture is the birth of a pure vision, a vision which is our own. Yet is is our own not only when we see Apollo, but see as Apollo as well.

Apollo can truly be seen as the Olympian deity he is only when we see as and through Apollo himself. Then we not only see his eyes but see with and through them as well, for openly to behold these eyes is to be drawn into a pure moment of Olympian calm. Then light is everywhere, and vision is all encompassing, a new vision which is a cosmic vision and which is realizing and releasing a new world. That world is comprehensively actualized in the fifth century, and not only in sculpture, painting, and architecture, but in poetry and drama, in philosophy, mathematics and science, and in the advent of democratic government as well. All of these revolutionary achievements of Greece were grounded in a visual revolution, one that is no doubt born with Homer and therefore initially realized through voice. But within three centuries a truly individual voice had realized itself in a universal vision, and a universal vision which is itself the realization of a new and individual center of consciousness. For the first time in history a unified and universal world is at hand. It is at hand in body itself, in the human eye, an eye that not only shines before us in the *Head of Apollo*, but draws us into its new world of sight.

Only in sculpture is this vision openly and unmistakably present, even if the most celebrated Greek sculpture is lost to us, and most of what we have is mutilated and often present to us only in Hellenistic copies of the originals. We can now see Myron's *Diskobolos* only through copies, but nevertheless it is apparent that something fundamental is present here, and present in a body that is movement and rest simultaneously, a body that is pulsating with a vibrant energy even as it is caught by the vision of the sculptor in an instant of repose. This is the instant immediately prior to the hurling of the discus, an instant which here engages us as the moment before the creation, for this is an instant which is the seed of all life and movement. Yet this instant of repose is itself a flowing moment. A cosmos of energy is present in this body, and here we can actually see an immediately bodily origin of a total energy and life. Now even if we are informed that such sculpture is worked with mathematically precise understanding of weight movements and counterpoise, we remain dazzled by the miracle at hand, for here a total energy is actually incarnate. Moreover, it is incarnate in a fully individual form and body, a body that itself is pure *energeia*, an *energeia* or pure actuality that Aristotle was later to conceive as the very identity of God as the Unmoved Mover.

Certainly the *Diskobolos* is an unmoved mover, but it is so only in an instantaneous moment immediately prior to a total release of energy, and thereby this is a moment of repose which is simultaneously an explosive and all consuming energy. And what is about to explode before us is body itself, a new body which is a total body and a total body because it wholly consumes all attention in its presence. That total absorption of attention is the realization of the birth of vision, of a pure vision, a vision which is a totally immanent vision, and a vision which is wholly focused upon the pure immediacy of an instantaneous moment. Thereby for the first time body appears and is real as body alone, a pure body which is pure energy, and in that energy a total life and actuality is present. Thus the birth of vision is the birth of body, a body which is just as new as the vision that makes it possible, and a body which draws into itself all that life and energy that were previously manifest in a numinous and archaic sacrality.

The new body, which is made manifest and actual by the way of a new vision and light, also brings with it a new tangibility or touch. This new touch is released by the full actualization of body, an actualization embodying a total opening to bodily presence itself. It is impossible simply and only to look and to look alone at these apparent objects of vision, as though nothing we represent here but visual objects. Objects as such are precisely what is absent in the actual presence of Greek sculpture, and absent not only because of the deep sensuality of this sculpture, but because this is an incarnate sensuality, a fully incarnate sensuality whose very presence consumes its beholder. Nowhere is this incarnate sensuality more fully present than in the pediment sculptures of the Parthenon, and most particularly so in the mutilated sculptures which remain to us from the east pediment of the Parthenon, which represented Athena's miraculous birth, which is to say the birth of Greece itself. Aphrodite is a primal witness of that birth, and here she is reclining next to and upon her mother Dione, as the goddesses themselves embody the ecstasy of the birth of deity. Perhaps it is fortuitous that the heads of these goddesses have perished, for now we are confronted only by the legs and torsos and partial arms of these deities, thereby being spared the full majesty of the Great Goddess, even if it is here present only in human and individual forms. But present it is, or rather its full incarnation, a presence that is not only overwhelming, but transfiguring as well.

And what an immeasurable distance lies between these figures and the remaining Paleolithic and Neolithic figurines of the Great Goddess, for while a full sensuality characterizes them all, the archaic figures are not actually present, or not bodily present. Their very aura of mystery precludes such presence, for that mystery establishes a distance between the Goddess and her beholder. No such distance is present between us and this Aphrodite. Indeed, all distance passes away in the presence of these bodies, but that perishing is not the perishing of death, which is the gift of the archaic Goddess; it is rather a perishing which is the advent of life, a dissolution or perishing of everything that is not a bodily presence. Even the garments of these goddesses are aflame with an immediate sensuality. The garments more fully embody the goddesses than does their visible flesh, for the folds of these celestial gowns are overflowing with energy, an energy that seems to derive from the sacred center of their breasts. No doubt that is an illusion, for no centers at all are present here, and cannot be present if only because all traces of center or ground disappear with the full release of bodily presence, a disappearance which is now incarnate before us.

How responsible the act of the iconoclast in response to such works of art, and how absurd the mere glance of the observer, for it is humanly impossible not to respond, and to respond by way of a bodily arousal, to the presence of these bodies. But no partial or fragmentary bodily response is possible in the presence of this energy, hence a merely genital sexual response cannot now be engaged, just as it would equally be impossible to respond only conceptually, or even only visually, for a consuming energy is here present which draws everything into itself. Yet this is not the presence of Dionysus, or of any other mystery deity, for it is a presence banishing both mystery and darkness, a banishment occurring in our very response to this bodily presence, a response in which we can only joyously touch. Perhaps thereby we touch for the very first time, or for the first time become capable of touching and only touching, or of touching a total presence.

A fullness of deity is present here, a deity which is present in no other historical horizon or world. This is a deity which actually can be touched, thereby releasing a real presence of deity which itself creates the touch by which it becomes incarnate. That touch is not simply occasioned by this sculpture, as though these figures were merely passive objects before us. It is fully embodied in these goddesses, and embodied in them so as to embody their beholders, who therein themselves become incarnate in their perception. Clearly this is a perception transcending all sensation. It transcends sensation because of the fullness of presence which it makes possible, a presence wherein and whereby consciousness is fully and totally awake. But this awakening of consciousness is not the awakening of a consciousness which is other than body, or which is consciousness alone. It is far rather the awakening of a world or horizon which is body and consciousness at once, a consciousness which is awake through a full bodily perception, a perception realizing a total presence of every source or center of consciousness and life. Such total presence is an incarnate presence, a presence which can actually be touched, and whose very epiphany releases and embodies that perception by which alone it is at hand.

These goddesses engulf us, as does the fullness of all Greek sculpture, but here we are ecstatically awakened, and not only by the birth of a goddess, but by the birth of ourselves. We are awakened by the birth of ourselves as incarnate perception, a perception whereby we become what we touch and behold. This point of space is truly a sacred enclosure, and thus it is an opening to another world. But that world is not other than our own, it is the full actuality of a bodily *energeia*, an *energeia* that is divine and bodily presence at once. Now this may well be a presence of the Great Goddess, but if so she is not present beyond us, or she is present beyond us only insofar as we are not fully present ourselves. For it is our own disengagement from full presence which this presence of deity promises to annul and erode. And that erosion occurs even as we behold Aphrodite and Dione, and it occurs as a gift of grace. This is a gift which is present in the actual energy of these bodies, an energy by which and through which we touch and see these bodies, and thereby are touched by them as well. For we can touch these bodies only as we are touched by them, for our touch is not only our own, it comes from far beyond our own life and power, and yet it comes as an energy and grace which is hereby our own.

It is from deeply within our own bodies that this grace draws us, thereby drawing forth an energy previously unknown. That energy dawns both before and within us, a before and within that is exterior and interior at once. This simultaneity of without and within embodies an organic vision and touch that is a whole and organic perception, a perception not only integrating seeing and touching, but integrating them so that here touching and seeing become one. Then the center of consciousness is not only within, it is simultaneously without. And it is without not only in the bodies of these goddesses, but without in the actuality of their touch, a touch that we not only feel in our bodies, but express and embody in our seeing and touching as well. In the grace of this moment of vision, the life of the Great Goddess is incarnate not only in the bodies of these goddesses, but in our bodies, too — an incarnation awakening our bodies as if from the dead — and awakening them to an incarnate perception, a perception in which the depth of our bodies is not only aroused but released and lived.

Inevitably such a moment of vision is both immediate and instantaneous. It can fully occur only in the immediacy of pure perception, and that perception must be momentary if only because it occurs so fully and so finally in the moment before us. That moment is an instantaneous moment precisely because it is a full and complete moment. Since everything within it is embodied and expressed, there is no potency or potentiality in such a moment that can be carried forward to another moment and time, and therefore no possibility here of the pure moment as either archetype or model. We know of the pervasive role of ritual in classical Greek life, but it was not sacred ritual as in other religious and historical worlds, it was rather a common or public or open ritual without a sacred or numinous aura, an aura then to be found in the mystery cults alone, which were practiced only by a minority of Greeks. We may be confident that by the fifth century the Olympian deities were never mysteriously present, or never numinously present, and this because they were actually and bodily present. Above all they were so present in sculpture, an immediate presence which never fully or truly befalls a mystery deity. Yet that immediate presence is an instantanious presence, and therefore a precarious presence, a presence that cannot be ritually repeated or renewed.

So it is that an integral and organic fullness of visual and bodily presence lasted but a moment in history. It is roughly confined within the fifth century B.C.E., and although it recurs in ever more diluted and artificial forms until the advent of Christianity, it never occurs or recurs thereafter, or never occurs in the full actuality of an incarnate moment. Nevertheless, it is possible to speak of an evolutionary metamorphosis of this incarnate moment, a transformation wherein bodily presence passes from the without to the within, or passes from a presence which is exterior and interior simultaneously to a presence where the without appears within, and appears so as to give full birth to an integral and organic face. The fourth century was the great period for portraiture in the ancient world, not until then do faces appear which are truly and uniquely individual, and we may surmise that it was not until then that it was even possible to see a uniquely individual face. This is possible, of course, only when face has established some distance from body, as a face appears which is face alone, a face which now has lost an integral union or harmony with its body.

Therein face stands forth so as to establish a new perspective, wherein the subject of consciousness stands forth so as to enounter and confront a new object of vision, a new object which is mirrored in the new prominence which is now given in portraiture to the eyes. These eyes are forcefully and irresistibly present in the *Bronze Youth from Anticythera* and the *Bronze Boy from Marathon*, for even though they are present in fully and organically realized bodies, the eyes are not simply an integral part of the bodies, as in earlier Classical sculpture, but stand out as eyes. Thereby they not only call attention to themselves, but establish themselves for the first time as the integral if interior center of body. This new interior center parallels if it does not embody the new role and identity of mind or *nous* in Greek philosophy. For the first time mind thinks as autonomous subject, and it thinks simply and only as mind, an interior subject apprehending and knowing the cosmos as objective world. Of course, no chasm or gulf lies between subject and object in Greek thinking and knowing, and thus no pure subject is here present which is wholly removed or isolated from its object. Nonetheless, a distinct and integral subject of consciousness appears in the fourth century, and in sculpture it appears by way of the advent of the truly individual face.

As opposed to ancient Near Eastern portraiture, the Classical and Hellenistic portraiture of the fourth century and thereafter presents us with a head that stands forth from its torso in such a way as to be manifest and real as head alone, a head standing autonomously forth from its own body, therein establishing and realizing a new autonomous center or subject of vision. We can see the contrast between this and earlier Greek portraiture by noting the head of the deity in the *Zeus from Cape Artemision*, one of the rare original Greek bronzes to have come down to us and one of the high points of fifth century Greek sculpture. The head of this Zeus radiates majesty and power, but it does not stand forth as head, if only becuse this head and face is in such integral harmony and union with the body of the god, a body that is an individual and organic whole. When the individual face as such appears in the fourth century, it is often integrally related to its body, but it is nevertheless manifest and real as a distinct and individual face, and as a face and a vision standing apart from even if within its own body. Now body itself is manifest as a full individual presence, but it is so only by way of an interiorization of vision.

This interiorization of vision realizes the center of consciousness as within body itself, a realization establishing a distance between body and consciousness, and an original harmony between body and consciousness ever more progressively becomes disrupted and annulled.

Nothing more fully embodies this disruption than the new autonomy of the eyes in Hellenistic sculpture, eyes which are perhaps most fully present in the *Bronze Portrait of "Lucius Junius Brutus"*, a Hellenistic bust that could be Etruscan, Roman, or Greek, but which is certainly a full descendant of fourth century Greek sculpture. Nowhere else in ancient art is such an intense inner life so fully manifest in portraiture. This interiority is centered in the eyes, and these eyes shine forth from an interior ground that is distant from the face that is here manifest. Now we have come full circle from the *Steward Ebil-el*, for those Sumerian eyes stand forth only to reflect a transcendent otherness, whereas the eyes of this Brutus give witness to the birth of an immanent distance, an interior distance which will become totally other with the birth of Christianity.

Chapter Two

Destiny, Deity and Death

Nothing is more exemplary of the identity of self-consciousness than is the Western literary tradition, and more particularly the Western epic tradition. The Western epic from Homer through Joyce not only gives witness to but itself embodies the historical origin, evolution, and embodiment of self-consciousness. Even if we have come to understand that this tradition has evolved out of primordial mythical and ritual traditions, and that it has a partial analogue or predecessor in the Gilgamesh epic, it is nevertheless undeniable that something truly new is born in the Homeric epics, which in their written form embody the origin of what we know as literature. At the time when the Homeric poems were born, probably the eighth century B.C.E., their language was free of any visual signs at all; it was associated with no letters, no characters, and no script. Homer himself was almost certainly illiterate; nevertheless, he is our first true author, the first poet or "writer" to create a sustained and integral literary work or works. For the first time in history, a literary work evolves out of its own center or ground, a ground deriving from a new center of consciousness that stands out from its own horizon and world. While the prophetic revolution in Israel occurred at this very time, and revolved about a radically new and individual form of faith, the oracles which are the primary expression of this revolution presented themselves as coming from afar and beyond, and could not in that context have been identified as having an individual or interior source. Not until the Homeric poems can we discover a voice and a speaker arising from a truly interior and individual ground.

But this interior and individual ground was not an isolated and solitary center, it was integrally related to its own world, a world that was realizing a revolutionary breakthrough from the archaic world to the birth of a full individual consciousness. Indeed, Homer is the Adam of our world, the first individual voice and speaker, or the first individual voice that had a revolutionary impact upon history. The impact of the Homeric epic was so revolutionary that it either gave birth to or initially embodied what we have subsequently come to know as consciousness and history. Only with Homer does a uniquely human consciousness and voice first appear and sound in history, a sounding distancing itself from both natural and divine realms, and so likewise effecting a revolutionary break from a society in which no full individual presence is possible. True metaphor was almost certainly born in Homer, for full metaphor is possible only when consciousness stands out from its ground in nature, thereby allowing a natural image to stand forth as natural even while integrally being associated with a human or divine movement or act. Full or true metaphor is an integral correlation of consciousness and its world, but it is a correlation that is possible only from the perspective of an interior and individual center, a center which by virtue of its distance from its world can enact a movement and activity embodying an integral and individual actor.

Yet a full and integral harmony between the natural, the human, and the divine realms is present in Homeric poetry. Such harmony can be found in no other historical or cultural world, and it is a deeper source or origin of the Classical and the Western worlds as a whole. Nothing is more characteristic of this Homeric harmony than the omnipresence of the divine, for the gods are present wherever there is life and movement, and again and again Homer attributes the instigation of important events either to particular deities or to "gods" in general (*theoi*) or to "god" (*theos*). Despite this immanent presence, however, and despite their recurrent epiphanies to chosen heroes, they ever remain Olympian or heavenly deities, and above all so by virtue of their immortal state, which is wholly opposed to humanity's inevitable fate or destiny of death. But this immortal state carries with it no true transcendent glory or majesty for Homer, and nothing is newer or more revolutionary in the Homeric epics than their portraits of the gods. For even if the Homeric gods embody more grace and beauty than any other gods, they are clearly morally inferior to the Homeric heroes, and they never inspire a genuinely numinous awe. Perhaps it is this very absence of divine majesty which makes possible such a unique and integral harmony between humanity and deity, a harmony which is the very arena and horizon of heroic virtue and power, for while gods and goddesses play a decisive role in the plot or action of these epics, never do they play a heroic role. That is wholly reserved for men and women, who are the real actors in these epics.

Goethe discovered an apotheosis of humanity in the Olympian gods, a deification of man rather than a humanization of deity, and a deification lying at the very center of classical Greece. Yet it is precisely because the Homeric gods are not truly anthropomorphic deities that the deification of humanity is alien to the Homeric world. Nothing is more characteristic of these gods than their distance from humanity, and above all a mortal humanity. In the Homeric Apollo, the most Greek of all the Homeric gods, this distance embodies a wholly impersonal or transpersonal presence, a presence never directing attention to itself and always oblivious to the interiority and individuality of the humanity to which it is manifest. Yet that impersonal presence is essential to the historical advent of individuality and interiority. The very fullness and ubiquity of a divine presence that remains a transhuman and therefore distant presence releases a radically new horizon and world for consciousness, a world in which consciousness can be present and actual to itself as an interior and individual consciousness. Here, the epiphany of deity to the individual hero is commonly manifest to that hero alone. It is an individual and interior epiphany that strengthens and sustains the virtue or *arete* of that hero, and does so not by an external infusion of power or mana but rather by way of an internal release of an individual center of consciousness, a center of consciousness that now for the first time can know the world or the cosmos as its own.

The omnipresence of deity is essential to the Homeric hero, but essential as a transhuman although not an alien presence that allows the hero to be himself, and to be interiorly and individually himself. The very ubiquity of this new divine presence brings an end to the darkness and chaos of an archaic world in which there can be no true standing forth of consciousness. The full presence of Olympian deity allows the Homeric hero to act through his own individual power or *arete*, that *arete* is truly his own, yet it is made possible only by a divine presence that is a full and actual presence, and therefore a presence banishing a primordial impotence and dread. Even if that presence is only a momentary presence, it is a full presence nonetheless, and therewith we discover the beginning of an actual and individual human presence, a presence embodying the advent of a full interior consciousness. That consciousness knows its own finitude and mortality as did perhaps no earlier form of consciousness, for even the greatest of the Homeric heroes cannot escape the fate of death, and the supreme heroism of Achilles is inseparably connected with an imminent death.

Just as death is impossible for Homeric deity, so likewise is heroic *arete*, for that *arete* is inseparable from death, a death that is the extinction of all life and power. Achilles, in Hades, declares to Odysseus that he would rather be a serf to a landless man on earth than king over all the exhausted dead (*The Odyssey*, XI, 465). Death is an essential and inescapable horizon for the hero, and his moments of triumph were simultaneously occasions for an awareness of the pathos of the human condition (for example, Achilles' speech to Priam, in *The Iliad*, XXIV, 19). That pathos is closed to the gods, for theirs is a bliss that knows no real or final pain, and cannot know such pain if only because they cannot know death. Homeric heroic destiny is possible only in the full context of real and actual death, a death that is the fate of every man, without exception, and a death that is the most poignant sign of a uniquely human condition. When we consider that a cult of the dead was perhaps the most powerful expression of Greek archaic religion, it is apparent that we may here observe the consequence of a radical religious revolution, and throughout Classical history the great majority of the Greeks did not believe in the possibility of a life after death.

Destiny is the deepest problem or mystery in the Classical world, a destiny that is inseparable from mortality, and one that is finally directed against humanity. Herodotus is representative of fifth century Greek thought in believing that deity is "jealous" and "interfering," that the gods resent any success or happiness which might come to man. Perhaps this theme is most powerfully expressed in a choral ode in Sophocles' *Antigone*:

> For time approaching, and time hereafter,
> and time forgotten, one rule stands:
> That greatness never
> Shall touch the life of man without destruction.
> Hope goes fast and far: to many it carries comfort,
> To many it is but the trick of light-witted desire —
> Blind we walk, till the unseen flame has trapped our footsteps.
> For old anonymous wisdom has left us a saying
> > 'Of a mind that God leads to destruction
> > The sign is this — that in the end
> > Its good is evil.'
> Not long shall that mind evade destruction.
> > > > (611–625., E. R. Dodds translation)

Here, it is manifest that an ancient gnomic tradition is one source of Greek tragedy, a tradition found elsewhere in the Near East, and particularly so in Mesopotamia, and one grounded in a primordial apprehension of a purely negative and alien power of the divine.

Already Aristotle noted that the development of tragedy did not attain its "natural form" until after having undergone a long series of changes. He asserted that tragedy certainly originated with improvisations upon the dithyramb (*Poetics* 1449a), a Greek choral lyric which in its earliest form was probably sung by a chorus of fifty men dressed as satyrs, to honor Dionysus. Modern scholars have traced the origin of Greek tragedy to archaic mythical and ritual cycles and have reconstructed the form of an ancient mystery play that brought salvation and immortality to the initiates who participated in its cycle of death and rebirth. The elements of this form are simple: a contest; a *pathos* or death or defeat; and a triumphant epiphany with an abrupt change from lamentation to rejoicing. But in tragedy this archaic form is radically transformed, as can be seen by the five components of Greek tragedy: (1) the *agon*, or contest between the hero and his adversaries; (2) the *pathos*, the suffering or death of the hero; (3) a messenger who relates the fate of the hero to the audience (the fact that Greek drama never depicts death on the stage is of deep significance); (4) a *threnos*, or lamentation; and (5) an *anagnorisis*, or a discovery and recognition of the ultimate state or destiny of the hero. In the archaic mystery play the anagnorisis was a discovery of the mutilated mystery god, which was followed by his resurrection; but in tragedy the victory of the resurrection of the god is transformed into the destruction, the abasement, or the elevation of the hero.

In Athens tragedy became established as a cult institution of the people, and the tragic poets were clearly the spiritual leaders of the state (see the debate between Aeschylus and Euripides in the *Frogs* of Aristophanes). Every tragedy was played by masked characters of superhuman majesty in a dramatic world heavy with religious awe, and not only was the Greek theater a sacred ritual center, but tragedy was enacted with a sacred music and dance that must have been of enormous power. If full Greek tragedy begins with the moral cosmos of Aeschylus, his characters are immersed in a world of archaic dread, a dread induced by the terrible power of fate. A cruel and destructive fate is primarily realized through *até*, the retributory and violent punishment meted out by the archaic chthonian powers, a retribution continually awaiting all human accomplishment. *Até* is the wrathful vengeance of the daemonic powers and deities, it is ever at the center of Greek tragedy, and it is commonly the fate of the tragic hero. Aristotle moralized this ground of Greek tragedy by maintaining that the peripety or reversal of the life and power of the hero was occasioned by a *harmatia*, a moral flaw or error on the part of the hero (*Poetics* 1453a). Although this Aristotelian understanding of the tragic hero long dominated our understanding of Greek tragedy, it was profoundly challenged by Nietzsche, and then virtually demolished by twentieth century criticism and scholarship.

What we now can clearly see is that the Greek tragic hero, with a few exceptions in Euripides, is assuredly not Aristotle's intermediate kind of individual, a man or woman not preeminently virtuous and just, whose misfortune arises not from vice and depravity but from an error of judgment. On the contrary, and most clearly so in Aeschylus and Sophocles, the tragic hero is a majestic figure, godlike in his or her power and strength, and challenging in his or her action and movement not only human adversaries but far more deeply the authority and the majesty of sacred and transcendent power. Above all it is in the greatest tragedies of Sophocles that we may observe an ultimate conflict between the human and the divine, and here we may also encounter the fullest embodiment of individual character and identity in Greek literature. For it is precisely the fullest realization of individual consciousness which occasions and calls forth a tragic destiny. Hence it is the virtue or *arete* of the Sophoclean hero which necessitates the wrathful vengeance of *ate*. Thus *ate* is invariably anticipated by the chorus, insofar as it is the chorus which sets the tragedy in the context of the archaic world, emphasizing the helplessness of man in the face of a hostile and mysterious cosmos and the inevitable destruction that awaits all human achievement.

Nowhere is the essential and integral relationship between *arete* and *ate* more fully present than in *Oedipus Tyrannus*. It is noteworthy that the plot of *Oedipus Tyrannus* is universally accepted as the purest plot in all tragedy, for every step in its development is a necessary realization of all that has happened before, as a wholly alien and cosmic *ananke* or necessity fully passes into tragic action. Finally, plot and character are one in this tragedy, a full union between interior consciousness and exterior action which is achieved nowhere else in drama or literature, as the realization of individual *arete* gradually but inevitably embodies the horror of *ate*, an *ate* which finally consumes all that *arete* that is realized and embodied in the acts of Oedipus. As a *tyrannos*,

Oedipus is a godlike if not a divine figure. In the opening scene of the play a priest of Zeus, who has come with other priests as suppliants to the palace of Thebes, declares to Oedipus that they are sitting in supplication at his altars. Soon Oedipus responds to the chorus's appeal to the gods with a godlike attitude, thereby establishing a semidivine status for himself which is only gradually eroded and reversed in the course of the drama. But that reversal of the divine and majestic status of Oedipus is the core of the tragic action. It is a reversal or peripety that is wholly impelled and realized by Oedipus himself, even if it is also a full actualization of a predestined fate.

It is this full coincidence between preordained fate and free individual act and decision which lies at the center of this tragedy. This center pervades the drama as a whole, for every movement of the action is at once a free and a predestined act, an act of *ananke* or necessity and a full and wholly human act of the individual actor. Indeed, it is precisely thereby that *arete* here becomes actual and real, as it becomes the dual consequence of a divine and cosmic necessity and individual decision and power. And even as Oedipus's initial majestic status is ever more fully eroded, it is just in accord with this abridgment and erosion of a divine power that an individual and interior identity and character appears and becomes real, as Oedipus ever more fully and finally becomes a man, and a man who is the full author of his destiny. It is this transformation of fate into destiny, into a freely chosen and willed necessity, which is embodied in this tragedy, a tragedy wherein the full horror of *até* becomes the consequence of a wholly and fully human decision and act. Now *arete* and *até* are one, and not simply in the archaic sense that *até* is a consequence of *arete*, but in the uniquely tragic sense that *arete* is *até*, that the highest and noblest human power is finally a purely negative and self-destructive power. Nowhere else in the ancient world do we find such a full embodiment of an actual and individual man. Here is a man who truly and fully becomes a man in the course of this tragic action and who most fully becomes a man when in the culminating moment of the tragedy he goes far beyond Jocasta's suicide by blinding himself, thereby striking out the source of both light and knowledge, and thus choosing a destiny that is even more dreadful than death.

Oedipus at Colonus is the final tragedy of Sophocles, and Colonus was not only the birthplace of Sophocles but also the site of the tomb-shrine of the hero-deity Oedipus, for Oedipus had long since become a god in Greek popular religion. In the opening of the play, a stranger confides to Oedipus that this place is both holy and forbidden, its ground may neither be touched nor lived upon, for most dreadful and feared are its divinities, daughters of darkness and mysterious earth. It is here that an oracle of Apollo has prophecied that Oedipus is to die, an aged Oedipus who has been instructed in contentment by suffering and time so vast that this Oedipus has almost ceased to be a man. Now Oedipus can declare that his murder of his father was a just extenuation, that before the law and before God, "I am innocent!" (549). If *Oedipus at Colonus* is a long, slow reversal of *Oedipus Tyrannus*, it is also a fully sacred and liturgical drama, but a tragic drama nonetheless, and tragic above all in the final disappearance of Oedipus. And in no other Greek tragedy, with the possible exception of *The Bacchae*, is the deep darkness of the archaic world more fully present. Thus the chorus can affirm that death is the end of man, and an end to be embraced:

> Not to be born surpasses thought and speech.
> The second best is to have seen the light
> And then to go back quickly whence we came.
> (1225, Robert Fitzgerald translation)

When Oedipus prays to the local deities, spirits or goddesses whose eyes are terrible, he recalls that when Apollo gave him oracles of evil he also spoke of this last country where Oedipus should find a home among the sacred Furies (90). Here it is that Oedipus can now insist to Creon that the calamities he suffered were by fate, and against his will, even if they were instigated by the gods (964). There are no evils in this Oedipus, an Oedipus who is driven by an insistent voice that comes from the divine realm, a realm awaiting him even now. Now is the time for Oedipus to pass into the dark underworld, an underworld of death, and as he passes into the night of death he prays for blessing upon the land he leaves. That blessing is as ambivalent as any passage in Greek tragedy, and if this is apotheosis, it is an apotheosis of eternal sleep. Accordingly, the chorus prays for a blessed descent and sleep of Oedipus in its final prayer:

> I pray you, even Death, offspring of Earth and Hell,
> To let the descent be clear
> As Oedipus goes down among the ghosts
> On those dim fields of underground that all men living fear.
> Eternal sleep, let Oedipus sleep well!
> (1574–78, Robert Fitzgerald translation)

A messenger then comes to report that what has happened to Oedipus is no simple thing, for although he left this place alone and thereby acted as a guide for all of us, he soon stopped to receive respite from his daughters, bid them a final farewell, and then called forth King Theseus to give his promise to be their guardian. Then he dismisses his daughters and allows Theseus alone to witness his ultimate destiny. And what is that destiny? A baffling and mysterious disappearance, and one inducing Theseus to shade his eyes as if from something awful and unendurable to see. But the messenger can nevertheless declare that the end of Oedipus was as wonderful as any mortal's ever was. Nonetheless, it induces weeping and bitter grief in his daughters, Antigone and Ismene, and Antigone can only confess that he has gone as one would wish him to and been swallowed up into an unseen space, where he is now shrouded in eternal darkness (1700). Antigone laments that her father's death was so lonely, just as Ismene grieves that he has no tomb. But Theseus returns and counsels that those to whom night gives benediction should not be mourned, and then insists that Oedipus in dying told him that no one should go near the place of his death nor tell of it, and this because it is a holy spot. Therefore it is an invisible place, or one open to no human vision, just as the end of Oedipus can be manifest only as a disappearance into darkness. But that disappearance into darkness is the highest destiny of the Greek tragic hero, one that is the tragic equivalent of an archaic resurrection, and that can finally induce a tragic chorus and audience to end all weeping and mourning.

This is the supreme catharsis of Greek tragedy, a catharsis anticipated and made possible by Homer, and a catharsis which is itself a passage into the depths of darkness. Whereas those depths are closed to Homer, not being present even in the eleventh book of *The Odyssey*, it was the negation and transcendence of these depths which made Homer possible, for the Homeric light arose from the deepest darkness, a darkness which returns in the mystery cults and in Greek tragedy. Nowhere in all art and literature is that darkness darker than in Greek tragedy, but here it is a spoken darkness, an enacted and embodied darkness, and therefore an enlightening darkness, and Oedipus in cutting out his eyes can scream: "Now you shall see only darkness!" (1273). And we see when the tragedy of Oedipus is resolved before us, for Oedipus can never be a ritual victim for us, a holy scapegoat who bears our pain and guilt. Finally, the character and action of Oedipus in *Oedipus Tyrannus* becomes a fully and wholly human action, one which summons us to become what we behold. Indeed, it summons us to embrace and affirm our destiny, and therefore our death. While humanly death can only be darkness, it is a darkness which is our end, and in *Oedipus at Colonus* that end becomes humanly realizable, and therefore present and real.

Nothing is more elusive in the Classical world than the meaning and identity of the divine. At no point is that world more alien to the historical world or worlds that succeeded it, and no hermeneutical problems are graver than those arising from attempts to interpret Classical texts which speak of the divine. Yet nowhere else is the unique genius of the Classical world more fully present. Certainly Homer and the great Greek tragedians are simply unintelligible if a postclassical meaning of deity is read into their texts, just as they are equally unintelligible if they are interpreted by way of a postclassical identity of man. From the later perspective of Christendom, what is most clearly missing from these texts is any presence of self-consciousness, whether of the heroes or of the gods, an absence which gives these figures an anonymous identity for us, although such a response could not have been possible in the Classical world. The Classical hero, whether epic or tragic, is never portrayed as being in conflict with himself. Never is there an interior *agon* or struggle, for interior presence is missing here, and therewith all self-presence or self-consciousness. Nothing so distances Shakespearean tragedy from Greek tragedy as does the uncrossable chasm not only between their tragic heroes but also between all the actors or characters in their respective worlds, a distance most obviously manifest in the absence of both the mask and the chorus from Shakespearean tragedy. But that distance is also fully present in the role and identity of deity in ancient and modern tragedy, for in Classical tragedy the characters are not only in conflict with each other but just as deeply if not more deeply in conflict with the divine.

The Homeric hero, unlike the Greek tragic hero, never engages in struggle or conflict with the divine as such. Even if he faces hostility and opposition from particular deities he just as surely is sustained and strengthened by deities with whom he is allied, and commonly Homeric moments realizing full *arete* are simultaneously moments of divine epiphany. Here there is a full coincidence between human and divine power and presence, one which is wholly missing in tragedy, as an epic harmony beteen the human and the divine is replaced in tragedy by an alien distance between the divine and the human realms. Now even if a real distance between man and the gods is present in the Homeric world, it is never an alien distance, so that here the gods never appear or act with a numinous identity. Such a numinous identity is present in Greek tragedy, and it comprehends not only the Olympian deities but all divine power whatsoever, and in tragedy, unlike in Homer, the pre-Olympian archaic world is present in its full and violent power. This power is profoundly directed against the *arete* of the hero, and tragic heroic *arete* unlike epic heroic *arete* can realize or embody itself only by struggling against divine power as such. Divine power is not only a foil of the tragic hero, but it must appear and be real to the hero himself as a purely negative power, or, ar least, it is invariably so in those moments or acts when tragic *arete* is becoming or realizing itself.

The Eumenides of Aeschylus is unique in Greek tragedy not only because it portrays a god, Apollo, who is fully allied with its hero, Orestes, but far more radically because it reaches a resolution in which the violent and hostile divine Furies are finally assuaged by Athena, and then settle in Attica as revered and beneficent powers. But in this tragedy it is Apollo and Athena and not Orestes who play heroic roles, and the play is a reenactment of the Olympian victory over the dark and hostile archaic and chthonian deities and powers, and thus it is more a liturgical celebration than a tragic drama. It is *Oedipus at Colonus* alone among Greek tragedies which gives us something approaching a truly affirmative epiphany of deity, even if its setting is the darkest of all in Greek tragedy, and even if its hero is the most fully divine of all tragic heroes. Yet here there is never either an individual or a personal epiphany or appearance of the divine. Moreover, all the concrete images of deity, such as those of the eyes of the local deities, are negative images, and negative images evoking negative identities. Indeed, grace in this tragedy is the presence but nonappearance of deity, its silence and invisibility, a pure silence and pure invisibility which is present in no other Greek tragedy, but whose presence here releases a unique heroic destiny that alone in Greek tragedy brings weeping and anguish to an end.

Thus it is the absence of deity in *Oedipus at Colonus* which plays an essential role in the positive or affirmative resolution of the tragedy. This absence of the actual presence of deity, and even the absence of the impact or effect of deity, is an essential ground of the transfiguration of Oedipus. It is precisely in the space or void established by the absence of deity that the aged Oedipus realizes something approaching apotheosis, but this is an apotheosis which is a silent and invisible epiphany, and therefore it is not an epiphany of anything which can actually be recognized as the divine. Nor can the triumphant Oedipus be recognized as a man. Everything that is either a human or a divine identity is missing in this resurrected Oedipus. Indeed, the only image we are given of this one who has finally received benediction from the night is a negative image, and a wholly negative image, for the resurrected Oedipus is quite simply the one who has disappeared into darkness. But that is grace, the highest and purest grace which is possible in Greek tragedy, a grace refusing and dissolving all fantasy and illusion, and a grace transcending, and wholly transcending, all mythical and religious identity.

At no point is Greek tragedy closer to its Homeric ground than in its political role and identity, for epic poetry and tragic drama were not simply accepted by the Greeks as embodying their own primal sagas. It was in and through these poetic instruments that the Greeks realized a unique historical destiny, and a destiny inseparable from the new community and new world which they established. Both the epic and the tragic heroes were exemplary models of and for their people, and above all so by way of their realization of *arete* through a passionate and violent conflict with an alien or hostile or inhuman destiny or fate. But nothing in Homeric or Greek tragic poetry is as profoundly political as Virgil's *Aeneid*, and nowhere else is the political identity of true epic poetry more fully manifest than in *The Aeneid*, for this poem is both the birthpang and the actual embodiment of a new political and historical world. If *The Aeneid* is the political epic par excellence, it is so first because it so fully embodies the Roman Empire, the first truly universal empire in history and politically the most powerful empire the world has ever know. Although Alexander the Great was the original creator of a political *ecumene*, it was Octavius Augustus who actually created or forged a universal empire; and if Aeneas is in significant measure a mythical and poetic persona of Augustus, then his is a unique heroic and epic identity, for no other epic hero is in any full sense both a historical and a political actor.

Perhaps no other epic is so politically and historically realistic as is *The Aeneid*, for even if this epic is a celebration of the universal peace of empire, it is a peace made possible not only by savage violence but also by a heroic and interior disengagement from passion, as most forefully enacted in Aenea's rejection of Dido's love. Aeneas may well be an Epicurean saint, but he is far more fundamentally a political saint, the only one in our epic literature, and as opposed to the political heroes of tragic poetry, he transcends all forms of truly individual conflict and discord. Therein Aeneas is a full political actor, as is no tragic political hero, and a political actor who is not only the founder of Rome but also the creator of a full and universal imperial power. Comprehensively present throughout *The Aeneid* are the new imperial virtues of *humanitas* and *pietas*, the one an internal solicitation for all human beings whatsoever and the other a fidelity to the deeper origins and grounds of a new universal society. At this point in antiquity all the Classical religious traditions were dead or dying, and so likewise were the moral traditions, and particularly so insofar as they were bound to a particular or individual community. The end of the Roman Republic was realized through a moral anarchy without precedence in ancient history, an anarchy unveiled in Shakespeare's *Antony and Cleopatra* before it was demonstrated by modern scholarship, and such anarchy had hitherto been followed by social and political disintegration.

Augustus created the Roman Empire out of this chaos, a chaos that continually lies beneath the surface of the action of *The Aeneid*, and which perhaps triumphs at the end of the poem. This is the chaos which only *humanitas* and *pietas* can arrest, the one by giving full human identity to political praxis, and the other by establishing a deep interior ground for that which is historically and actually groundless. One of the most striking differences between *The Aeneid* and the Homeric epics is the new role and identity of the gods. Apparently the same pantheon is present once again, differing only in its Roman dress. But the truth is that a whole new religious world is here at hand, for if the Homeric gods could be treated by the heroes with ironic humor and disdain that is because they are so fully integrated with a human world, whereas the deities of *The Aeneid* are not integrated with this Hellenistic world at all, and cannot be if only because they inspire a numinous awe. This is an awe which always preserves an alien distance of the gods, a distance never passing into interior presence, as it does so marvellously in the Homeric epics. For the deities of *The Aeneid* maintain not only their transcendence but also their mystery, a mystery which in Juno is directed wholly against the human world. Such religious realism is foreign to Homer, but it is present throughout *The Aeneid*, as the Classical world has now fully passed into the Hellenistic world and therein comes to an end a humanly ordered and harmonious cosmos. And newly present is a new form and identity of the human individual, an individual living in two worlds, one the new civil world of the empire and the other a new world of the private individual. For the first time in history a full distinction is established between public and private identity, as the peace and the power of a triumphant empire opened up the space for a private individual and interior consciousness, an interior space sustained not only by the ubiquity of imperial power but also by a reverent awe for transcendent mystery.

Although such awe had long been present as an interior ground of imperial power, never before had it been directed to a faceless and nameless transcendence, an anonymous transcendence fully engulfing human identity, and yet a transcendence releasing an interior distance which made possible the birth of private individuality. The Roman imperial citizen was a citizen of a truly universal and cosmopolitan world, and while the universality of that world made possible the advent of private individuality, this advent was inseparable from a new *pietas* establishing the transcendence of a universal human origin and destiny. Aeneas even as Augustus is the embodiment of an anonymous transcendence; a transcendence sanctioning and hallowing a new universal world, but a nameless and faceless transcendence nonetheless. Indeed, an anonymous transcendence was essential to the establishment of a truly universal empire. Roman imperial portraits and sculpture record the presence of a new and individual face, but it is a cold and vacuous face, as is most strikingly present in the extant portraits of Augustus himself, a face making incarnate that interior emptiness which seems to characterize Aeneas.

Yet such interior emptiness is surely necessary for total political praxis, a praxis which in Augustus triumphantly vanquished social and political anarchy. In Aeneas it embodies a heroic virtue that can fully and totally give itself to Roman destiny even in the absence of every previously established source of meaning and identity. Aeneas is a masked hero, the most fully masked hero in the Western epic tradition, and a hero who seems to have no interior presence, no character, no internal identity, no truly human name. But he is the first hero to act in a world in which the gods are humanly and interiorly absent, in which justice and order are preserved by force and violence alone, and in which political praxis is universal and all consuming. Medieval Christendom did not venerate Virgil simply because of its misreading of the *Ecologues*, nor did Dante and Milton choose Virgil as their primary model and source of epic inspiration because of a misjudgment of his poetic weight. It is far rather because Virgil and Virgil alone first created an epic poem making incarnate a universal and historical destiny, and a destiny which is universal precisely because it is free of all actual and embodied interior presence.

Chapter Three

Israel and the Birth of Scripture

If a radically new and all-encompassing vision is the unique creation of classical Greece, a vision underlying all the revolutionary breakthroughs of the Greek world, so likewise a radically new and all-encompassing voice is the unique creation of ancient Israel, a voice which itself embodies a new and total identity. While that identity is a transcendent identity, and a totally transcendent identity, nevertheless it is here manifest and real as the sole source and ground of all identity whatsoever. And it is so manifest at the innermost center of voice itself, a new voice which for the first time in history can itself embody an absolute origin and ground. Although it is true that prophecy is not unique to ancient Israel, not even in its overwhelming and revolutionary power, as witness Taoist prophecy in ancient China, it is nevertheless true that no other prophetic tradition knows and embodies an ultimate and primal ground that actually speaks, and speaks in the fullness of voice itself. Nor does it simply speak in a cryptic or gnomic utterance, but rather in the plenitude of language itself, a plenitude which itself becomes a ground and source of a whole new mode and identity of speech and voice. The prophetic oracle presents itself as being the very speech of Yahweh. The voice of its "I" is the "I" of "I AM," an "I" which is absolutely invisible, and thus "I AM" is the absolute antithesis of vision. But the pure invisibility of "I AM" is the source of a new and total voice, a voice whose full sounding brings a final end to an original silence, and thus an end to all unspeakable and unrealizable identity.

There is no greater mystery to us than the historical problem of the origin of Israel. What most clearly distinguishes the people of Israel from all other peoples is the ultimacy with which their own traditions focus upon the question of origin, an origin or genesis which here alone is total and all-encompassing. Now, and for the first time, genesis is total because it is a once-and-for-all event. It can never be repeated or renewed, and cannot undergo repetition or return because it is an absolutely unique event. So likewise the people who are grounded in this event are a truly unique people, a uniqueness reflecting and embodying the absolute uniqueness of "I AM." There is no deity even remotely comparable to "I AM" prior to the advent of Israel: for even those deities in the ancient Near East which are Yahweh's apparent predecessors have left no sign or evidence of an absolutely transcendent and majestic power that is the sole source and origin of all and everything. But such an absolute power and ground is directly or indirectly recorded in all Biblical epiphanies of Yahweh, and is so most fully and most clearly when these epiphanies erase and reverse all seeing and naming as such. Indeed, it is in that very erasure and reversal that the full and actual naming of Yahweh occurs, a naming embodying a totally immediate and absolute Otherness. For Yahweh is that absolute Other who is immediately present and manifest at the center of the fullness and the immediacy of voice.

Certainly Greece and Israel are sites of our beginning, sites embodying the origin of our actual identity and speech. Now a new speech and identity actualizes and realizes itself by naming or speaking, by naming a new center of identity as "I" or "I AM." In one sense, no forms of language are further apart than are the Homeric epics and the Biblical epics: for the one establishes a new immanent consciousness as the center and ground of a new world, and the other establishes and speaks an absolutely transcendent "I AM" as the origin and ground of all identity. Each of these epic creations and traditions released and embodied a new consciousness and a new humanity which were destined wholly to transform the worlds and horizons in which they were sung and enacted. Yet at no point are the Homeric and the Biblical epic traditions closer than in a deep aversion which they share to the domain of the dead. Nothing is more forbidden in either tradition than intercourse with the realm of death, and this condemnation deepened as each tradition developed. For it was a negation and transcendence of the archaic world which made possible the revolutions of both Greece and Israel. In Israel and Greece alike, regressions from their revolutionary beginnings commonly occurred by way of a renewed communion with death, a communion made possible by the rebirth or preservation of archaic rites and myths, as can be observed in Baalism and the mystery cults, each of which were regressive returns to a now forbidden world. Yahweh stands forth most clearly in his antithetical relationship to the archaic religious world, and even if his historical roots lie in storm gods of nomadic peoples, unlike such deities, Yahweh never became the consort of the Great Goddess. Indeed, the Great Goddess is more profoundly forbidden in the Biblical tradition than in any other tradition in the world. And even if she appears and speaks in the personified Wisdom of the Book of Proverbs and the Bride of the Song of Songs, she is far more disguised and hidden in these figures than she is in any other epiphany. The Great Goddess is the Mother of Death, or the primal source of a life that can be realized only through death, and even if that life can be known by its devotees as immortality, it is a life wholly alien to the life promised by Yahweh. For the redemptive promise of Yahweh is indissolubly united with earth and time.

Such an absolute condemnation of communion with death is another significant sign of the ubiquity of the otherness of Yahweh, an otherness which is all in all. Even if the realm of death is wholly removed from Yahweh's majestic authority, it is not removed from Yahweh's transcendent otherness, for the realm of death becomes unspeakable in the Hebrew Bible, and therefore and thereby becomes unreal. Now the state of death is unconsciousness, forgetfulness, and silence, as it is to a significant but lesser degree in the Homeric and Apollonian tradition. But in Israel death is commonly given a purely negative identity, and particularly so in the prophetic tradition, which in the Book

of Jeremiah can pose an absolute antithesis between the way of life
and the way of death (21:8). Above all, death is the realm of silence,
a silence enacted by Yahweh. Just as Yahweh's Torah brings an end
to the presence of the Goddess, thereby ending the presence of the
gods, so likewise the Torah and its traditions silence the realm of death,
so that death can only be greeted with an aversion which itself makes
possible a new life.

This new life is wholly other than that life which is manifest in the
archaic world, thus necessitating an iconoclastic shattering of that life
and world. Again and again this shattering is most fully manifest in
the prophetic tradition, which continually proclaims and enacts an
absolute silencing of the archaic world. Nowhere is this shattering more
forcefully present than in the prophetic assault upon all earthly power,
for even if that assault is anarchistic and apolitical, it nevertheless directs
its assault upon all power as such, thus attacking not only social,
political, and economic power, but the whole social and cultural world
of the ancient Near East. Now all worldly power whatsoever becomes
manifest as being antithetically related to the transcendent majesty
of Yahweh, and only a turning from all such power and all such authority makes possible a turning to Yahweh. This concurrent and coincident turning, a turning from worldly power and to a now wholly
transcendent Yahweh, gives birth to a radically new interior and
individual faith, a faith which is possible and real only for one who
steps forth and away from all archaic identity. Accordingly, family,
clan, priesthood, and state cease to be sources of primal authority as
a consequence of the prophetic revolution. For it is precisely the standing forth of a new interior and individual faith which is the clearest
and most decisive expression of the Yahwist revolution.

Originally, the oracles of the canonical prophets were eschatological
oracles, which is to say that they were enacted and pronounced in
the eschatological context of the end of Israel, or the end of Israel
as a nation or society. While this eschaton or end is a consequence
of Yahweh's just judgment — for Israel in Canaan had been reborn
as an archaic people and nation — it is this ending alone which makes

possible a full turning to Yahweh. For this ending realizes a full ending of all pre-Yahwist identity, and only an ending or transformation of the archaic world makes possible a full communion with Yahweh. So it is that the people of Yahweh are fully or truly born only through exile, only through the utter destruction of their nation or nations and the seemingly irretrievable loss of their land and cultus. Therewith came to an end everything that has been the source of life and identity to an ancient people, but nevertheless the people of Yahweh if not the people of a former Israel survived. That survival made possible for the first time in history the advent of an autonomous people, a people who as a people were landless, nationless, and cultless, and yet a people who thereby and only thereby embodied a new and revolutionary society, for it was a society freed of the primal presence or ground of any earthly or natural power or authority.

Yet Israel was an autonomous society only by being a theonomous or theocentric society. Even as Israel only now became a truly new people, so only now does Yahweh become fully manifest as the God who alone is God. While this epiphany either accompanies or actually brings the nation of Israel to an end — an epiphany most purely and most imaginatively recorded and expressed in the wholly alien El Shaddai of the Book of Job — it is precisely this wholly eschatological epiphany which makes possible and real the birth of a people transcending both a historical and a natural source or ground. Now a primal ground can only be a covenant with Yahweh, and an eternal covenant with Yahweh, and therefore a covenant that is independent and free of all worldly power and authority. So it is that a post-exilic covenant can only be the renewal of an absolute beginning, a beginning wholly transcending all natural and historical cycles, and thus a beginning or genesis wholly other than any conceivable or imaginable or mythical identity.

Only as a consequence of exile does a fully Biblical or revelatory naming or speaking of creation occur in Israel. This is most purely present in Deutero-Isaiah and Job, and here it is a consequence of a new naming of God. This naming liberates creation from all mythological and cosmological meaning by apprehending the Creation as an absolutely transcendent ground and source. Now beginning or origin is absolute and total. Nothing less than that beginning can be a true origin or source, therefore every natural and human origin is an illusion, and a blasphemous and demonic illusion when it is known and apprehended as a true source. Thereby every sacred and mythical origin is annulled, but so likewise is every natural and human origin, or is so annulled when it is not celebrated and comprehended as an act or epiphany of Yahweh. Not only is Yahweh or "I AM" the God who alone is God, but Yahweh or El Shaddai is the Creator, the Creator who alone is creator, the Creator who is the sole source and ground of everything whatsoever. Now origin ends as a human or natural source, for "I AM" is the sole source of every "I," and the only source of every true or primal ground of meaning and identity. But only an interior and exterior loss of every given and manifest source or origin makes possible this radical and revolutionary opening to a wholly and totally transcendent ground.

The self-identity of Israel is a re-saying of "I AM," and even if that re-saying is a silent re-saying, it is a re-saying nonetheless, a re-saying re-versing all given identity, and reversing it so that identity or self-identity now becomes the other of itself. It is when the manifold of the given in all its comprehensiveness falls under a total and imminent judgment that identity as such becomes other than itself. Then the center of identity itself is actualized as self-judgment, and deep or primordial ground becomes manifest and real as transcendent and absolute otherness. Only in the catastrophic situation of the ending of the nation or nations of Israel does Yahewh dawn within Israel as absolute otherness, an otherness that is not only the source of an immediate eschatological judgment, but is itself the actuality and embodiment of that judgment. Now the original light and promise of the Day of the Lord wholly passes into darkness (Amos 5:18), and Behemoth or the primordial monster of chaos becomes manifest and real as the archetype of an absolutely transcendent power (Job 40:15). Then and only then is Yahweh truly and fully manifest at the Creator, the Creator before whom all nations are as nothing, and who knows all nations as less than nothingness and emptiness (Isaiah 40:17).

Israel can name Yahweh as the Creator only when it can know and speak "I AM" as absolute sovereignty, a sovereignty before which all other identity becomes empty and nameless, and a sovereignty whose manifestation and actualization assaults and subverts everything that stands forth in its presence. The full presence of "I AM" is the absolute reversal of all other presence and power, the de-construction or de-presencing of presence as such, as the fully actual presence of absolute otherness enacts and brings forth a fully negative identity to everything that exists and stands forth. To know Yahweh as the Creator is to know the groundlessness, and the absolute and total groundlessness, of ex-istence as such, and therefore to know and to realize ex-istence as exile, and not only as exile, but as exile which is exiled from itself. Now identity becomes its own other, and realizes itself as the otherness of itself, an otherness which is actualized with the pronunciation of "I AM." Survival in exile is then possible only by way of the silent pronunciation of the Divine Name, a silent pronunciation which nevertheless speaks in the very writing of the text of the Bible, as Bible itself is born in response to the silence of the people of Israel.

The People of the Book are an exilic people, the only exilic people who have survived throughout recorded history, and the only people who created a text or scripture which is the sole ground of all constituted and sanctioned authority. For the first and only time in history a people is born which is free of the ultimacy and sacrality of the given in all its forms: nature now recedes and withers away except insofar as it reflects the glory of the Creator, a new mono-Yahwism creates exclusivist institutions which divorce their people from all deep or integral participation in the grounding centers of archaic life, and the once overwhelming power of the archaic sacrificial cultus is now internalized and interiorized in a new individual even if communal life. This is a life transcending the sacrality of land and kingdom, and therefore a life freed of the ultimacy and finality of all forms of earthly and natural power. Thereby a new conscience and consciousness is born, a fully individual conscience and consciousness, but nonetheless a communal or corporate consciousness constituting a truly new people, a people for whom and in whom the Torah of Yahweh is both the grounding center and the final judge of all life.

Torah, even as all primal words, is untranslatable, and despite the Pauline tradition it must not and cannot be understood as a pure imperative, and this because it is known by the people of Israel as both the source and the embodiment of an ultimate energy and life. Only a negation and refusal of that energy and life can make possible an apprehension of Torah as Law, or as Law in the Pauline and Christian sense. For it was Torah that made possible the very survival of Israel, a survival without known historical precedent, and a survival inaugurating the very possibility of a fully corporate and communal life and body which is free of all given and established forms of power. The Buddhist Sangha, which was also born during this period, is perhaps the first independent human community of any kind, and its radical iconoclasm no doubt played a social, cultural, and religious role comparable to that of Israel's. But the Sangha never became a nation or a people, except much later in Tibet, nor did the Sangha ever historically become the sole despository and embodiment of an ultimate and primal ground that otherwise is absent or unheard.

The People of the Book are guardians of the Torah, and guardians because they are the people of the Book, the first people actually to write a whole scripture, a writing whose very words are celebrated and preserved as revelation. Originally *torah* meant oral instruction or direction, but during the monarchic period of Israel it assumed the form of a written code, later it became a comprehensive term for the Pentateuch as a whole, and eventually became indistinguishable from Scripture or Bible. Torah is quite simply the revelation of Yahweh or "I AM," and the revelation of the words of "I AM," as for the first time integral and individual words embody the fullness and the finality of revelation. Significantly enough, Torah only became manifest and real as Bible at a time when the pronunciation of the name of Yahweh had become absolutely forbidden, so that here revelation as Bible and the absolute silence of the source of revelation go hand in hand. That silence now becomes a sign of revelation, perhaps the sign of revelation, and with the epiphany of Bible as revelation all prophecy becomes consigned to the past. Both Christianity and Islam followed this path in their canonization of Scripture, so that in this tradition or way the birth of text as revelation coincides with the end of voice as revelation, and only that ending makes possible the absolute authority of Scripture.

Therefore Scripture is the written record and voice of absolute origin, an origin which is manifest and real as absolute and final only with and through the birth of Scripture, so that the advent of Scripture is simultaneously the advent or epiphany of absolute origin or beginning. All too naturally the Bible opens with the beginning of the world, an absolute and unique beginning, and a unique and absolute beginning both recording and embodying a unique and absolute origin and ground. No genuine cosmogony or cosmology is present here, or not insofar as archaic traditions of origin have been transformed by the legal, the prophetic, and the wisdom traditions of Israel. For the Biblical record of origin is finally non-mythical or anti-mythical insofar as it fully speaks only of the Creator. Unlike all mythical accounts of origin, Genesis speaks of a unique and absolute beginning: that beginning is the sole act of the Creator, and it is that one act which is the absolute origin of all life and existence. If all ancient Near Eastern nations celebrated their origins in the most solemn liturgical festivals, festivals which enacted and renewed not only the origin of a people but the origin of the world, Israel in exile transformed an archaic sacrificial cultus into text, thereby making possible the birth of Scripture not only as witness to but as embodiment of Creation. For even if creation is now a once-and-for-all event, so likewise is Bible the once-and-for-all revelation of the Creator.

Only after the exile does Israel fully come to know Moses as the giver or mediator of the Torah, for Moses is not even mentioned in a preexilic prophetic oracle, and he is absent from the wisdom tradition of Israel as well. But now Moses becomes the grounding center of Torah, even as Torah becomes Scripture or Bible, for even if this new identity of Moses is a consequence of the Deuteronomic reformation of the seventh century B.C.E., it is thereby a product of the disintegration of monarchic Israel. Thus the new Moses and the new identity of Torah are a product of a new Israel, as a people who are being freed or liberated from the violence and the terror of all earthly power now become open to the absolute otherness of that power. Therefore the exodus from "Egypt" is at bottom an exodus from worldly power. If pre-monarchic Israel could know Yah or Yahweh as a Warrior, a Warrior whose majestic holiness is terrible in its deeds of power, as in the earliest recorded Hebrew poetry (Exodus 15:1–18 and Judges 5), a post-exilic Israel knows Yahweh or "I AM" as an absolutely sovereign and absolutely transcendent Lord, a Lord whose sovereignty transcends and reverses all forms of worldly power. Nowhere else in history does such a comprehensive reversal of a primal deity occur, for nowhere else in history does a divine or ultimate identity become manifest and real as a consequence of an exodus from the will to power. True, the Buddhist Nirvana or Emptiness is a consequence of a fully comparable exodus, but it is an exodus realized in the interior depths of meditation rather than in the actualities of history.

When Bible is manifest as Torah, and Torah as Bible as well, then all laws finally derive from the Creator, and all authority, too. Monarchic Israel could know the King as the Messiah, the anointed One of Israel, and hence the instrument of Yahweh in establishing and maintaining the sacrality and order of Torah. With the destruction of the monarchies, and the end of Israel as an ancient nation, Torah alone now exercises the former role of the monarch, and not only of the monarch but of virtually all the ancient or archaic centers of authority, thereby giving birth to Torah as the sole embodiment of an absolute and unique authority. Now Torah is the Word of Yahweh, and the word or words as well, words therefore embodying the absolute transcendence of the Creation. Accordingly, covenant now becomes an eternal covenant, a covenant issuing from the Creation. Israel, too, becomes reborn as the people of the beginning, the one people whose very life and identity not only gives witness to but itself embodies both the sign and the seal of a unique and absolute beginning.

That absolute beginning, a beginning which is a once-and-for-all event, is an event which is Yahweh's alone, and therefore is absolutely other than all other events. Thereby and therein absolute otherness first fully enters history and consciousness. This entrance decisively transforms that consciousness and history in which it is enacted and embodied, thus making possible and releasing the sole time and site in history in which an integral and intrinsic otherness is fully born and thereby is fully real. Although the full historical and internal realization of this otherness does not dawn until the birth of Christianity, its possibility and its potentiality were established by Israel. While Israel knows the ultimacy and the totality of absolute otherness, this knowledge then and now demands a refusal of the pronunciation of the Divine Name, a refusal which is a primal source of the life of the people of Israel, and a refusal which becomes affirmation and celebration in the observance of Torah. If the people of Israel are the people of Torah, the People of the Book, that is because here and here alone origin is manifest and real as both absolute and unique: an origin which actually and fully speaks in Scripture or Torah, even if that speech must become silence to actualize its witness and sign.

Not until the advent of exilic Israel is sign or Scripture fully born. This birth is inseparable from the embodiment of absolute otherness in consciousness and history, an embodiment realizing for the first time in history both the possibility and the actuality of a pure writing or system of signs that is wholly dissociated and removed from all natural or given identity and meaning. With the full birth of text as Scripture, voice fully passes into writing, and every natural or human source of voice therein perishes. For the text of Scripture is liberated from every possible source, from every actual or natural or human origin. It is so liberated because it is the embodiment of absolute otherness, a pure otherness whose source can only be itself. The Israel who knows Torah as both the voice and the speech of the Creator, is the Israel who hears and celebrates a Torah which is absolutely silent. That silence, the first such silence in history, is the decisive sign and seal of the presence, and of the full and embodied presence, of the absolute otherness of the Creator. Now voice and speech become silence, an absolute and total silence, and that pure silence is the revelation of "I AM." But that pure silence is incarnate in Scripture, a Scripture which is the Word of the Creator, but it is a silent word and Word, a silence which is itself an embodiment of the Creator. So it is that Israel came to know Torah as the very model or archetype of the Creation. For Torah is the primordial ground of the Creator, and thus Torah itself is the archetype and source of everything whatsoever which exists and is real. But it is so only as an absolutely silent Word, a Word and words transcending every real and actual source, for thereby and only thereby is Torah itself the sole and only Source.

Torah or Scripture is at once both absolutely other and absolutely the same: it is absolutely other than creation or world, even while being the sole ground and origin of world or Creation. So likewise the text or writing of Scripture is now simultaneously both absolutely other and absolutely the same: it is infinitely removed from the actuality of speech even while being the sole ground of speech, it is wholly other than the actual center and voice of speech even while thereby being the primal source and the final archetype of speech. Now sign as sign is wholly other and wholly the same: it is wholly other than all given or natural identity even while being the sole source and ground of all identity and meaning. The birth of Scripture is the birth of symbol as sign, of primordial ground and source as writing or text, of a new and revolutionary transcendence that is wholly other precisely by being wholly present. For it is fully present in a writing or text that absolutely negates every possible origin or source. Consequently, Scripture or Torah is an absolute presence which is an absolute absence: for it is absolutely present as total and only source only by negating and annulling every possible human or natural source. This negation speaks and fully speaks in the total silence of the text of Scripture, a silence marking and embodying the total presence of Torah.

Only in Mahayana Buddhism is there present such an integral and total coinherence or coincidence of absolute otherness and absolute identity. But only in Israel does such a *coincidentia oppositorum* actually realize itself in text or scripture, a scripture which thereby becomes an unending writing or script. For not only is Torah the sole embodiment of the Creator, but that embodiment ever repeats and renews itself in commentary and tradition, a repetition which is at once a renewal of the original act of Creation and a rebirth of the original covenant and revelation at Sinai. Thereby Creation and revelation are one, even as Genesis and Exodus are one, for Sinai is the site of "I AM" alone, and therefore Sinai and Creation are indistinguishable. So it is that Sinai is absolute Source, a source that is continually repeated and renewed in the life of the people of Israel. While this repetition and renewal is a silent and invisible repetition, it is nonetheless a repetition, and a repetition that speaks or is manifest and real in Torah alone. Yet Torah is actual and manifest only in script or in writing, for the oral Torah of rabbinic Judaism fully and finally passed into the writing or script of Talmud. If scripture and tradition or Scripture and Tradition are one in the Talmud, this is a unity which is maintained even when it passes into meditation and contemplation in the Kabbalah, for Scripture or Torah is one in Israel, a oneness or unity that is present only in the People of the Book.

No people in history has taken writing and therefore reading with such total seriousness as has Israel, and it could even be said that full or pure reading begins only with the exile of Israel. The first known text of Homer is no earlier than the fifth century B.C.E., the period which witnessed the birth of the library in Greece, and also the period when Ezra brought the first written text of Torah out of exile into Jerusalem. But those scribal traditions which Ezra and his school recorded, and recorded in a text which is text and text alone, have no counterpart in the Classical world until the Hellenistic age. For not until then do books appear in the Classical world that are books and only books, and this most fully occurs at Alexandria, a city which at least in its composition was just as Jewish as it was Greek. The text as an object of study and meditation was born in Israel, and as such it is certainly a product of exile. Only now does text become Text, and therein it becomes all and everything, for every deep and primal source of meaning now passes into text. Thus with the historical advent of the new Israel, an Israel born only in and through exile, all ancient and archaic sources of meaning are transformed and reversed, as land, kingship, temple, and state undergo a metamorphosis into text, and text as text for the first time in history becomes Scripture. This birth of Scripture is the birth of a new and revolutionary totality, a Totality which finally becomes wholly embodied in writing or text. Therefore it is a silent Totality, even if the silence of Scripture is the embodiment of an Origin and Voice which hereby becomes all in all.

Chapter Four

Paul and the Birth of Self-Consciousness

N ot until the time of Philo and Paul did the Hebraic tradition make a decisive impact beyond the community of Israel, and it is of overwhelming importance that to this day it is Paul and in Paul alone that the worlds of sacred history and individual self-consciousness appear and stand forth together in their own integral and distinct identities. For it is only in the letters of Paul that Biblical language or Scripture is manifest and real as Biblical language even while being spoken and resaid in the language of a full and active self-consciousness. This coinherence and coincidence, a coincidence which is a *coincidentia oppositorum*, became an essential ground of the Christian epic tradition, and it is unquestionably a primal ground of Western Christendom as a whole. Yet nowhere else in our tradition and traditions do self-consciousness and revelation stand so isolated and apart. For Pauline language, and Pauline language alone, commonly and almost continually embodies a dichotomy between "I" language and revelatory language. This dichotomy realizes an integral and internal contradiction between the language of revelation and the language of self-consciousness. A full and actual language of self-consciousness first historically appears in Paul's letters. Here it is a negative language, indeed, a self-negating language, as the "I" of self-consciousness knows itself as a sinful and guilty conscience and consciousness, a carnal or fleshy "I" that is wholly and totally imprisoned by sin (Romans 7:14–20.). For the first time in history a full and total impotence of the will is now manifest and actual at the center of consciousness, and that impotence is the site of the dawning voice of self-consciousness, a lacerated and self-lacerating voice which can speak only by speaking against itself.

Nothing is more controversial either in the interpretation of Paul or in the problematics of Christian anthropology itself than the identity of the deeper or the inner man. A classical text here is Romans 7:22, where Paul declares that he delights in the Law of God, *kata ton eso anthropon*, in my inner man or my inmost self or my inner depths. These depths can be and have been identified with the Law of my *nous* (7:23), thereby identifying the real or authentic self with *nous* or mind rather than with *soma* or body. On the other hand, these depths can also be interpreted as the "mind" of sin or unregenerate man, for even *sarkic* or carnal man exists in a center or ground that "knows" the Law of God. Indeed, it is here and only here that Law dawns and is real as a pure and absolute imperative. And despite the traditions of Christian scholasticism, whether Catholic or Protestant, the *nous* of Paul is far removed from the *nous* of Plato and Aristotle, and is so above all because of the absence in Paul of any sense of the purely contemplative or purely cognitive mind.

For Paul, the *nous* or mind of *sarkic* or sinful man is hostile to God (Romans 8:7), it not only does not but cannot submit to God's Law, and therefore it is under the condemnation of death. Such an understanding of *nous* is totally foreign to the Greek philosophical tradition, and is far closer to Paul's contemporary opponents, the Christian Gnostics, than it is to any philosophical understanding of mind before Kierkegaard and Nietzsche. Nevertheless, this is not a Gnostic understanding of the natural mind if only because it understands that mind not as earthly matter but as sin. For the wisdom of this world is folly with God (I Corinthians 3:18), and Paul can only mean the deepest wisdom of this world, a world which in its totality now stands under the judgment of eternal death. The mind of this world or old aeon is a sinful or fallen mind; it is wholly other than Spirit, even if it is the only mind that naturally or spontaneously can be known as my own. So it is that in the life of faith we are the Lord's, none of us either lives or dies to himself (Romans 14:7), for in the life of the Spirit we are not our own (I Corinthians 6:19). Here, we are not our own because what is my own is sin and death. At most I can wish or desire to serve the Law of God with my mind, but actual obedience is closed to me so long as I live according to the flesh, and I live in bondage to the flesh insofar as I live as my own.

Now ownness in this sense could not even have been upon the horizon of Plato or Aristotle, nor of any other thinker who is innocent of apocalyptic judgment, and therefore innocent of a total and interior guilt. The fully interior or self-conscious ego is the ego of sin. Historically it never appears apart from a Pauline language and consciousness, which is to say a guilty conscience, a consciousness that knows itself as sin. Within this tradition or mode of consciousness there can be no spiritual "I," or no spiritual "I" which is my own, for it is the ownness of self-conscious ego which is the antithesis of Spirit. Yet, it is also true that within the historical world of self-consciousness, Spirit never appears or is real apart from that "I" which is only its own. That "I," an independent and unique "I," an "I" which knows itself as its own intrinsic other, is the site of a historically unique form of Spirit; a Spirit that is not only itself and only itself, but is itself only insofar as it is not another, and is absolutely itself only by being absolutely other. The God whom Paul could know as being "for us," can be for us only as being against us, only by being a God of final and total judgment.

A dialectic is present here, an integral and genuine dialectic, a dialectic that simultaneously knows God as a God of salvation and judgment, of life and death. Thereby it also knows the innermost self as death and life, as guilty and justified, as flesh and Spirit. The "I" of that deep selfhood is an "I" of life and death, for it is precisely the total and free gift of life which issues in an interior realization of total guilt and death, a death which is the necessary and inevitable consequence of an eschatological actuality that is life and death at once. Now that we are ever more fully coming to realize that Paul's deepest struggles were not with Jewish Christianity as such but rather with a Christian or Jewish Christian Gnosticism, it is ever more fully clear that nothing is more antithetical to Pauline faith than a purely pneumatic or spiritual life in the Spirit, a life that knows Spirit only insofar as it is literally or substantially free of flesh and death. Thereby Resurrection is wholly dissociated from Crucifixion, the Christ of glory wholly transcends the Christ of the cross, and life in the Spirit is even now wholly free of death and guilt. Also thereby and precisely thereby the inner man becomes known and manifest as the spiritual "I," an "I" that is free of flesh and guilt, and an "I" wholly transcending any integral relationship to world or flesh.

Nothing could be further from the real Paul than a Christian Gnosticism. It was just by way of his profound opposition to Gnosticism that Paul created the language of Christian theology, a language wherein and whereby revelatory language passes into self and world understanding, and where world and self understanding are one. Pauline theological language is anthropological and cosmological at once, for the creator of the language of original sin is also the creator of the language of the guilty conscience. Just as Paul knows death as the consequence of sin rather than of creation, so he knows the actuality of self-consciousness as the actuality of sin. Thus self-consciousness as such initially appears as a dichotomous consciousness, a doubled and divided consciousness which is itself only insofar as it is not itself, which is for itself or manifest to itself only insofar as it is against itself, only insofar as it is a pure and total negativity. But that negativity is not simply and only an interior negativity. It is also and even thereby a cosmic negativity, for the full actualization of an interior negativity brings with it a new negative identity to everything that stands forth in consciousness.

Even the Law of Israel is now manifest as a law of sin, for while the Law is holy, and the commandment is holy and just and good (Romans 7:12), the ultimate purpose of the Law is to lead us to death, the death of both an interior and an eschatological judgment, a death in which eternal and interior judgment are one. The Law was given only in response to the advent of sin (Galatians 3:19), and positively it can only serve as a guardian until the coming of Christ. But Christ is the end of the Law (Romans 10:4), or the end of the Law for those who live in Christ. A radical new meaning of the Law dawns with the full advent of self-consciousness. Now for the first time consciousness can know the coming of the Law as the advent of death, for while "I" was once alive apart from the Law, when the commandment came, sin was reborn, and "I died" (Romans 7:9). So it is that sin itself is dead or unreal apart from the Law, a Law which is intended to make us conscious of sin. It makes us conscious of sin by realizing within us an eternal death, even if that death cannot be fully actual and real until the coming of Christ. That coming brings with it a total and apocalyptic judgment, and with that judgment the Law itself becomes manifest as a Law which is not only revealed in Torah but is universally present in conscience and consciousness (Romans 1:18–23). So it is that the Law of Israel is now manifest as a law of sin, for not only is the Law given to make us conscious of sin, but sin itself is dead or unreal apart from the Law, a Law which is not only revealed in Torah but is deeply and universally present in conscience and consciousness.

Accordingly, sin is for the first time manifest as a totality, as the curse of sin is not only within but in the groaning of the cosmos as a whole, and all stand under the judgment of eternal death. It is just the apprehension of the universality and the totality of sin and death that here makes possible the birth of theological language. For genuine theological language, even as genuine philosophical language, is a fully comprehensive language, a language that can establish real identity only by establishing a universal identity, an identity which is manifest and real in every object and category of consciousness. But now every object of consciousness is inseparable from a divided and doubled subject of consciousness, as for the first time the subject of consciousness becomes manifest as the source and ground of consciousness itself. Hence the fallenness of the world is not only inseparable from the actualization of a self-negating consciousness, but is itself the consequence of that divided consciousness, for apart from the self-division and self-alienation of consciousness there can be no real or actual identity of Fall. But once full self-negation is actualized in consciousness then all identity that is manifest and real to that consciousness will be a negative identity, an identity which is negative not only in its appearance or manifestation but also in its center or core.

While only the beginning of an actualization of self-negation is present in Paul, that beginning is irrevocably and irreversibly established, or is so until the self-consciousness which it inaugurated itself comes to an end. Integrally related to the advent of self-consciousness in Paul is a new sense of universal history, a new apprehension of history as a unitary and organic whole, even if that whole only becomes manifest and real as the consequence of the dawning of a final and apocalyptic judgment. The totality of history is thereby unveiled by way of the purely negative symbolic identity of "old aeon" or "old creation." Now a final judgment is inseparable from and is indeed the reverse expression of the actual advent of the Kingdom of God, an advent which triumphs in the Resurrection of Christ, thereby inaugurating the final age of the Spirit. Only in the perspective of this advent does history appear as an integral whole, for then history or the Old Adam is manifest as the absolute otherness of the New Adam or Christ, an otherness which itself becomes actual or real only through the advent of that total grace which is the fruit of the cosmic victory of the Resurrection.

Accordingly, both history and selfhood or self-consciousness are totally negative actualities for Paul. But their negativity is the polar or dialectical consequence of the new and final grace of Christ or Spirit, a grace whose very ultimacy or totality is inseparable from the total negativity of its recipient. Indeed, it is the advent of eschatological grace which effects or embodies eschatological judgment. So it is that the birth of a self-lacerating self-consciousness is a gift of grace, the final grace of the age of the Spirit, and a grace which promises to bring an immediate end to the Old Adam. Nothing is more characteristic or distinctive of Paul's faith than its apocalyptic immediacy, its participation even now in the final and total grace of the eon of the Spirit, a grace which is actually realized or enacted in the eschatological events of the Crucifixion and the Resurrection of Christ. For the first time the symbolic identity of an eschatological event is fully realized in consciousness itself, and this is a final event with all the ultimacy and finality of a primordial event, which is to say the original act or event of the Creation itself.

The Crucifixion and the Resurrection of Christ now stand manifest as one final and eschatological event, but it is an event which is not yet consummated, and not consummated because Old Adam and Old Creation have not yet come to an end. But they have come to an end in the new life of the Spirit, and it is precisely for that reason that history and consciousness now stand forth as totally negative identities, negative identities and negative actualities which are fruits of the Resurrection of Christ, a resurrection which brings an end to the life of the "old eon" or "old creation." That end is immediately manifest in the new identity of history and consciousness, a totally negative identity which actualizes the eschatological event of death, a final and ultimate death which is the interior and historical identity of Resurrection. Now darkness descends upon all actual identity whatsoever. This is a new darkness which is the cosmic and historical identity of eschatological light, and a darkness which is the necessary and inevitable consequence of the final victory of the Resurrection. Paul's very discovery of Resurrection as the polar or dialectical identity of Crucifixion is inseparable from a discovery of death as the dialectical or polar identity of life. Thereby cosmos and history pass under the eschatological judgment of death, and death becomes the new identity of world and humanity, a death whereby and wherein the world will come to an end in an apocalypse of grace.

For the first time in Western history death itself passes into an ultimate and final symbolic identity. Now death is the integral otherness or the dialectical opposite of Christ, an identity of death which is possible and real only by way of the eschatological manifestation and actualization of the eternal life of Christ, a life which is realized in consciousness or self-consciousness only through the interior actualization of the eschatological judgment of death. Even as sin came into the world through the act of one man and death through sin, and so death spread to all men because all men sinned, so one man's act of justification leads to acquittal and life for all men. That act of justification is the death of Christ Jesus, whom God put forward as an expiation by his blood: only by that "blood" does justification occur, for redemption or reconciliation to God is realized only by and in the death of God's Son (Romans 5). And Christ died for the ungodly, for even while we were enemies of God Christ died for us, and it is precisely our realization of the redemptive identity and actuality of that death which makes manifest and real to us our own eternal death in sin.

Accordingly, we can know that Christ's death is "for us" only by knowing our own eternal death, only by realizing and actualizing a total impotence of the will, an impotence whereby and wherein our "I" passes into a totality of sin. This is that "I" that speaks for the first time in history in the voice of self-consciousness, a voice that can speak only by way of a newly realized negativity, an interior negativity reflecting the advent of an interior otherness. Thus an absolute or total otherness is the necessary and inevitable consequence of the eschatological advent of a free and total grace. The death of the Second Adam is a repetition of the death of the First Adam, and repetition because each death is both an originating and a total event. But the actual repetition of original death negates the negativity of original sin, as this negation of negation realizes a new eon or new creation. Thus the new creation or new eon which triumphs in the Resurrection of Christ is inseparable from the birth of an absolutely new identity and actuality of the old eon or old creation. For the first time an absolutely guilty or absolutely active negative identity is realized as the full or total identity of consciousness itself, and that identity actually speaks in the historical birth of self-consciousness.

Self-consciousness is the voice of the negation of negation, the interior voice of the death of sin. Thereby it is a repetition of the Crucifixion, a repetition whereby the ultimacy and actuality of eternal death passes into consciousness. Thus self-consciousness is established and realized as the interior repetition of the Crucifixion, a repetition wherein death is conquered by calling forth the totally negative identity of death. That totally negative identity here becomes actual and real in the new and internal birth of the absolutely negative "I." While that "I" is the innermost voice of consciousness itself, it is so only insofar and inasmuch as consciousness has become other than itself. For it is the advent of interior otherness which releases the self-identity of self-consciousness, thereby embodying the otherness of consciousness as the identity of itself. Death is the name of our innermost self-identity, an identity that is manifest or that realizes itself only in the event of Crucifixion. Crucifixion is that eschatological event which calls forth and makes real the totality of Fall, but also and even thereby it is that eschatological event which issues in the end or reversal of that fallen totality in Resurrection.

Paul establishes Crucifixion and Resurrection as the polar identities of each other. They are eschatological events that are not only enacted by Christ but are repeated or renewed in the new life of the Spirit, a life wherein and whereby a new eon or new creation is realized and established. If death is swallowed up in victory, the victory of the Resurrection, it is thereby and only thereby that death is most fully itself, and not only most fully itself but also most actual and real. The full actuality of the "blood" of Christ internally issues in the self-alienation of consciousness, a doubling of consciousness wherein consciousness appears and is real to itself as its own other. That doubling of consciousness is consciousness's own resurrection, as the self-alienation of consciousness becomes the arena and the world wherein consciousness not only first becomes aware of itself, but wherein it actualizes or makes real a new eon or new totality of interior actuality. The advent of the interior totality of Spirit is actualized by the eschatological event of the Crucifixion. That actualization is realized in the Resurrection of Christ, as the expiation effected by the death of Christ annuls the finality of sin and guilt.

Thereby sin and guilt pass into the center of consciousness, but they do so only as negated or self-negated actualities, for "one man's act of justification" (Romans 5:18) is the self-negation of the guilt of all, a self-negation eschatologically realizing the negation of the original negation of death. Only thereby does the original actuality and totality of death first stand forth in consciousness, and it stands forth in consciousness as a negated actuality, and as a self-negated actuality, as Resurrection transforms death into life by calling life from death itself. Resurrection can only actually be realized in consciousness as Crucifixion, as a real and actual death, even if that death is the death of death itself. But that death is the self-negation of death, a death realizing itself in the birth of self-alienation, a self-alienation wherein the pure and integral otherness of consciousness realizes itself as the innermost center or "I" of consciousness itself. Consciousness then realizes itself as the otherness of itself. Only as that otherness is consciousness resurrected from death, for then death ceases to be alien and apart by passing into the center of self-identity itself.

It is noteworthy that there is no record in the prophetic tradition of a full interior awareness or consciousness of sin. Jeremiah's reference to an "evil heart" (7:24) falls far short of a Pauline consciousness of sin, just as Jeremiah's confessions and dialogues with the Lord always sustain the integrity and strength of the prophetic "I." For even if the greater strength of the Lord has deceived that "I" (20:7), and the word of the Lord has become a reproach and derision all day long for the prophet, the mocking to which the prophet is submitted is simply the consequence of a genuinely prophetic call. Most remarkably of all, the "I" of Jeremiah can stand forth in the presence of the Lord, and stand forth in dignity and strength, calling upon the Lord as its refuge in the day of evil. For the words of the Lord became to that "I" a joy and a delight to its heart (15:16). While Jeremiah knows that the "heart" is deceitful above all things and desperately corrupt (17:9), so that none can understand it, the "I" of the Lord searches the mind and tries the heart, to give to every man according to his ways and the fruit of his actions. Then cursed is the man who trusts in man and blessed is the man who trusts in the Lord. Such blessing is closed to Paul, for whom an interior trust in the Lord is impossible, and impossible because the interior "I" is an "I" of sin.

Nevertheless, it is significant that the Book of Jeremiah records a fuller presence of self-consciousness than does any other prophetic book, for here one also finds the clearest awareness of the sinful "heart." But there is no sign in the Book of Jeremiah of genuine self-laceration, the curse to which Jeremiah is submitted is the curse of a prophetic calling, and while the devastating weight of that calling undoubtedly contributes to a new sense of the depth and independence of the "I," that "I" itself never here appears as guilty. Nowhere in the world before Paul is there a record of an interior conscioiusness which knows itself as guilty. Its nearest counterpart is perhaps the Buddhist understanding of the chain of causation or dependent origination, which expresses the doctrine that all physical and psychical phenomena are conditioned by antecedent factors, thereby making possible a realization of the illusion of a permanently or continually existing ego. The Buddhist can know that all existence is pain, suffering, and evil (*dukkha*); but the full realization of this knowledge releases its knower from the actuality of selfhood, an actuality which is here illusory and unreal. Paul, too, can know interior selfhood to be unreal, but it is spiritually unreal, and spiritually unreal because of the overwhelming actuality of the carnal "I" of sin.

The Pauline dichotomy between "flesh" and Spirit is the arena of the guilty conscience: here is where the indicative and the imperative now for the first time stand forth as opposites, and here is where sin and death first become manifest as the totality of existence. An ever more fully dawning apocalyptic judgment is the source of the realization of this dichotomy. In response to this all-consuming judgment the strength and righteousness of the "I" collapses, thereby unveiling the fleshly "I" as the "I" of sin. But this unveiling is possible only by way of the actual presence of apocalyptic judgment. This is a judgment effecting a sentence of eternal death upon the Old Adam, a sentence which even now is present in our guilty conscience. In this perspective, the guilty conscience is the consequence of the real presence of apocalyptic judgment, apart from that presence consciousness cannot know itself as guilty, nor could the guilty conscience as such exist. The actual presence of final or eternal judgment is a negative presence; indeed, it is a fully and totally negative presence, a presence before which all actual existence becomes guilty. Paul knows that presence as the consequence of Crucifixion and Resurrection, the inevitable consequence of the actualization of redemption, a redemption through which and in which the Old Adam comes to an end.

Thus to know the "I" as the "I" of sin is to know the presence of redemption. Only the actual presence of the New Adam makes manifest the totality of the Old Adam of sin and death, a presence which is actually present in the consuming fire of apocalyptic judgment. Total judgment is the interior identity of final redemption, a judgment interiorly calling forth or fully actualizing sin and guilt, for Resurrection is the interior actualization of eternal death. Hence the Resurrection of Christ is the consummation of the Crucifixion, a consummation in which the justifying act of Christ's death fully annuls the guilt of original sin, but does so only where the full actuality of original sin is actual and real in consciousness itself. The guilty conscience is the fruit of Resurrection, the internalization and interiorization of justification. The "I" released by Resurrection is the "I" who has been crucified with Christ, and if it is no longer "I" who lives but Christ who lives in me (Galatians 2:20), this is because the "I" has fully passed into death and is now manifest and real only as the carnal "I" of sin.

Consequently, sin and guilt are the self-embodiment of death, and total sin and eternal death are the self-embodiment of the atoning death of Christ. The forgiveness of sin is the birth or actual advent of Spirit. But the birth of Spirit is the death of the Old Adam or "I," a birth and death which for the first time establishes and makes actual and real an absolute dichotomy between self-consciousness and grace. The birth of self-consciousness, of a full and actual self-consciousness, is a consequence of the advent of the new aeon of the Spirit. It is the full and interior advent of Spirit which actualizes an absolute dichotomy between flesh and Spirit, and for the first time flesh or the old creation is manifest and real as a totality of death, a death that speaks in the new voice of self-consciousness. Now an apocalyptic war rages between flesh and Spirit, a war never hitherto present, and only the approach or the presence of that war makes manifest or real the new identity of sin and death as "I." Only now am I fully impotent and guilty, a guilt and an impotence which never before had been realized in consciousness, for only the internalization and interiorization of death makes possible that self-division and doubling of consciousness which issues in the birth of self-consciousness.

The advent of self-consciousness is a consequence of the Crucifixion of Christ. For if our "old man" was crucified with him so that sin might be destroyed, we are thereby united with him and fashioned into the likeness of his death, and only thereby are we united with his Resurrection (Romans 6:5). Only one who is dead is set free from sin, and we live with Christ only by having died with Christ, for only crucifixion with Christ actualizes the death of sin, the death of death itself. Now the death of death is the death of our "old man," the death of the "I" of sin, and that death and only that death is Resurrection. Resurrection is the advent of the death of death. For it is that advent and that advent alone which makes manifest and real the totality of death, a totality which becomes real for us when we are crucified with Christ, and only then is our "old man" actual for us as our "I." Then our "I" is actual and real as the absolute otherness of our new life in Christ, and it is the full and interior presence of absolute otherness which actualizes a total dichotomy within the very center of consciousness. Then and only then is the "I" manifest and real to itself as the "I" of sin, for then and only then is there an "I" which knows itself, and knows itself as the absolute otherness of the new life of Resurrection.

If the motif of crucifixion with Christ determines Paul's theology, it no less determines his anthropology, an anthropology wherein we know ourselves by knowing and realizing our death in Christ. Our union with Christ is the baptism of death (Romans 6:4), and only by being baptized into his death do we know ourselves, and know ourselves as the "I" of death. Thus self-knowledge is the knowledge of death, and self-consciousness is the consciousness of death, for self-knowledge and self-consciousness can be actual and real only when selfhood knows its absolute otherness as its own. And we know our otherness as our own by knowing a new life in Christ or Spirit. Anyone who is in Christ is a new creation, the old has passed away, and the new has come (II Corinthians 5:17). Only by way of the death of the "old man" does the new creation come: it is the full actualization of the voidness, nothingness, emptiness, or guilt of the "I" of sin that inaugurates the new creation. But that actualization realizes a full and actual identity of the "old man," and that identity actually speaks in and through the new carnal "I," as death and guilt now knows itself as its own "I." Thereby eternal death or absolute otherness comes to an end as an alien and exterior otherness. Death in itself has passed away, now death is fully actual and real only as an internal and interior reality, only as self-consciousness itself.

When pure negativity passes into the very center of consciousness, it realizes itself as consciousness itself, as a doubled and divided consciousness, a self-alienated consciousness whose alienation lies at the center of itself. Then self-alienation becomes manifest and real as the source and ground of consciousness itself, and the otherness of death and guilt become real as the otherness of consciousness itself, an otherness which knows itself as its own "I." Now absolute otherness is "I" myself, it is wholly internalized and interiorized as the integral otherness of itself. Finally otherness is itself only insofar as it is within itself, only insofar as it is finally and irrevocably within. Thereby a within is fully actualized which is its own otherness, an otherness which is itself, which is "I." The actualization of this dichotomy is the actualization of a pure internal and interior dichotomy, a self-dichotomy which is self-consciousness. For consciousness can be conscious of itself only by being other than itself, only by realizing itself as its own otherness, an otherness which is the object of consciousness, but simultaneously the subject as well.

Although it was Paul who first understood Resurrection as the polar or dialectical identity of Crucifixion, and thereby unveiled Crucifixion and Resurrection as one eschatological event, Paul also employed a triumphant and non-dialectical identity of Spirit which is dissociated from the weakness and suffering of the crucified Christ, a non-dialectical and non-eschatological form of Spirit that soon was to dominate the faith of the Church. Nowhere is this more evident than in the first letter of Paul to the Corinthians — and ironically so, since Paul's Corinthian opponents were Hellenistic Christians who believed that even now they were living the full glory of the Resurrection, a glory transcending both a future resurrection and the passion of the cross. The "spiritual men" of Corinth live in a Lord of glory who delivers them from the tribulations of the flesh. But Paul in his opening chapter to these spiritual Christians insists that God chose what is foolish, weak, and low in the world, even things that are not, to bring to nothing the things that are. God alone is the source of life in Christ, therefore there can be no boasting, and Paul declares that he decided to know nothing among the Corinthians except Jesus Christ and him crucified. The theme of Crucifixion dominates the first two chapters of this letter, and no mention of Resurrection occurs here, but when Resurrection becomes the center of the letter in the fifteenth chapter, the theme of Crucifixion is muted, and there is present only a Christ or Lord of glory.

Paul's disjunction of the crucified Christ and the Christ of glory is not a mere literary accident in this letter, for that disjunction soon overwhelmed the Church, and it is the spiritual Corinthians and not the apocalyptic Paul who would have been most at home in the fully developed Christian Church of the second century. One consequence of Paul's dissociation of Crucifixion and Resurrection in the conclusion of this letter is that death assumes a spiritual and dualistic meaning, as mortality is wholly distinguished from immortality and death is distinguished from sin. Although sin has been overcome by Christ, death remains the last enemy to be destroyed (I Corinthians 15:26). Thus it is conquered not by the Crucifixion and Resurrection of Christ but only by the final resurrection, a resurrection of a wholly spiritual and imperishable body, and a resurrection that cannot be inherited by flesh and blood. Here, it would appear that Paul has been vanquished by the "spiritual" Christians, for while he has postponed a wholly spiritual life of the Christian until the final resurrection, then that life will fully triumph, and the appointed time has grown very short (7:29). Now despite the fact that this portrait of life in the Spirit is wholly transcended by Paul's somewhat later and far more mature understanding in Romans 8, a dialectical understanding which unites both the events and the identities of Crucifixion and Resurrection, it is nonetheless true that it is the earlier and non-dialectical and non-eschatological vision of Spirit in I Corinthians 15 which was destined to become both the orthodox doctrine of the Church and the dominant image of death and immortality in Christendom.

Thereby a foundation is established for a spiritual life and identity that is wholly dissociated from death, a resurrected life of the Spirit that simply and literally transcends sin and guilt, as Christ becomes the spiritual Adam from heaven who is totally dissociated from the physical Adam from earth and dust. Therein Resurrection becomes simply and only exaltation, an ascension into heaven, and Christ becomes simply and only the Christ of glory who reigns in heaven. Even if nothing could be further from the real Paul who is clearly and openly manifest in the greater portion of his genuine letters, this is the Paul who was accepted as the apostle to the Gentiles by the Patristic Church, a Paul who again and again had to be deconstructed and reversed throughout all the later history of the West. Yet it was the original and radical and apocalyptic Paul who is the father of self-consciousness, a self-consciousness which became the driving energy in the West, and a self-consciousness which from Augustine through Joyce has been the primary site for the realization of the Western Christian identity of God.

Chapter Five

Augustine and the Foundation of Western Christendom

There is no more profound insight into the historical actuality of Christianity and the Christian Church than Nietzsche's aphorism that Christianity is the stone upon the grave of Jesus. Certainly the history of religions records no reversal of an original way as deep and comprehensive as that effected by the Christian Church in the first three generations of its existence. But not until the explosive advent of Islam does the birth of a religion so rapidly issue in a full historical triumph. Such a triumph surely would not have been possible for a Jewish apocalyptic sect, or not possible unless that sect undergoes a radical metamorphosis, a metamorphosis so radical that historically considered it is not possible to see any genuine continuity between the original Jewish sect and the Hellenistic Catholic church. At no point is this transformation more total than in the celebration of immortality or eternal life in the Patristic Church, a celebration seemingly dominating the life of a persecuted and underground Christianity, and then becoming all in all in the post-Constantinian but pre-Gothic Church. Of course, so far as artifacts and monuments are concerned our knowledge of the life of the pre-Constantinian Church is almost wholly based on memorials to the dead, but this fact itself is not without significance, and the language and iconography of the catacombs is in full continuity with Patristic Christian literature.

Once it was common to interpret Patristic Christianity as the

Hellenization of a primitive and Jewish Christianity, but no Hellenistic mystery cult so centers its life upon death and immortality as does the Patristic Church, and while persecution and martyrdom could understandably issue in an acceptance of death, nowhere else in history can one discover such a comprehensive and passionate longing for death, a passion that although checked was not reversed by the Constantinian triumph of the Church. Already in baptism the Christian is not only initiated but is also incorporated into eternal life, a life which is continually renewed in the mystery of the Eucharist, and is not interrupted by the event of death. Such redemption is eternal peace in the celestial paradise of Christ, a Christ who in the earliest Christian art is the Shepherd of souls and the Teacher of Eternal Life, and after Constantine this early esoteric figure passes into the Teacher of True Wisdom. There is no sign throughout this iconographic tradition of a suffering or crucified Christ, and it is not until the fifth century that representations of the Crucifixion occur in Christian art, but then they are virtually shapeless, for only in the sixth century does the Crucifixion actually become present in Christian art.

One of the many ironies of the Constantinian victory of the Church was the movement to the East of the center and the capital of the Roman Empire, henceforth the city of Rome lay completely outside of the sphere of imperial administration and culture, and the Western Church was destined to a peripheral and provincial life until the birth of the Carolingian age. Nevertheless, this was the period that witnessed the full establishment of the Western Church, even if dogmatically it was so largely a reflection of the Eastern Church. But it was not wholly an echo of Byzantine Christianity, and above all so not in its interior consciouisness and sensibility, as manifest not only in its art and architecture, but far more fundamentally in its theological thinking. And then and only then in the history of Western thought was theological thinking the fount and origin of thinking as a whole, as a new and radical theological thinking soon established itself as a primary center and ground of Western Christendom, a thinking that has not wholly or even substantially been dislodged in the intervening centuries. Augustine can truly be said to be the real fouunder of Western Christendom, for his thinking not only decisively established the doctrinal contours of the Western Church, it more fundamentally gave birth to a theological thinking that was interior and cosmic at once, a thinking that was simultaneously a universal and a fully individual thinking, thereby establishing for the first time in history the subject of consciousness as the sole ground for a universal horizon and world.

Not until Augustine's *Confessions* does self-consciousness first fully realize itself in any form, for not only is the *Confessions* the first extant autobiography, and therefore may justly be said to be the creator of that genre, it is also the first full work of any kind in which self-consciousness is present and realized as a grounding center, a center which was destined to become a primal ground of Western culture and society as a whole. The Augustinian "I" is a truly new selfhood, for even if it is a rebirth of a Pauline self-consciousness, that rebirth did not occur until Augustine, and only with and in Augustine does that rebirth become universal and all comprehensive. Of course, the Augustinian "I" is not a solitary ego, this is an "I" that knows itself only insofar as it is known by God (*Confessions*, X, i), for even if the "I" is one alone (X, vii), it nevertheless knows about itself only through the light and grace of God (X, v). Accordingly, the Augustinian 'I" or self-consciousness is a response to and even an immanent reflection of a truly new transcendence of God, for it is just as fully present and real in its immanent presence in consciousness as it is in its transcendent presence in Heaven.

Nothing is more revolutionary in Augustinian thinking than its apprehension of the self-consciousness of God. This first occurs theologically in the final book of the *Confessions*, which calls forth the Trinitarian identity of the Creator, and then becomes a major theme of the treatises on the Trinity and the City of God. While it could be said that an awareness of the self-consciousness of God is an inevitable consequence of the birth of the Augustinian self-consciousness, such an awareness is wholly alien to Augustine's Pauline source, just as it is to all pre-Augustinian Christian traditions, therefore it may be said to be decisive for the Augustinian revolution. Moreover, there is no trace of such a self-consciousness in Augustine's Plotinian and Neoplatonic sources, nor in any expression of the Classical tradition, whether pre- or post-Christian. Not until Augustine does the "I" of God become manifest as an immanent as well as a transcendent identity, indeed, an immanent identity that is simultaneously and even thereby a transcendent identity, as for the first time a subjective identity is realized as a universal identity, a universal identity that is the essential and integral source of all identity whatsoever.

Moreover, it is the immanent source of our deepest identity, of our self-identity, which calls forth a recognition of an image of God in ourselves. And this is an image of the divine Trinity itself, for as Augustine declares in the City of God: "We resemble the divine Trinity in that we exist; we know that we exist, and we are glad of this existence and this knowledge" (XI, 26, Bettenson translation). Above all this image establishes its reality for us, and its ultimate reality, in our certainty of our existence, "the certainty that I exist, that I know it, and that I am glad of it" (XI, 26), a certainty that is independent of any imaginary and deceptive fantasies. Such a certainty is only born with the Augustinian self-consciousness, for this is a self-consciousness that is integrally and simultaneously conscious of God and the soul, wherein the depths of the soul or of the "I" are a true even if distant image of God, and of the depths of God. Hence this image both mirrors and embodies the Trinity. That embodiment speaks and realizes itself in our certainty of our own existence, a certainty which the "I" truly and fully knows, and a certainty which rejoices in this very knowledge, for it summons us to become close to the fullness of God in our resemblance.

Perhaps at no point is Augustine more distant from the Classical world than in his certainty that no one would wish himself not to exist. Our fear of death is a consequence of our deep revulsion from annihilation, and Augustine is persuaded that even the most wretched would certainly be overjoyed to choose perpetual misery rather than to perish utterly, a persuasion that is not unrelated to his obsession with Hell and damnation. Nothing is deeper within us than our dread of annihilation, a dread that is present even in our love of knowledge, for Augustine believes that anyone would rather remain rational and be sorrowful than to lose one's reason and be joyful. Indeed, this dread of annihilation proceeds from the presence of God within us, a presence awakening a sense of our own lost immortality. Nothing is so bitter as that sense, for the certainty of this sense is the reverse of our certainty of existence. Here lies the supreme paradox of the Augustinian consciousness and sensibility, for nothing is closer to us than the presence of God, a presence that is closer to us than the presence of ourselves. Indeed, it is only the divine presence that makes possible and actualizes the fullness of self-presence. Yet self-presence and the certainty of self-presence is a negative presence, for it inevitably evokes an awareness of the contingency and mortality of our existence, a mortality that is the true otherness of the goodness of existence, and yet a mortality which is inseparable from everything which we can actually know as existence.

No thinker in history has been so driven by conflicting and opposing currents and influences, both internal and external, as was Augustine. At no other point is he so clearly a transitional figure between the ancient and the modern world. Nothing could be further apart than are the Plotinian and Pauline poles which most decisively shaped his thinking, and nothing could be more interiorly distant than Augustine's polar consciousness of sin and grace. Existence is at once both wholly good and wholly fallen, it is the product of the goodness and grace of God alone, and yet it is wholly turned against its Creator. No genuine thinker has been so profoundly other-worldly as Augustine, and yet no other thinker has had such a profound sense of the goodness of being. This is a goodness even issuing from the contingency of existence, for that contingency is a consequence not only of the Creation but also of the eternal and continual presence of God, a presence apart from which nothing whatsoever would or could exist. This sense of contingency is not fully born until Augustine, for not until Augustine is there an interior consciousness of the absolute immanence of God, an immanence which is present and which is fully present in existence itself. This is why we rejoice in the knowledge of the certainty of our existence, for thereby we know the presence of God, a presence which is the deepest ground of existence or being.

But the nearness of God is also the distance of God, for if God is present in every fleeting moment of existence, and if apart from this presence there would be no existence, God is also distant in that very presence. A decisive sign of that distance is the unrest and turbulence of existence, a turbulence reflecting and embodying a profound discord at the very center of existence. There are Augustinian moments in which this discord, and the very actuality of movement and motion itself, is declared to be finally unreal, as witness this comment in the *City of God*, which is intended to bring his beloved Plato within the compass of Scripture:

> But what impresses me most, and almost brings me to agree that Plato cannot have been unacquainted with the sacred books, is that when the angels gave Moses the message from God, and Moses asked the name of him who gave the command to go and free the Hebrew people from Egypt, he received his reply, "I AM HE WHO IS, and you will say to the sons of Israel, HE WHO IS has sent me to you." This implies that in comparison with him who really *is*, because he is unchangeable, the things created changeable have no real existence. This truth Plato vigorously maintained and diligently taught.
>
> (VIII, 11 Bettenson translation)

Needless to say, Augustine's Plato is a Neoplatonic Plato. But it is not only this tradition that can lead Augustine on occasion to divorce time and eternity, but also his very apprehension of the absolute existence of God.

Already in his seminal discussion of time in the eleventh book of the *Confessions*, Augustine maintains that we cannot rightly say what time *is*, except by reason of its impending state of *not being* (14). This is why in eternity all is present, whereas in time all is never present at once (11). Accordingly, the creation is not a new act, and there is no new will in the creation, for God wills all that He wills simultaneously, in one act, and eternally (XII, 15). This understanding of time and eternity evolves into a doctrine of providence in the *City of God* wherein God has foreknowlege of all future events, knowing unchangeably all which shall be, and even our wills have just as much power as God willed and foreknew (V, 9). This leads inevitably to the central Augustinian problem of the freedom of the will, perhaps the real center of Western theological thinking, and a center that becomes real only in the context of the simultaneous presence of the fullness of the will itself and the finality of the eternal act of God.

God's will and God's act, just as God's will and God's being, are one. In that unity of will and being or act and will God is immanent and transcendent at once, so that His immanence is therein and thereby indistinguishable from His transcendence. A fully comparable coincidence is present and real in the depths of our consciousness, for as those depths realize themselves in the fullness of self-consciousness, we realize ourselves to be simultaneously an embodiment of sin and grace. We are a consequence of grace by virtue of the very presence of existence itself, an existence which of itself and in itself is only and wholly good, and yet which in its interior presence for us is turned against itself, by virtue of our rebellious will, a perverse and fallen will which at its very center rebels against its Creator. That fallen will is inevitably present and manifest in the fullness of self-consciousness, for the fullness of individual selfhood is for us the fullness of the individual will. Our will is the antithesis of the will of God, for whereas God's will is one with His being, our will is turned against our being, our true and essential being, because we will to be the sole source and author of our own individual existence.

Pride is the beginning of all sin, it is the source of the fall of both humanity and of the fallen angels, and both in preferring themselves to God chose a lower degree of existence, and therefore sank to a lower state of being. But if pride is the source of this sin or evil it is not its cause. For nothing causes an evil will, since it is the evil will itself which causes the evil act, and an evil choice proceeds not from a nature or being, but rather from a deficiency of being deriving from our having been created from nothing (*City of God*, XII, 6). An evil choice never consists in a defection to things which are evil in themselves, it is the defection in itself that is evil, for there is nothing whose existence or nature is evil. Evil choice and evil itself consists solely in falling away from God and deserting Him. Although evil diminishes and corrupts the goodness of nature or being, it does so only in the consequent deficiency of its own will, a deficiency which is itself an absence or privation of goodness or being, so that sin or evil in itself gives witness to the intrinsic goodness of existence. That goodness is not even compromised by the birth of "flesh," for flesh for Augustine is that lust of the body which is in opposition to spirit, a lust that is born with original sin, whereby and wherein the original disobedience of the will fulfills itself in the body's disobedience to the soul.

So it is that the first act of Adam and Eve after the Fall is to cover their *pudenda*, their organs of shame, for while these organs remain physically the same, now for the first time they become shameful. This is a shame reflecting the disobedience of the "flesh," a disobedience which immediately seizes power over the whole man. And the most decisive sign of this ultimately and fatally pathological condition is the advent of sexual orgasm. Sexual orgasm did not exist before the Fall, for it is a consequence of a new dichotomy between the body and the soul, a violently discordant state in which passion and mind are wholly unlike but wholly commingled, thus making possible a pleasure surpassing all physical delight, a pleasure culminating in a climax wherein the mind is overwhelmed (*City of God*, XIV, 16). This is the very moment and condition that makes possible the transmission of original sin, the one moment in which mind is wholly absent, a moment of lust in its purest form, and also the moment in which the will is least free. Each of us has our origin in this moment of pure lust, whereby the sin of Adam becomes the sin of all, and our actual origin becomes the very opposite of our origin in the Creation.

Nothing more fully embodies Augustine's understanding of the radical deficiency of evil or the sinful will than his conception of sexual orgasm. Here his theological genius is at is fullest height, for not only does he fully conjoin his Plotinian and his Pauline roots in this conception, but thereby and precisely thereby he fully brings together an interior and psychological language and understanding with an ontological and theological understanding. Theology will not again realize such an integral and unitary mode of understanding until Kierkegaard and Nietzsche, nor is it elsewhere present in Augustine's work, even if his work as a whole continually strives for some such resolution. That resolution was denied Augustine himself, save at this one point, and it is not insignificant that the Christendom which he founded became the most sexually repressive culture and society in history. But Augustine believed that the Great Mother surpassed all the gods, her sons, in the enormity of her wickedness, a wickedness present above all in that sexual mutilation which she demands of her devotees. Nothing so arouses Augustine's horror as this mutilation (*City of God*, VII, 26), for compared with this ultimate horror all the crimes of the gods fade into nothing. The greatness of this horror is appropriate only to the Great Mother, and precisely as Mother, for thereby she is the sexual origin or womb of the world. Not until Freud's discovery of the Oedipus complex will thinking once again realize the sexual origin, and the pathologically sexual origin, of a fallen or repressed consciousness and identity.

It is not until Augustine that sexual passion or lust is realized and portrayed as being simultaneously an external and an internal bondage. At no other point is Augustine further from his great Classical predecessor, Euripides. Moreover, it is in his understanding of lust or concupiscence that Augustine most clearly and most decisively realizes his revolutionary psychological understanding, for here he makes fully concrete his conception of the will as being wholly enslaved and yet nevertheless free. For he incorporates this understanding not only in his self-portrait in the *Confessions*, but again and again throughout his work. In the *Confessions*, Augustine most decisively moves toward conversion when he realizes that we do evil because we choose to do so of our own free will. But initially he thinks that if we do anything against our will it seems to be something which happens to us rather than something which we actually do (VII, 3). And that which happens to us which most draws us away from the beauty of God and transcendence is the weight that we carry in the habit of our flesh, and even when Augustine in an instant of awe knew in his mind the light and sight of the God who IS, he recoiled and fell back into his old ways, carrying with him nothing but the memory of the God whom he had loved and longed for (VII, 17). Yet gradually he comes to realize that it is his own will that enchains him:

> For my will was perverse and lust had grown from it, and when I gave in to lust habit was born, and when I did not resist the habit it became a necessity. These were the links which together formed what I have called my chain, and it held me fast in the duress of servitude. But the new will which had come to life in me and made me wish to serve you freely and enjoy you, my God, who are our only certain joy, was not yet strong enough to overcome the old, hardened as it was by the passage of time. So these two wills within me, one old, one new, one the servant of the flesh, the other of the spirit, were in conflict and between them they tore my soul apart. (VIII, 5 Pine-Coffin translation)

Thus his inner self was a house divided against itself, although he was beside himself with a madness that would bring him sanity, and dying a death that would bring him life.

No more was required for that sanity and life than an act of the will, a resolute and total act of the will, and one that will realize what it wills. But that is just what is impossible for him in this moment of agony. Whereas the mind can give an order to the body and it is at once obeyed, when it gives an order to itself, it is resisted. Then the mind does not carry out its own command, and this because it does not fully will to do this, and insofar as it does not will the order is not carried out. Now the reason why the command is not obeyed is that it is not given with the full will, for if the will were full, it would not command itself to be full, since it would be so already (VIII, 9).

This is a disease of the mind, wherein there are two wills within us, a carnal and a spiritual will, neither by itself is the whole will, and each possesses what the other lacks. Augustine's deliverance from this bondage is a true miracle of grace, one that would thereafter imprint upon him the never wavering conviction that justification is by grace, and by grace alone, for only the grace of God can deliver us from that innermost disease of our mind and will. And this disease is most fully and most clearly manifest in our lust, a lust that overwhelms us by its power and delight, and a lust that we will even when we would resist it. For our resistance to lust can never be a full resistance, and this because that "spiritual" will which wills this resistance is not and cannot be for us a full will, and the decisive sign of this is the very "will" of the spiritual will.

For Augustine the most remarkable feature of the sexual sphere is its involuntariness. Nevertheless we know from within that we will concupiscence with our own free will. So far from simply happening to us as though it visited us from without, it is present at the very center of the activity of the will, and is so most firmly when it occurs most involuntarily. This is precisely the point at which Augustine realizes the overwhelming reality of original sin, and its consequence that *massa perditionis*, which is sin and judgment at once. For it is the judgment of sin that we do the evil we would not. This is the judgment that is eternal death, and it is a judgment that we enact within ourselves in every moment of concupiscence, for each such moment is at once an involuntary and a freely willed moment, a moment in which our own wills are unquestionably present, as witness that unique delight released by lust, a delight which is so fully our own, and yet the very power of lust is wholly beyond us even if wholly within us, and this beyondness of lust is what most enslaves us, and does so even if it is our own immediate ground and source. Now we can fully recognize that we are born of lust, that lust is that which we most passionately will, and that such a will in its innermost center is a divided will. For it is a will that can never will concupiscence without willing against itself, and therefore can never will concupiscence without internally realizing its own guilt, and yet it can never will not to lust, or not do so fully and decisively, and this because the divided will is by necessity an incomplete or partial will, and therefore can never fully and wholly will.

The Augustinian God is at the very center of our life, our consciousness, and our existence. Yet it is that Unchangeable Light which is wholly other than our everchanging and deeply mortal contingency. And we are at once the image of that Unchangeable Light and its very opposite, the eternal death of the *massa perditionis*. Indeed, the eternal death of divine judgment is a necessary and inevitable consequence of our rebellion against God. For that rebellion realizes an inversion of the image of God, an inversion wherein our nature and identity retains that image but only in an inverse form, so that the center of our existence is simultaneously wholly good and wholly damned. For we are integrally and essentially good simply insofar as we exist, and yet we are actually mortal and totally corrupt in the actuality of our fallen will, as above all manifest in the inevitability with which we sin. Now that sin is truly sin, it is the product and consequence of our will, and of our free will, for it is a will that remains free even in its bondage. Therein most deeply lies the presence of the image of God within us even now, and that is a presence which we can never escape, even if it is also a presence which is the most immediate source of our damnation. But the presence of the fallen will is presence and absence at once. It is a will which actually exists and acts, and yet it acts only by way of a deficiency of the will, a deficiency which is simultaneously a deficiency of goodness and being, and it is in and as that very deficiency that our full actuality inevitably and necessarily sins. Augustine fully prepared the way for those later Augustinians who will discover glory in our damnation, for damnation is possible only for those who exist in and as the image of God, and Augustine can close the *City of God* with the affirmation that the redeemed saints in the Heavenly City, while having no sensible recollection of past evils, will nevertheless know the eternal misery of the damned, for how else could they sing the mercies of the Lord?

Augustine opens the ninth book of the *Confessions* rejoicing that his Lord has broken the chains that bound him, chains that impelled him to will every possible evil, and all that a merciful Lord asked of this sinner was that he deny his own will and accept the will of the Lord. That will is goodness itself, a goodness which is simply and only itself and no other, for the *summum bonum* is the *summum esse*, the Supreme Being is the Supreme Good. That is an identity which Augustine does not realize until his conversion, for not until then does he live in a "will" that is goodness and reality at once, a "will" that is fully and only itself, and therefore a "will" that can and does fully, and totally, and actually, will. At all these points that "will" is wholly other than our own; and its full presence simultaneously both demands and effects the transformation or conversion of our will, for an acceptance of the will of the Lord is necessarily a denial of our own. Now such a presence of God is at once an eternal and a momentary presence. It is eternal in the one and only act of God, an act whereby God is and only is Himself, and an act whereby and wherein He is eternally present. But that eternal presence actualizes itself as a momentary presence to us in the moment in which our fallen will decisively enacts its "deficiency," an enactment occurring when we freely accept the will of the Lord.

But that acceptance is a denial of ourselves, a denial of ourselves as a divided will, a will that in warring against itself is impotent in that very war, and therefore a will that *is* only insofar as it is not, a will whose very willing inevitably embodies its alienation from itself. This is that willing and that will which is free and impotent at once: free insofar as it is and exists as will, impotent insofar as it wills to be itself or to be. It is as a fallen and rebellious will that it is an impotent will, for in originally refusing and defying the will of God it therein and thereby turns away from the goodness and reality of God. This is that fall immediately issuing in a privation or deficiency of reality and goodness, a deficiency lying at the core of the divided and therefore impotent will. So it is that the impotent will cannot will even to be itself, for it cannot actually will so as to enact what it wills, and thus cannot fully will. Nothing else so manifestly embodies its deficiency, a deficiency which is never absent when we will, and is fully absent only in that moment when we accept the will of the Lord by denying our own. For that denial is our fulfillment, that death is our life, for only then can a will to be or to exist be fully present within us, and that presence can only be the inner or interior presence of God.

This is a presence and a conversion which founds the Christian mysticism of the West, for it is a divine presence which is inseparable from existence and will itself, from a will which is and only is existence and life. And that will is inseparable from its opposite, inseparable from the absolutely impotent and divided will, a will which is only insofar as it is not, and which is free only insofar as it is enslaved. Yet enslaved it is, and totally and eternally enslaved. But its enslavement is wholly other than the necessity of nature, for it is an enslavement which wills to be enslaved or impotent, and does so and necessarily does so in the very deficiency or emptiness of its nature or being. This is a deficiency or emptiness which is not found outside of the image of God, not found outside of that person who is alone an image of the Trinity itself, and therefore not found outside of or apart from the interior and immanent presence of God. If God wills all that He wills simultaneously, in one act, and eternally, our divided will simultaneously wills itself as an isolated will and as life or existence. But our will as a wholly isolated will is therein and thereby nonexistence or nonwill, and is so because there is no life or existence apart from God. Therefore our isolated will is only insofar as it is not itself, only insofar as it is the creation of God. Consequently, the one and eternal act of God becomes, in the fallen image of God, a divided and a dichotomous act, an act which is only insofar as it is not and which lives and acts only insofar as it is a lacerating and wounding act, and a self-lacerating and self-wounding act that acts only by acting against itself.

The ontological name of pride is quite simply nothingness or nonexistence. Thus the act of pride is a nihilating act, and it acts only by willing or intending nothingness, that very nothingness out of which

God created the world. This is a nothingness which we know as selfhood and selfhood alone, a selfhood isolated from God and creation, and therefore a selfhood which does not and cannot exist. Nevertheless, it is present and actual in the radical deficiency or emptiness of our will, an emptiness which is the essence of the wholly isolated and purely individual will, and an emptiness which manifests its emptiness in the actual bondage of our will. Such an ontological emptiness is identical with sin, and the origin or actual beginning of emptiness is the origin of sin or original sin. Now original sin does not and cannot affect existence or being, because sin neither is nor exists insofar as it is the absence or privation of being. Or, rather, it exists only in the isolated and divided will of the fallen and falling image of God, a perpetually falling inverse image of God, which falls and is falling in every act of its divided and impotent will. Nonetheless, an image of God is present in that division and impotence, and present in the very freedom of the impotent and divided will, a will that is responsible, and wholly responsible, for its every act, a responsibility calling forth, and necessarily and justly calling forth, an eternal judgment of death.

Nothing is more overwhelming in Augustine than his continual affirmation of the freedom of the will, for even if that freedom is illusory in sin, it is freedom nevertheless, as witness the judgment of damnation. So it is that the divided will is free and impotent at once. It freely wills and knows itself to freely will even in its impotence, for the agony of the divided will is possible and actual only by virtue of the presence of the freedom of the will, a presence apart from which guilt would be absent. If only Western culture and society has known a radical and interior guilt, it is only here that we can historically discover a self-consciousness of the freedom of the will. For historically self-consciousness has never occurred apart from a guilty conscience. A guilty conscience has never been more fully present than in Augustine, but it is precisely that presence that made possible Augustine's revolutionary understanding of freedom and grace, an understanding wherein grace is predestination and freedom at once. As Augustine remarks in the *Predestination of the Saints* (Chapter XIX), the only difference between grace and predestination is that predestination is the preparation for grace, while grace is the gift itself. It is predestination which makes grace possible, for apart from predestination the sinner would be wholly closed to grace, and necessarily so by virtue of the very nothingness of his fallen and rebellious will. Predestination alone is the source of the power and the actuality of the conversion and transformation of the sinful will, the potentiality for which is in no way whatsoever present in the empty nothingness of the fallen will. Above all predestination is the primary sign and symbol of the freedom of the will, for not only does it make possible the final freedom of the saints, but it overwhelmingly makes manifest the freedom of the damned, who alone are responsible for their eternal judgment (*The Enchiridion*, XCV-CV), a responsibility which could only be theirs by way of the total absence of the grace of God. That absence is actual in all sin, which is precisely why sin is sin, and it is just because the knowledge of predestination teaches us that no one is saved except by undeserved mercy that we can realize the utter vacuity of sin.

But to know the pure nothingness or the utter vacuity of sin is to know the totality of grace. This is a totality that is absolutely free and absolutely all in all. It is at once the sole source and ground of all life and existence, and nevertheless the absolutely free Will, and a Will that in its very absoluteness is love and being at once. For to know the totality of grace is to know the totality of love, a love that is fully and actually present in predestination, and a predestination that is itself the eternal act of God. Predestination to eternal life is wholly of God's free grace, and thus it is an act of mercy and love, but its corollary, "the permission of what is evil" (*The Enchiridion* XCVI), is permitted only in the justice of God's judgment, and certainly all that is just is good. Consequently, the predestination to eternal life and to eternal death is an act of love and grace. Indeed, it is the act of grace and love, for it is the eternal act of God. Love and justice are one in God's act, so that justice and love are finally and eternally one, and this final unity of justice and love is realized by us when we realize the pure nothingness of evil and sin. Nothing could be further from genuine Manichaeism than this primal Augustinian doctrine of the nothingness of evil, and nothing is a deeper ground of the Augustinian doctrine of the freedom of the will. For that deficiency of will which is the evil will is ours alone, and while permitted by God, it is enacted only by ourselves.

It is in Paul and Augustine that we can discover the roots of that absolute dichotomy which lies at the very center of the Western consciousness. This dichotomy is symbolically present in the uniquely Western Christian antithesis of Heaven and Hell, but internally and interiorly present in an individual will that is wholly imprisoned and yet actually free, and a will that knows itself to be actually free only in those moments when it realizes its total bondage. Augustine's revolutionary understanding of a free and total grace that can be total and free only as a predestinating grace is a full manifestation of a uniquely Western internal identity and will, a will that is profoundly and internally divided against itself, and yet a will whose overwhelming energy proceeds out of that very division. The guilty conscience, indeed, the totally guilty conscience, is quite simply the interior realization of self-consciousness, for that realization can only be a self-embodiment of self-division, a self-embodiment of that dichotomy lying at the center of self-consciousness. And that self-embodiment is inevitably an explosive embodiment, even if only potentially so, for it is an interior realization of a violent polarity of consciousness, a polarity that is in deep opposition to itself, and is so in its very center and ground.

Augustine created a system of religious thought and practise that was destined to be the integral foundation of Western culture and society for well over a thousand years. Anselm of Canterbury will pride himself on saying nothing that Augustine had not said before him, and all of the great medieval Christian schoolmen, including Thomas Aquinas and Meister Eckhart, were religiously and theologically Augustinian, just as were the medieval Christian mystics, and even the founders of the Protestant Reformation. So likewise all the explosive creative and revolutionary currents of Christendom have an

Augustinian ground, a ground that was ironically shared by their conservative and reactionary opponents, for Augustine was the Church theologian par excellence. Never before or since in history has one thinker been the primal source of such violently conflicting forces and movements. Augustine is alone among thinkers, at least until Hegel, in so fully and so purely centering his thinking upon an absolute and internal dichotomy, a dichotomy between God and the soul, yes, but also a dichotomy in which the absolute sovereignty and love of God is internally and interiorly manifest only in the absolute abasement of the subject. That abasement made possible a full self-realization of the subject, a self-realization embodying the explosive energy of the West. But this is a self-realization which is inseparable from a dichotomous ground, and that ground will not become silent or unreal so long as Western culture and society continue to exist.

Chapter Six

Dante and the Gothic Revolution

At no other point was Augustine's influence both more profound and more ambivalent than in his understanding of the two cities in the *City of God*, one city choosing to live by the standard of the "flesh," the other by the standard of the Spirit. The second society is predestined to reign with God for all eternity, while the first is doomed to undergo eternal punishment with Satan (XV, 1), so that the earthly city needs only generation, whereas the heavenly City also needs regeneration to escape the guilt that is the fallen consequence of generation (XV, 16). Augustine himself rarely identifies the City of God with the Catholic Church, but he is capable of identifying the Church with the Kingdom of God and Kingdom of Heaven (XX, 9). Thereby he transposes an originally apocalyptic realm into an ecclesiastical realm, for even if the temporal Church comprehends both saints and sinners, it "even now" is the Kingdom of Christ. Augustine conceived a parallel history of the two cities, and at no point is this parallel so close as it is between the city of Rome and the Catholic Church: for even if Rome is the second Babylon, it was also God's design to conquer the world through her, to unite the world into the single community of the Roman Empire, and so to impose peace throughout its length and breadth (XVIII, 22). All this, of course, is a preparation for the coming of Christ, and it is not insignificant that the *City of God* was Augustine's most widely read and influential book throughout the Middle Ages.

Certainly one of the founders of the Christian Middle Ages was that Augustinian pope, Gregory the Great, who founded the Papal

States in 590, thereby not only making the papal state independent of the Byzantine exarch at Ravenna, but also fully establishing the independence of the Church of Rome from all temporal authority. Although this was possible only in the context of the dissolution of imperial authority in the West, and would be compromised again and again in the future, it nevertheless made possible the advent of the most powerful religious institution in history. But never before or since has a major religious institution arisen in the midst of such darkness and horror, a horror not truly to be matched elsewhere until the twentieth century, and not to be transcended in Western Christendom for some five hundred years. Population figures give us some sense of this catastrophe: during the late Roman Empire the city of Rome contained some 250,000 people, but it had dwindled by Charlemagne's time to no more than 20,000, and Rome was then the most populous city in the West. So likewise the Roman Empire at its height in 200 C.E. had some 46 million subjects, including 28 million of the 36 million people in Europe; by 600 the European total had dropped to 26 million, a 25 percent decline, and it is clear that this drop in population was far greater in the Mediterranean countries than in the north of Europe. Thereafter a transformation occurred, for at the beginning of the fourteenth century the population of Europe was an unprecedented 80 million, thus preparing the way for a violent and comprehensive explosion of Europe.

Carolingian society is the center of the history of the Dark Ages and its one all too isolated and precarious source of light, but this is a totally insular and agrarian society, and the first Christian society which had broken away from the ancient and Classical worlds. If Charlemagne was both the most powerful and the most devout of all Christian monarchs, his reign occurred in a world in which there was no real distinction between Church and State. This was the most clerical society in Western history, and it was also the most militaristic, or the most successfully so, and no other major ruler was so continually occupied with war as was Charlemagne. Throughout the Dark Ages the profession of arms was the sole criterion of nobility, for the nobles were quite simply professional warriors, and thereby was established the three orders or estates of medieval society, those who fought, those who prayed, and those who worked. Yet there were only two social classes in the Dark Ages, the free and the nonfree, only the nobility were free, including the ennobled clergy; and daily life for the vast majority was a continual round of misery, as brutality and violence dominated this world, and virtually everywhere there was indifference to human life and suffering.

Charlemagne's biographer, Einhard, reports that he took great pleasure in listening to recitations from the books of Augustine, and especially so from the *City of God*, for he worshipped morning and evening with great regularity, and throughout his reign nothing was nearer to his heart than that by his own efforts the city of Rome should regain its former proud position. This greatest of Christian monarchs cared more for the church of the holy Apostle Peter in Rome than for any other sacred place, even including the cathedral which he built at Aachen, but he visited Rome only four times in a reign of forty-seven years, perhaps in reaction against being involuntarily crowned Emperor and Augustus by Leo the Great in 800. No Western Empire was created in that coronation, nor a revival of the Roman Empire in the West, and the Carolingian Empire was followed by the greatest chaos in the history of the West. For Western Europe was then decimated by the invasions of Vikings, Saracens, and Magyars, and the Carolingian world disintegrated. Yet out of that disintegration there gradually issued forth the birth of Europe.

Europe was born with the birth of feudalism, a birth that occurred out of the violent dissolution of older societies, and as a consequence of the profound weakening of the authority and the power of the State. Feudalism created or sustained a vast gulf between the impotent masses and a ruling elite, and it entailed the rigorous economic subjugation of a subject peasantry to a ruling class of warrior chiefs, a class which is itself held together only by ties of obedience and protection that bind man to man, thus creating the uniquely European form of vassalage. While vassalage was limited to the upper levels of society, its authority and symbolism permeated the whole of social life, even including religious life, for the ancient attitude of prayer, with arms outstretched, was replaced in the feudal world with the gesture of the joined hands, a gesture clearly borrowed from the feudal ceremony called "homage", in which a man becomes the "man" of another man by swearing an oath of homage. This was a society in which war was the *raison d'être* of every position of social and political authority, and the vassal is simply the lieutenant of a great warrior, at least originally, for it was military authority alone which prevailed in the chaos of the ninth and tenth centuries.

Until the eleventh century, poverty ruled Europe as never before the collapse of the Roman Empire: plague, famine, destruction, and commercial atrophy dominated a thinly populated West, with no towns of more than a few thousand inhabitants, with no significant industries, and with a rural population practising agriculture in adverse circumstances. The vast majority of men were simply powerless, and for them the visible world was either meaningless or filled with evil, except insofar as it gave some sign of eternity. Stability was sought through some physical association with eternity, hence the enormous importance placed upon contact with the relics of saints, and even the Pope in practice owed most of his authority to the fact that he was the guardian of the body of St. Peter. After the Carolingian renaissance Western art regressed for two hundred years, and European art throughout this period was in effect an art of icons. Yet the advent of Romanesque sculpture in the eleventh and twelfth centuries was not simply a rebirth of art in the West. It was a decisive sign of a joyful awakening of society as a whole, an awakening no less present in an enormous commercial revival, as ancient Europe was reborn in a new urban life. For this was the moment of the birth of the European bourgeoisie.

The birth of the European bourgeoisie was quite simply the birth of the medieval city, for whereas cities had dominated the ancient world, they had been virtually absent in the Dark Ages. From its beginning the Roman Empire has been a Mediterranean commonwealth, but with the victory of Islam the Mediterranean largely passed into the Muslim world and Europe became an almost wholly insular and agricultural society. All this was changed with the revival of Europe in the eleventh century, and perhaps the most significant result of the crusades was that shipping passed into Christian control, and the Mediterranean became once again but now far more powerfully a Christian world. The birth or rebirth of the medieval city heralded the advent of a new class in history, the European bourgeoisie, one that appeared seemingly out of nowhere, and one with no actual precedent in either Church or State. Of course, the birth of this class cannot be dissociated from the rebirth of monasticism in the eleventh and twelfth centuries, for following the collapse of the Benedictine monopoly in the late eleventh century, there occurred the founding and comprehensive growth of a wide variety of religious orders that within a hundred years created a new form of Christianity. In the twelfth century, the Cistercians created the first autonomous religious world in the West, equipped with a new interior discipline, a thorough organization for internal supervision, and isolated from external interference. But something very like this new monastic system occurred in the new medieval city, and it was here that even monasticism realized a new form with the birth of the Dominican and Franciscan friars in the thirteenth century.

A new distinction between secular and religious authority arose in the eleventh century, one that had not existed in the Dark Ages, and certainly not in the Carolingian Empire, but one that was destined to create a truly new civilization. Although present in the new monastic life, it was even more comprehensively present in the new cities, and not least because the medieval city was a strictly urban entity. For the first time in history an overwhelming gulf was established between the social and economic organizations of the cities and their distant counterparts in the rural areas. The new merchant communities in the cities created new social and economic organizations, and with the birth of the commune in Cambrai in 1087 a new political organization was created which soon prevailed throughout the urban world.

Both commune cities and other cities realized a new political community, a *universitas*, a *communitas*, a *communio*, all the members of which were united by being answerable to one another, thereby establishing a new political world. True, this world was limited to a small class, but whereas the medieval world had previously recognized only two active orders, the nobility and the clergy, now the middle class was established as a legal and privileged order.

The greatest demand of the new middle class was for personal liberty, a liberty to be sustained by new special tribunals, and one that was soon to become a natural attribute of the full citizen. Already in the twelfth century the new cities had become new states, with their own comprehensive administration and jurisprudence, and sheltered within a fortified enclosure. But this new world was not confined to the city, for a new peasantry was born during this period, as free labor was gradually substituted for serf labor, and before the end of the thirteenth century feudalism was virtually dead in Western Europe. What we have come to call the Gothic world is the world of Western Europe during the twelfth, thirteenth, and early fourteenth centuries, and it is just as fully present in the urban life of the cities as it is in the new architecture and art. Indeed, it is present everywhere in the social, the cultural, and the religious life of this world, for now a new Western civilization is fully born. But unlike the birth of Classical civilization this birth was also the rebirth of an ancient world, a world which is Classical and Christian at once, for it was only with the advent of the Gothic world that the Classical and Christian worlds become united.

Of course, a union between a Biblical faith and community and Classical culture had previously been realized in Islam, and it was through Islam that Western Europe, both Jewish and Christian, was truly initiated into Classical culture. For even if the Carolingian scribes succeeded in preserving the great bulk of what remains to us as Latin literature, the Roman world only actually entered the Carolingian world through the Roman Catholic Church, and the Catholic Church between the late sixth and late eleventh centuries was innocent of all but the rudiments of Classical culture. John Scotus Erigena does appear as a light shining in the darkness of the ninth century, but his writings were condemned and recondemned to destruction, and thereafter exercised only an underground and all but hidden influence. Medieval philosophy as a living tradition is only born with Anselm of Canterbury, and the evolution of Christian medieval philosophy remained at least two centuries behind its Islamic counterpart. Nothing was more alien to the dominant medieval Christian mind than Greek *theoria*, even if medieval speculation as a whole, Islamic, Jewish, and Christian, is unthinkable apart from its ground in that *theoria*.

Nevertheless, Greek *theoria* does enter the medieval Christian mind, and in the Gothic age it does so far more fully and decisively than it had done so in Augustine. For now it does so far more profoundly through Aristotle rather than Plato, and even if this was for the most part an Islamic and Jewish Aristotle, it was Aristotle nonetheless, and Aristotle was surely the purest and most profound secular thinker who ever lived. We need not wonder that the entrance of Aristotelianism into the medieval Christian world created such a violent furor, the wonder is rather that it was so quickly accepted and absorbed, thereafter becoming in effect the official philosophy of the Roman Catholic Church. Nothing like this happened in the Islamic or Jewish world, or to the extent that it happened it became hidden from view, for the Roman Catholic Church is alone among religious bodies throughout the world in fully integrating a truly secular mode and body of thinking with a purely religious world and language of revelation. This was accomplished by Thomas Aquinas, who is surely one of the most revolutionary thinkers who ever lived, and he is most revolutionary precisely as a systematic thinker, the first truly and comprehensively systematic thinker since Aristotle, and the last before Hegel. Neither Islamic nor Jewish thinkers even attempted an integration of reason and revelation, for if this attempt was initiated by Philo, Philo even as Spinoza, became a model of the ultimate heretic in Judaism, and there has never been a Philonic tradition of any kind. So likewise there is no real integration between reason and revelation in Augustine, there is rather a profound dichotomy between the two, a dichotomy which passes into harmony in Thomism, and that is precisely the real theological difference between Augustinianism and Thomism.

The golden age of medieval Christian scholasticism occurred in one generation, between 1255 and 1274, and in that generation the Neoplatonic Augustinianism which had dominated twelfth century Christian thinkers passed into a new Christian Aristotelianism. Aristotelian philosophy became Aristotelian theology in Thomas Aquinas, and this in a truly new sense, for unlike his Aristotelian Islamic and Jewish predecessors, Aquinas united the whole body of theology into an organic whole, all of whose parts are united by a new theological notion of being. This new notion of being is in large measure a consequence of a new understanding of creation, and Aquinas most clearly differs both from Aristotle and the Islamic Aristotelians by understanding the world itself as a new world rather than an eternal world, even if the *novitas mundi* or newness of the world is known only by revelation (*Summa Theologica* I, 46, 2). For if Aquinas was a monk who could affirm that what chiefly befits a religious is to study those letters that pertain to the learning that is according to godliness, he was also an embodiment of the new Gothic world. Indeed, he is the conceptual center of that world, and not least in his discovery of the *novitas mundi.* That was a conceptual discovery it is true, and a conceptual discovery that was a metaphysical discovery, a metaphysical discovery that revolutionized the medieval philosophical tradition. Now Being itself or *esse* is identified with the very core of being. It is that "act-of-being" lying at the root of the real, and thus it is identical with actual or real or pure existence. Thomas can now say what Aristotle could never say, that God is the pure Act-of-Being, and this "act-of-being" is the actuality of being as being. Aristotle's pure actuality or *energeia* is the divine or metaphysical activity of pure thought (*nous*) eternally contemplating itself, but Aquinas's actuality is the actuality of being *per se*, an actuality which is not the act of contemplation, but an actuality lying at the very center of the real as real.

It could be said that Aquinas called forth the purely conceptual identity of the "newness" of the world, a *novitas mundi* that never was upon the horizon of Greek *theoria*, nor upon the horizon of an Islamic Aristotelianism that could identify the common truth of reason and revelation but not their common actuality.

Once pure actuality is no longer the actuality of pure thinking alone as in Aristotle, but rather the actuality of existence itself, then existence itself acquires a whole new meaning, a *novitas* reflecting the unique and absolute act of God. For the first time in the history of thinking existence can be conceived as existence itself. Then existence can be known, and actually known, as the creation of existence itself (*ipsum esse*), for the so-called "natural theology" of Aquinas is made possible by the act of creation alone, an act that can be known only by revelation. There is no disjunction between natural and revealed theology in the system of Thomas Aquinas, that is a disjunction which arose with the birth of nominalism, and is wholly foreign to the "realism" of Aquinas. And nominalism is a consequence of the disintegration of the Gothic world, a disintegration which is realized in the fourteenth century. But at the height of the Gothic period, the very time and world in which Aquinas lived and thought, existence could be celebrated and known as God's creation, and therefore known as the very "newness" of the world. That "newness" is possible and actual only through the act of God, the unique and absolute act of God. But the act of creation is the act of pure actuality or pure act, an act which is God's alone, but which is nevertheless and even thereby the act of existence itself (*ipsum esse*).

We cannot understand the original and historical Thomas Aquinas without understanding the Gothic world in which he lived, and more particularly understanding that world as a new world, a world which never previously existed in Christendom, and a world which has never been actually existent since. But that world made possible the later worlds of the West, and not least in discovering the pure actuality of existence itself. That actuality is virtually unspeakable in an analogical language that is not the language of the Gothic world, for already in the fourteenth century the root meaning of the Thomistic *analogia entis* had collapsed. While modern scholars have employed Aquinas as a way into the original meaning of Gothic architecture and Gothic poetry, it is also possible to employ Gothic art as a way into the original meaning of the theological language of Aquinas, and if it is all too clear that Gothic architecture, sculpture, painting, and poetry were profoundly revolutionary, then it will not appear odd to identify Thomas Aquinas as a revolutionary thinker. For Aquinas' new metaphysical language is but one expression of a new Gothic language, a new language that reversed a millenium of Christianity by actually celebrating the world, a celebration that was a consequence of a discovery of a new glory embodied in the very texture of the world. While that glory is, indeed, the glory of God, it is not simply a dim reflection or a fragile and fleeting image of an infinitely distant divine Majesty and Glory, but rather a glory that fully and decisively enters and becomes embodied in the very language of the world, and thus a glory that here and now is immanent and transcendent at once.

Nothing is more characteristic or revealing of the revolution effected by Gothic art than the rediscovery of the body in the cathedral sculpture of the twelfth century. It is true this rediscovery evolved out of Romanesque sculpture, but a decisive break occurs now nonetheless, a break issuing in the Christian advent of the whole and integral human body. Perhaps nothing was more alien to the ancient Christian sensibility than the human body. Not only is it virtually absent from Patristic and Byzantine art, but Augustine could speak for the whole ancient Christian world in lamenting the corruption of our body which is the punishment for original sin. The rarity of the Crucifixion in Western Christian art until the Gothic period is also mute testimony to an ancient and persistent Christian reluctance and refusal to associate the Incarnation with the body. Suddenly the body fully breaks forth in Gothic sculpture, as though it were seen by Christian eyes for the very first time. Perhaps it was then first seen as a gift of grace, indeed, as a gift of the Creation. For the first time in Christian history the body can now stand forth and be manifest as a truly human and natural body, for even if a resurrection of the body is now only partially manifest and real, it is real nevertheless, and real even as a sensuous presence. Most startling of all, Christ himself appears incarnate in the body in the sculpture of *Christ Teaching* in the south portal of Chartres Cathedral, carved about 1215. And not only is this a bodily Christ, but also a fully human Christ, a Christ who here appears as the very antithesis of the Christ of Glory who had dominated Byzantine and even Romanesque art. Now the Incarnation is actualized in the Christian consciousness as an incarnation in the body, and the human body itself can now for the first time stand forth and be real as the Body of God.

Gothic cathedral statuary is the first Christian art to portray the human body as fully natural and truly holy at once. At no other point in the Gothic world does a resurrection of the Classical world occur more decisively, and at no other point is that resurrection more vibrant as a transfiguring power. If this is not a birth of vision, it may justly be spoken of as a resurrection of vision, as that truly infinite light which dawned in the Gothic cathedral becomes embodied in the eye that beholds it, and the Eye of God is no longer an infinitely distant point upon our horizon, but an Eye that sees in our own. The first builder of a Gothic structure, Abbot Suger of St.-Denis, was also the first to formulate a theory of anagogical vision, a vision which is a full ecstatic experience of God, and an immediate vision of God, a vision released and made possible by the advent of the Gothic world. A scholastic theological term which was reformulated and exactly defined during this period gives clear evidence of the breakthrough which occurred. The term is *aevum*, and it now signifies that duration which participates simultaneously in time and eternity, and while *aevum* has multiple meanings, it can and does signify that ultimate state of the human soul when it realizes an actual contact with the divine presence. This present or immanent eternity which was defined by twelfth century scholastics is visibly present in the fullness of twelfth and thirteenth century architecture and art, and even if such an epiphany of *aevum* would have been humanly alien to an Augustine, it now becomes comprehensively present throughout the Western Christian world, and present for all to see and behold.

The Byzantine Christ is predominantly if not wholly Christ the Pantocrater, and this is the Christ who initially appears in medieval Christian art, but already in the late tenth century the crucified Christ is carved in wood in the *Gero Crucifix* in the Cologne Cathedral, and this is probably the oldest monumental crucifix in Europe. While it stands alone in the cruel darkness of that world, it stands before us nevertheless, and it also inaugurates a truly new movement of Western spirituality, and one that will explode in the Lutheran reformation of the sixteenth century. A distinctive sign of the dead Christ on the Cross is that his eyes are closed, as are the eyes in the *Gero Crucifix*, and the dead eyes accompany a broken body, a Christ who is fully a Christ of Passion. Accustomed as the Western Christian has become to images of the crucified Christ, it is important to recognize that this image only very slowly and gradually entered Christian art. Significantly enough it does not become fully established in the Western Christian sensibility until the fifteenth century, by which time it brings a final end to all Western images of Christ the Pantocrater. Among earlier images of the Crucifixion, the *Gero Crucifix* is distinctive if not unique, because this truly is a Christ of Passion, whereas other early crucifixes, such as most of the Spanish crucifixes of the twelfth and thirteenth centuries, portray a Christ with open eyes, and a Christ who remains a Christ of majesty. That majesty is not truly shattered until the late fourteenth century, a shattering accompanying the end of Gothic art, but in the thirteenth and early fourteenth centuries, and perhaps during that period alone, Christ is both fully human and fully divine in the most decisive expressions of Western Christian art.

Giotto is the most revolutionary artist in the history of art, an artist so revolutionary that it still remains impossible to understand how such a revolution could have occurred, and occurred with such extraordinary rapidity and comprehensiveness. One is tempted to speak of Giotto as the very creator of Western painting, and certainly it is not until Giotto that a Western painting appears which is a universe removed from Eastern painting. And one cannot say of Giotto, as one can of Gothic sculpture and architecture, that here Greek art is reborn, and while this may be due to the fact that most Greek painting is lost to us, it would appear to be far more likely that a painting truly resembling Giotto's had simply never before existed. Of course, Giotto was probably an apprentice of Cimabue's, and there is genuine continuity between the painting of Cimabue and Giotto, but there is also a radical break, and that break constitutes the advent of the fullest actuality of Western painting, an actuality embodying an absolutely dazzling presence. In Giotto's painting, that presence is human and divine at once, and above all so in the cycle of paintings in the Arena Chapel at Padua, which along with his paintings in The Church of Santa Croce, Florence, is one of the two major blocks of his undisputed work which survive. The Arena or Scrovegni Chapel paintings are frescoes which are universally regarded as marking the peak of Giotto's maturity. Created during the early years of the fourteenth century, they center in a series of three cycles of thirty-eight frescoes painted systematically upon three walls of the chapel, and balanced with a portrait of the Majestic God and His legion of angels on the east wall and of Christ and the Last Judgment upon the whole of the west wall opposite the altar. The thirty-eight frescoes depict the life of Christ in strict chronological order from events heralding his birth until Pentecost, frescoes which aptly can be said to be the first narrative and epic portrait of the life of Christ.

These frescoes can also be said to be the culmination of a mimetic revival in the West, one that dawned in the eleventh century, beginning as a mimed performance by monks showing the Easter story, but gradually coming to include the nativity of Christ, and thence evolving into vernacular mystery plays, which were dramatic enactments of New Testament events. These liturgical dramas conjoined the primal events of the Gospels with the events of daily life, thereby initiating a *coincidentia oppositorum* of divine and earthly events, a *coincidentia* which is finally fully realized in Giotto's frescoes and Dante's *Commedia*. For the fullest frescoes of Giotto, even as the *Commedia* of

Dante, create an integral and organic human world, but also and even thereby a world which is the domain and eternity of God. It has often been noted that the new Gothic style revolved about a sudden revelation of a new order in the world, a truly logical order which is just as fully present in the scholastic *summae* as it is in Gothic architecture, and which is overwhelming not only in its comprehensiveness but also in its clarity and unitary form. Surely that order is present in the Arena frescoes, but now it is present in new human figures, each of whom embodies a new individuality. Yet these individual figures comprise a unitary cosmos, and one which is centered in the integral movement and the full actuality of Christ. One source of this new cosmos is the advent of three-dimensional painting, which occurs in Giotto for the first time, and this makes possible the realization of a new center, a center which is center and periphery at once. Already in the twelfth century, Alan of Lille had revived Plotinus' notion of the Monad or the One, a Monad which manifests itself as a principle and end, even while itself having neither priniciple nor end. As principle and end, the Monad can be called a circle, but since everything evolves from the Monad, the Monad is a circle encompassing all. Hence the new maxim of Alan of Lille: "God is an intelligible sphere, whose center is everywhere and the circumference nowhere." In Giotto's Arena frescoes, that Neoplatonic intelligibe sphere passes into the full sensuous reality of painting, and a purely transcendent One becomes a totally immanent and comprehensive center.

That center in the Arena frescoes is Christ. But this is a new center which is fully present in every human figure in this world, for each human figure or actor is not only himself or herself and no other, but also a center fully participating in the presence and movement of Christ, and enacting and embodying this new universal presence of Christ in his or her own integral and individual center. Thus a new individual and integral presence is fully realized in this painting, just as it is in the poetry of the *Commedia*. That presence is simultaneously an individual and a cosmic presence, and a cosmic and individual presence which is centered in a new epiphany of Christ. That epiphany does not occur in Heaven as it does in Byzantine and Romanesque painting, but rather on earth, so that for the first time in Christian painting the world stand forth as a real and actual world. Thus it might be said that this new actual presence of the world and this new and universal epiphany of Christ are one event, as a new body of Christ not only is incarnate in a new world, but is finally indistinguishable from that world, and indistinguishable because of the ultimacy and full and present actuality of the new human centers of this truly new world. For those centers are not only themselves, just as they are not only earthly centers, they are also divine or ultimate centers. Each one not only reflects but also embodies a new presence of Christ. Thereby every human center now becomes a center of the world, and that center is everywhere, thus for the first time making possible a dissolution of the limit or circumference of the world.

Giotto's Arena frescoes are probably the first painted portraits realizing genuine likenesses of human beings, and whether this is truly so or not, there can be no doubt that a new human being is present in these portraits, one made possible by the pure immediacy of painting, and fully released by the new spatial and temporal dimensions of this series of frescoes. There is a narrative unity in these frescoes which is unique in Western painting, a uniqueness establishing Giotto as our supreme epic painter, and this temporal unity is integrally related to the new organic space which is present in this world. While the horizon of this world is just as infinite as the new infinite space of the Gothic cathedral, now that macrocosmic world dawns in the microcosmic world of this chapel. Thereby it dawns in this new human being, an individual being who is fully human even while reflecting and embodying the light and love of Christ. A traditional iconographic isolation of Christ ends in these paintings, as Christ's presence and actuality is now inseparable from this new human world, and it is the action and movement of Christ which energizes and enlivens this world. Indeed, the only truly immobile figure in these frescoes is the dead body of Christ in the *Crucifixion*. The very lifelessness of that body brings a realistic center to this narrative that is absent in tragedy, but that realistic center firmly unites this epiphany of Christ with the center of the world. Although painting was the last art to be reborn in the Gothic world, there is an absolute originality present in early fourteenth century Italian painting which is found nowhere else in history except in Homer. Just as Homer realizes the birth of a fully individual consciousness, Giotto and his followers realized the immediate presence of a center that is everywhere.

Giotto is perhaps best known for the cycle of frescoes portraying the life of St. Francis in the Upper Basilica in Assisi, and while some scholars have doubted that Giotto painted these frescoes, it is nevertheless impossible to dissociate the names of Giotto and St. Francis. For St. Francis almost immediately was considered by many to be a second incarnation of Christ, and such an incarnation would appear to be present in the painting of Giotto and his followers. Moreover, both Giotto and St. Francis transformed the world of the Christian Middle Ages, for even if the Poverello had been preceded as an apostle of poverty by Peter Waldo and the Waldensians, it was St. Francis and his disciples who decisively established Lady Poverty as the truest image and presence of Christ, a presence which in the early fourteenth century became a profound assault upon the established power of the Church by the Franciscan Spirituals. Popular heresy was born in the West in the eleventh century, and in the twelfth century there was a wave of heretical movements, a time when lay preachers suddenly became numerous and important. It was in the twelfth century that the technical term *heresy* came to be employed to speak of all forms of dissent from the personal to the political, and many churchmen believed that this sudden growth of heresy was an assault by Satan upon the Christian world. It certainly was an assault upon the established religious and political power of that world, and most particularly so upon the newly realized political and economic power of the Church, for it was in the context of the new identity of the temporal power and sovereignty of the Church as Church that there arose the newly realized identity of the crucified body of Christ.

A truly new identity of the Roman Catholic Church was born in the late eleventh century, and born with a new imperial role of the Papacy, one which was decisively established by Hildebrand or Gregory VII. In 1075 Gregory VII privately wrote his famous *Dictatus Papae*, consisting of twenty-seven lapidary sentences embodying the revolutionary principles upon which Gregory was prepared to act. The most fundamental one of these is that the Pope's authority is the authority of Christ, so that the Church and society itself are to be transformed so as to institute the universal imperial authority of Christ in the monarchic rule of the Pope, a Pope who has the authority to depose emperors, for all worldly and ecclesiastical authority is subordinate to the authority of the Pope. In the following year Gregory VII formally deposed the Emperor Henry IV, and forced him to do public penance at Canossa in 1077, and even if this led to a political and ecclesiastical defeat for Gregory VII, it nevertheless was of enormous importance in establishing the new authority and power of the Papacy. Thereafter the popes commonly claimed and attempted to exercise imperial power, and the Papacy became perhaps the dominant political and social institution in the Gothic world. Of course, episcopal sees had gained enormous power in the late Dark Ages, and there was little to distinguish an ecclesiastical and a lay nobility, but only in the Gothic period does the Church as institution become a real political and economic power, and one which was directed to establishing its universal and sovereign power.

No more profound reversal of this new sovereignty of the Church occurred than in the lives of the Poverello and his disciples. For it was the Franciscan movement which most fully discovered the poor and the humble as the actual body of Christ, and thereafter poverty and humility gained a truly new identity which had never previously been actually present in the world, an identity which again and again was to realize a revolutionary force throughout the world. Already in the late thirteenth century, Peter John Olivi, who was the intellectual and charismatic center of the Franciscan Spirituals, and who was believed by the radical Franciscans to be second only to St. Francis himself, believed that a new spiritualized Church would rule the world before the final end of history. This would occur by way of its embodying the very order of the universe, an order and law revealed in the Word and the Person of Christ. As Peter declared in his letter to the Sons of Charles II:

> By means of this law the potency of matter passes from the un-formed to the formed state; even more remarkably, the very lack of form serves at the same time as the stable source and foundation of forms. In imperial fashion, every external act of God has its beginning from this law . . . This is why the root of all grace, both in the celestial and the terrestrial Church, stands in the center, that is, in humility. If I may so speak, it receives its foundation and its increase in the central nothing. (McGinn translation)

For this divine law of humility is simultaneously the law of creation out of nothing and the law of redemption out of the kenotic emptying and suffering of Christ. Thus it is that an image of the "central nothing" is unveiled as the very ground of reality itself.

This is the ground that becomes the center of the mystical theology of Meister Eckhart, and even if Eckhart like the radical Franciscans was condemned by the imperial authority of the Church, it was precisely this new mystical vision which established the practical and theoretical foundations of revolution in the West. The very heart of this revolutionary foundation is a mystical notion of God or the Godhead who is pure of all being (*puritas essendi*) but is nevertheless the sole cause and source of all being. This divine abyss or ground (*grunt*) is the hidden source from which all evolves and to which it will finally return, but unlike the Neoplatonic One, which appears to be its identity, this is a ground that is actually and interiorly born in the individual human soul. For that birth is the source of a new goal of an absolute union between the soul and God. Eckhart's disciple Suso could report that the departed soul of Eckhart came to him and revealed that it was now living in glory because it was "purely divinized" in God, divinized by the way of a profound self-abandonment, a self-abandonment that was the very center of this new mystical way.

Remarkably enough, Eckhart could declare that the man who has truly abandoned or annihilated himself, and therein abandoned both God and the world, will thereby take possession of the lowest point, and then God "must" pour the whole of Himself into this man or God is not God (sermon 48). But in what what Peter Olivi called the "central nothing" God is not God, for before the creation God was not "God," and after the creation God is not "God" in Himself but only in and to the creation.

> Now I say that God, so far as He is "God," is not the perfect end of created beings. The least of these beings possesses in God as much as He possesses. If it could be that a fly had reason and could with its reason seek out the eternal depths of the divine being from which it issued, I say that God, with all that He has as He is "God," could not fulfill or satisfy the fly. So therefore let us pray to God that we may be free of "God," and that we may apprehend and rejoice in that everlasting truth in which the highest angel and the fly and the soul are equal — there where I was established, where I wanted what I was and was what I wanted. So I say: If a man is to become poor in his will, he must want and desire as little as he wanted and desired when he did not exist. And in this way a man is poor who wants nothing. (Sermon 52, Colledge translation)

Only the man who is actually free and poor possesses poverty. A man who is truly poor cannot be anywhere where God could work, for that man has broken through both the Creator and the creation, and become one with the God who is beyond God and being.

The Eckhartian "I" or *Istigkeit* is an "I" whom God must become, even as "I" must become God (sermon 83). But this occurs only when the creature and the Creator are mutually annihilated, even if it is precisely by that kenotic annihilation that each most truly and most actually becomes itself. Therefore the creature is nothing in itself, and this nothingness or poverty of the creature is that ultimate state in which it is fully united with God. Accordingly, the nothingness of the creature is pure of all being (*puritas essendi*), even if this is a nothingness which is not less than being, but rather beyond being. That beyond-ness is realized in absolute poverty, a poverty of actual self-annihilation, but a self-annihilation which realizes a birth of God in the soul: "He gives birth not only to me, His Son, but He gives birth to me as Himself and Himself as me and to me as His being and nature" (sermon 6, Colledge translation). Thus it is that "I" am the Son of God, but I am the Son of God only when I am not, only when I am truly poor and abandoned, and therein am identified with the Passion and the Poverty of God. While the writings of Eckhart that remain to us say little of the Passion of Christ, they nevertheless are profoundly grounded in the kenotic self-emptying and self-abandonment of God. This self-emptying becomes realized in us when we are poor and abandoned, for then the fullness of God must be born in us, and God gives birth to me as Himself.

The official Bull which condemned Eckhart in 1329 could assert that Eckhart had been led astray by a Satan who turned himself into an angel of light in order to replace the light of truth with the cloud of the senses. Among twenty-eight articles which the Bull condemns, and which it asserts that Eckhart preached, taught, and wrote, we find the doctrine that we shall all be transformed totally into God in the same way that the sacramental bread is changed into Christ's Body. So it is that Eckhart is likewise accused of asserting that what Scripture says of Christ is also true of every good and divine man, and that man performs whatever God performs, even including the creation of heaven and earth. For the Father gives birth to "me," His Son, and the same Son without distinction, for no distinction can exist or be understood in God Himself. Eckhart's refusal to allow distinctions in the Godhead lies at the very heart of his heresy, so that the eternal generation of the Son of God now becomes the eternal generation of all. Finally there can be no distinction between the *bullitio*, the boiling within the Godhead before the creation, and the *ebullitio*, the emanation of the creation from its primordial and divine ground. For this energy and life of the Godhead is ultimately the energy and life of all. That is precisely why the Creator and the creature are finally "nothing," for a divine nothingness or emptiness is the ultimate identity of reality itself, and an identity which becomes actual and present in the movement of self-abandonment or self-annihilation. Now this is a movement Catholic orthodoxy would deny to God Himself, so it is that Thomas Aquinas asserts that Christ's Passion did not concern or affect His Godhead (*Summa Theologica* III, 46, 12), for God's nature eternally remains impassible, and can neither be wounded nor suffer any change. Christ only suffered in His "lower powers," His "higher reason" did not suffer thereby, so that Christ's whole soul suffered only insofar as it was allied with the body of Jesus (*Summa Theologica* III, 46, 8).

Even if this would appear to be a reversal of the Arianism which the medieval Church identified as the center of all heresy, it is far rather the way by which Catholic orthodoxy could preserve the absolute being of God. One may surmise that even Thomas Aquinas was unable to preserve and sustain his revolutionary metaphysical understanding in the final part of the *Summa Theologica*, and certainly not if this was the part that was most affected by his corporate life in the Church, for this was the very time when the Catholic Church faced the deepest opposition in its history. But this was wholly an internal opposition, and one that reached its profoundest depths in that deepest of all medieval "heretics," Dante Alighieri. Dante's one full and open theological treatise, the *De Monarchia*, was condemned to the flames and placed on the Index by the Pope himself, and this in the year of Eckhart's condemnation, 1329. That coincidence gives only a slight if revealing sense of what the Church faced in the most revolutionary prophet and visionary of the Christian Middle Ages. Nevertheless, this treatise presents a seminal point at which to enter Dante's world, for the period of its preparation and composition, 1309–1313, was the crucial period of Dante's own transformation as an artist and visionary. And it was immediately followed by the beginning of the composition of the *Commedia* which continued until shortly before Dante's death in 1321. When he wrote *De Monarchia*, Dante was virtually obsessed by a radically new messianic vision, for as he declared in an open letter of 1310, a "new day" is now dawning, a messianic day that will usher in a universal era of peace and justice, a final and ultimate day made possible by the rebirth of the Holy Roman Empire.

Dante believed that this rebirth occurred with the coronation of the Emperor Henry VII, whom Dante speaks of in this treatise as the anointed One of God, and whom he could address in an open letter to Henry VII as the new son of Jesse and the Lamb of God. In large measure, *De Monarchia* is an expression of Dante's new messianic hope, and one measure of the distance separating *De Monarchia* from the *Commedia* is the death of Henry VII on August 24, 1313. But before that untimely death, Dante believed that the very arrival of the new Roman Prince and anointed One embodied a new providential order, an order which will fully be realized only in the future, although an order that was initiated in the ancient past. This occurred with the advent of the first Roman Emperor, Augustus Caesar, whose victories by God's will brought universal peace to the world, and whose empire was sanctioned by Christ Himself when he "chose" to be born under the edict of Roman authority, thus demonstrating by "deed" that Caesar's authority was just (II, 11). Dante believed that the Roman Emperor was the Emperor of the world, for it is precisely the rule of one emperor that makes possible the unity of humanity, a unity which alone can realize a universal unity of humanity, and thereby embody a universal peace and justice. Indeed, Dante's articulation in this treatise of "the universal community of the human race" (*universalis civilitas humani generis*), or simply "the human community" (*humana civilitas*), established for the first time in the West the ideal of a universal temporal order.

De Monarchia is perhaps the first theological treatise which gives an ultimate role to praxis or action, for even if action is spoken of here as secondary to speculation, it nevertheless is by action that the Messianic Empire will be established, and the establishment of that Empire is itself an ultimate goal. Thus in Book III of *De Monarchia* Dante formulates two ultimate goals (*in duo ultima*), this was his first grave heresy, for these goals correspond to two forms of beautitude, as opposed to the one and only eternal beautitude which is the ortho-dox doctrine of the Catholic Church. These two goals demand two rulers, a temporal and a spiritual ruler, the Emperor and the Pope, each has an authority independent of the other, and that authority for each comes immediately from God. Dante refused to recognize the legality of the Donation of Constantine, a curial forgery which was not yet recognized as such in Dante's time. He insisted that the Pope has no temporal or political authority as such, thus directly opposing the doctrine of Aquinas who maintained in *De regimine principum* that all Christian monarchs owe the same submission to the Pope that they owe to Christ Himself, and that the Pope possesses both spiritual and temporal sovereignty. The Dante of *De Monarchia* insisted on the contrary that we owe the Supreme Pontiff the obedience that is due Peter and not Christ, a position that is radicalized in the *Paradiso* when St. Peter declares that his place on earth has become usurped and is now empty in the sight of the Son of God (XXVII, 20ff.). This was Dante's second grave heresy, and it was far more threatening to the medieval Church than was Eckhart's heresy, for it is simply a negation of the temporal authority of the Church.

That negation is itself the expression of a new and radical affirmation of the world, and a world which in itself as time and nature embodies an ultimate and eschatological goal. This goal derives, of course, from the will of God, but now that eternal end which is willed by God has both a temporal and an eternal intention and direction. God by means of "nature" or the creation has established an end for the whole human race (*De Monarchia* I, 3). For humanity was created to realize supreme goodness, and it is the will of God that such a perfect order be realized in the actuality of time and history. Nothing could be further from the *City of God* than this affirmation, even if Dante does carry forward, and carry forward to a radical conclusion, Augustine's theological understanding of the Roman Empire. Now the City of Man becomes the equal of the City of God, at least insofar as the latter is the temporal Church, just as the Empire has a theological and divine authority which is equal to that of the Church. For that temporal goal or beautitude which is the end of the Empire is no longer subordinate to the eternal or spiritual end of the Church. Dante can even assert that nature, being the work of God, lacks no perfection, and therefore it deliberately "chooses" every means towards the fulfillment of its intentions (II, 6). Yet such a teleological understanding of nature or the creation is here grounded in an intense messianic hope, a hope and even assurance that "nature" is now realizing its deepest intention, and that a new order of perfect peace and justice is about to be established in the world. It is not without importance that the greatest of medieval apocalyptic theologians, Joachim of Fiore, appears as a redeemed and shining prophet in the *Paradiso* (XII, 140), and ironically appears with St. Bonaventura, the Franciscan minister general who successfully opposed the Franciscan Spirituals who were so largely inspired by Joachim. But in Dante Joachim's third *status* or age of the Spirit is realized as a continual and coordinate temporal and eternal order.

It is baffling that so little of the *De Monarchia* appears to be absent from the *Commedia*, and this despite the fact that Henry VII died before any of the *Commedia* was written. Did the wholly unexpected death of the promised Messiah impel the creation of the *Commedia*? What we can say is that the *Commedia* is a truly new apocalyptic epic, an epic just as original as *The Iliad*, and just as important in terms of its celebration and embodiment of a new world. That world is not simply the world of the Catholic Church, just as it is not only the world of the Holy Roman Empire. It is rather a world in which Church and Empire are parallel and coordinate poles of a City of Man which is the City of God, a new world which is the consequence of an integral and unified vision of nature, humanity, and God. No such unified vision and understanding is present anywhere else in the Western world. Nor is it elsewhere present in the Middle Ages, even if the *Commedia* can justly be said to be the *summa* of the Christian Middle Ages. Certainly it is a *summa* which is far more comprehensive than the *Summa Theologica*, for Dante realized what no purer philosopher or theologian has ever achieved, a truly unified mode of cosmological, anthropological, and theological understanding. While it is true that this unified mode of understanding is the product of a revolutionary imaginative vision, it is a genuine conceptual understanding nonetheless, for the *Commedia* is the only work in the world in which the imagination and thinking are wholly integrated.

Dante even as Giotto discovered the unity and wholeness of the concrete individual. For the first time an actual individual becomes a poetic speaker, and the individual quest and journey of that speaker is realized in the *Commedia* as a cosmic and universal ralization of eternity. For Dante is himself the epic hero of the *Commedia*, even if he is also thereby a universal humanity, and a universal humanity which is fully universal and fully individual at once. For the first time the fullness and actuality of self-consciousness passes into poetic language itself, thus effecting a revolutionary transformation of Western poetry, a transformation paralleling Giotto's transformation of Western painting. The *Inferno* is the first full poetic actualization of self-consciousness, and it is an actualization realizing a new human being. This is a human being it is true portrayed by Giotto, and portrayed as a unique and individual human being, but now that human being speaks for the first time, and speaks through the "*io sol uno*," the "I myself alone" of Dante (*Inferno* II, 3). This initial poetic realization of self-consciousness is far more total and comprehensive than it will ever be again, for not only does the *Commedia* embrace over five hundred individuals, but most of these are present as particular and historical individuals, and a great many of them as individuals with their own distinctive voice.

Nevertheless, the *Commedia* is also a resurrection of the ancient world. Now a book is born which is simultaneously a Classical and a Christian book, and not only insofar as Christian and Classical poetry now become one, but also insofar and inasmuch as Classical and Biblical mythologies now enter their first genuine synthesis. Not only is Virgil Dante's primary guide and shepherd in the *Commedia*, but *The Aeneid* itself is reborn in the *Commedia*, and not least in the presence of the new Caesars, as Aeneas undergoes a metamorphosis into the Christian Emperor. Dante can seemingly conjoin the names of Jove and

Jehovah when he speaks most cryptically of the Crucified God (*Purgatorio* VI, 118), for here the reign of Zeus or Jupiter is comprehended within the reign of God, and the authority of Caesar parallels the authority of Christ. Nothing else could account for the fact that at the end of the *Inferno* Brutus and Cassius are equated with Judas Iscariot as traitors of God. Even if all pagans are denied salvation in the world of the *Commedia*, Dante reverses Augustine's refusal and reversal of pagan virtue, and Cato, who in the Middle Ages was the legendary ideal of pagan virtue, appears in the first two cantos of the *Purgatorio* as a guardian of salvation. Not only Virgil but also *The Aeneid* are continually present throughout the *Inferno* and the *Purgatorio*, and most particularly so its sixth book recording Aeneas' descent into the underworld, a descent which is reenacted in the *Inferno*, and then reversed in the *Purgatorio*. But most fundamentally of all, *The Aeneid* is reborn as a political and historical epic in the *Commedia*, as Aeneas's triumph is finally realized in a Christian Empire.

However, Augustine's discovery of the integral and individual will is also reborn in the *Commedia*. But now that will realizes a new identity, and a new personal and individual identity, by being present in a new actuality and act. Nothing is more overwhelming in the *Inferno* than the advent of a single human act that is decisive for all eternity, as the damned embody in Hell the ultimate destiny of a single act, an act which itself embodies and reveals the deepest character and identity of the individual human being. Now act is destiny, and a full individual act is eternal destiny, a destiny which is freely chosen and predestined at once. Nowhere is this act more fully present in the *Commedia* than in Francesca's words recalling her fall from grace:

> "One day, to pass the time away, we read Of Lancelot — how love had overcome him. We were alone, and we suspected nothing.
> And time and time again that reading led our eyes to meet, and made our faces pale, and yet one point alone defeated us.
> When we had read how the desired smile was kissed by one who was so true a lover, this one, who never shall be parted from me, while all his body trembled, kissed my mouth. A Gallehault

indeed, that book and he who wrote it, too; that day we read no
more."

(Inferno V, 127–138, Mandelbaum translation)

The innocent simplicity and spontaneity of these lines is nevertheless
the voice of one who is eternally damned, and damned for the very
act that at first glance appears to be a wholly spontaneous and
unpremeditated act. But that act is Francesca's own: here she most
decisively and finally realizes her deepest identity, an identity which
is simultaneously an eternal identity and a unique and concrete act.

If we conceive the Gothic world as a historical world that fully conjoins and unites time and eternity, then nowhere is that world more
fully present than in the *Commedia*, as the full and actual reality of
time is not only preserved in eternity, but is therein fully realized as
a unique and full actuality. The Gothic world transformed an entire
millennium of Christian history, and transformed it by discovering
the transcendence of eternity in time itself, as time once again becomes
an eschatological time, a time in which eternity is here and now. Now
time itself is simultaneously an earthly and chronological time and
a sacred and eternal time, a simultaneity revealed in the very
chronology of the *Commedia*. For its epic action occurs during Easter-
tide in the year 1300 and lasts just a week, from the night of Maundy
Thursday when Dante finds himself astray in the Dark Wood, until
noon on the Wednesday after Easter, when Dante is transfigured in
Heaven. The period of Dante's descent into Hell repeats and renews
the time of Christ's death and burial, just as his journey through
Purgatory renews and repeats the time of Christ's entombment, and
his entrance into Paradise coincides with the dawn of Easter Sunday.
A Pauline and ancient Christian partiicpation even now in the Crucifixion and Resurrection of Christ is now fully realized in the earthly reality
of time and history, in the spring of the year 1300, and in the actual
life and experience of Dante Alighieri, and at a chronological point
in his life when he was very age that was reputed to be the age of
the Crucified and Resurrected Christ.

Yet nothing is more theologically revealing of the *Commedia* than the virtual absence of the temporal and historical Christ. Now even if his name cannot be spoken in Hell, and thus is absent from the *Inferno*, it is remarkable that the thirty-nine times in which the name of Christ is mentioned in the *Commedia* there is never a reference to the earthly or historical Jesuis but always instead an invocation and celebration of the Son of God: the Son of God who is Lord, Emperor, Light, Word, Wisdom, and Power. While Christ is our Redeemer and our Bliss, Bridegroom of Poverty and the Church, He is so always as the true God, the God of pure transcendence. The one full reference to the Crucified God speaks not of Christ but of "Jove supreme" (*Purgatorio* VI, 118), and even the single reference to the "breast of our Pelican" (*Paradiso* XXV, 113) is simply a way of identifying Mary as being closest to Christ. At no other point is Dante further from Giotto, or further from St. Francis himself, even if the story of Christ is told in the *Commedia* only through the story of St. Francis (*Paradiso* XI). And it is significant that when he tells this story, he adds no images or insights of his own, but simply transcribes into verse a few passages from St. Bonaventura's *Legend of the Blessed Francis*. The simple truth is that the human and historical Christ is not and cannot be present in the *Commedia*, and cannot be present because Dante knows Christ only as the true God, a God who cannot become incarnate, or cannot suffer and die as God.

Christ's person appears at only a single point in the *Commedia*, that is in canto XXIII of the *Paradiso*, when Dante led by Beatrice sees the eighth heaven of the Fixed Stars and the Church Triumphant, and then for an instant sees Christ as the "One Sun" which enlightens all the stars, a clear and shining "Substance" so bright that even his transfigured eyes could not bear it. Beatrice reveals to Dante that this Light which has overcome him is a power from which there is no defense, then Dante's mind or soul is carried wholly away from itself, and Beatrice summons him for the first time to open his eyes and to look at her as she is (27–48). But even when Dante now enters the beautific vision he cannot actually see Christ but only Beatrice, and his fragmentary glimpse of an absolutely exalted Christ is what makes possible his full vision of Beatrice, a vision which realizes Dante's full and actual entry into Eternity. Then a transfigured earth and time is present only in Beatrice, the Beatrice who had initially summoned Virgil to rescue Dante from the Dark Wood, and who appears in glory at the end of the *Purgatorio* to replace a now disappeared Virgil as Dante's guide and shepherd in Paradise. But this is the same Beatrice whom Dante had first met as a young Florentine girl in 1274, and who had died in 1290, a death which inspired *La Vita Nuova*, where Dante first identifies Beatrice as the heaven of light. Beatrice gave Dante, if only in vision, a real initiation into an individual experience of eternity, thereby releasing an anagogical vision which is truly and only Dante's own. That experience finally made possible a new language of uniquely Beatrician love, a language arising from a unique historical world, and from a uniquely singular Beatrice, and a Beatrice who maintains and preserves that unique singularity even in her epiphany and voice in Heaven. Beatrice for Dante was the very embodiment of grace, indeed, the instrument, and, for Dante, the sole instrument of redeeming grace. Consequently, for the epic hero and creator of the *Commedia*, Beatrice is the sole full image and the only intimate presence of the incarnate Christ, of the Christ in whom and by whom time and eternity are one.

Dante's third and gravest heresy was the identification of Beatrice as the incarnate Christ, for even if this made possible the imaginative revolution of the *Commedia*, it is absolutely opposed to the dogma of the Church, and is a universe removed from the theological and ecclesiastical system of Thomas Aquinas. Yet medieval Christianity did not even notice this seemingly ultimate heresy. It could not notice it, for the birth of the Gothic world occurred with a new epiphany of the Mother of God as the immanent source of grace. The Gothic cathedrals themselves were erected as sanctuaries and embodiments of the divine Mother, and for the first time in Christian history worship and devotion were far more fully directed to the Mother of God than to the Son of God, as the Annunciation replaced the Nativity as the primary

icon in Christian art, a transformation which is completed and fulfilled
in the *Commedia*. At no other point is a resurrection of the ancient
world more fully present in the Gothic world. But this is not a rebirth
of an archaic or Oriental Goddess, it is all too clearly a rebirth of the
Greek Goddess, and not the awesome and numinous Goddess of an
Euripides, but rather the absolutely gracious Goddess of the highest
moments of Greek sculpture. Of course, there is little more than a
hint of such a figure in the New Testament, and even if the Mother
of God is present in the personified Wisdom of the Book of Proverbs
and the Bride of the Song of Songs, she is never so present as an actual
goddess. Who can doubt that the Queen of Heaven who appears in
the highest heaven of Dante's Paradise is a Goddess? After entering
the beautific vision, Dante has three visions of the eternal Virgin, and
in the last vision he sees the face that most resembles Christ, and only
its radiance can grant Dante the power to look upon Christ (XXXII,
86). The final canto of the *Paradiso* opens with a prayer of St. Bernard
of Clairvaux to the Virgin Mother, a prayer which declares:

> "Virgin mother, daughter of thy son,
> humble and exalted more than any creature,
> goal established by Eternal Counsel,
> thou art the one by whom human nature
> was so ennobled that its Maker
> did not disdain to become its creature.
> (Huse translation)

The Italian of the last clause has a sound and meaning that cannot
be reproduced in translation — *che 'l suo fattore non disdegno di farsi sua
fattura* — but it is nonetheless clear that it is the Mother of God who
has transformed humanity so as to make possible the Incarnation.
Thus the real work of redemption occurs in the womb of Mary rather
than upon the Cross. It is the mediation of the love that is realized
there that opens humanity to the presence of the Redeemer, a mediation that is effected for Dante by Beatrice.

Accordingly, Beatrice is the embodiment of the Mother of God, the actual and individual one who embodies Her love for Dante, and the one and only avenue of salvation for Dante. Only in Beatrice is incarnate deity present for Dante, for she and she alone embodies for Dante a heavenly and redemptive light. While this light may ultimately be the light of the Son or Sun, it is humanly and actually recognizable to Dante only in a feminine form, the very form and figure who is the human source of the Incarnation, but a human source who undergoes a divine metamorphosis in the full realization of the Incarnation. Unlike Giotto, unlike St. Francis, unlike Meister Eckhart, Dante could know a sanctifying or redeeming grace only through an actual embodiment of the Mother of God. The only deity that even a transfigured and beatified Dante can actually see is the Goddess, first present in the Beatrice who Dante can finally and fully see, and then present in the Virgin, whom Dante can now see even if he cannot truly see Christ. Or, rather, a beatified Dante does see Christ by seeing the Mother of God. That is the only vision of God that is possible even in the highest heaven of the Empyrean, and that is precisely that highest Gothic and anagogic vision which realizes a union of time and eternity, a vision revealing the love and the glory of the Godhead which moves all. That divine love which permeates and moves the universe is openly manifest and interiorly actual only through vision, an anagogic vision of absolute grace, and a grace that is here present only through the actual presence of the Mother of God, an actual presence that is actually present for Dante only through Beatrice.

Beatrice is first unveiled in canto XXXI of the *Purgatorio*: this is the most intimate canto of the *Commedia*, and the only one in which Dante mentions his own name. Here, Beatrice discloses to Dante that never did either nature or art set before him beauty so great as was present in her body. Her body has now crumbled in the dust, but the desire Beatrice released in Dante was ultimately directed to a love of that good beyond which there is nothing to be longed for. Above all it is in Beatrice that a *quia* or "thatness" is actual and manifest, a *quia* which is the very heart of the real, and which is given us even in the absence of a total understanding which would have precluded the necessity of the Incarnation (*Purgatorio*, III, 37). Finally, *quia* is unspeakable, but it is nevertheless indubitably real, and it is indubitably real as a present and intimate reality, a reality which is the ground of full vision, and a reality which is actual here and now. In Virgil's discourse on love in the XVIIIth canto of the *Purgatorio*, love is unveiled as the very center of the creation:

> Your perception takes from outward reality an impression and unfolds it within you, so that it makes the mind turn to it; and if the mind, so turned, inclines to it, that inclination is love, that is nature, which by pleasure is bound on you afresh. Then, as fire moves upward by its form, being born to mount where it most abides in its matter, so the mind thus seized enters into desire, which is a spiritual movement, and never rests till the thing loved makes it rejoice.   (22–33, Sinclair translation)

Perception itself unfolds within us an interior reality, and our interior turning to that reality is the movement of love, a love which is a response to a reality or creation that is finally "isness" and love at once. That is the *quia* which is manifest to Dante in Beatrice, for its purity is the fullness of beauty itself, a beauty which as love moves the sun and the stars, but also a beauty which is latently present in every act of perception.

Already in the early eleventh century Ibn Sinna or Avicenna could know that love is the prime moving force of the universe, and know it as Aristotle had never known it, for the Prime Mover of Aristotle who affects the cosmos through *eros* (*Metaphysics* 1072b.3), is an Unmoved Mover who acts upon the cosmos only through the world's longing for the divine. It was not until the triumph of Islam that love could become manifest as an actual force and power in the universe as such, a universe whose sole ground is in the creative act of God, and which continues to exist only through the sustaining presence of God. But it is not until the advent of the Gothic world that love becomes manifest at the center of consciousness. Even if that romantic love which was born in the Gothic period historically derives from an

Islamic influence upon Southwestern Europe, it is nevertheless true that it is only in the Gothic world that we can discover a full interior realization and actualization of the universal presence and power of love. Nowhere is that love more fully present than in the *Commedia*, but there it is inseparable from a violence and hatred that would seem to be its opposite, for if the *Paradiso* and the concluding cantos of the *Purgatorio* are our fullest visions of love, nowhere else in Western literature are hatred and discord more fully present than in the *Inferno*. And the truth is that this hatred is present in the *Paradiso*, and specifically so in its condemnation of the Church, a condemnation that is so radical that St. Peter can declare that his tomb has become a sewer of blood and filth, and that only Satan can now take comfort in the rulers of the Church (XXVII, 25). It was the temporal power of the Church which aroused Dante's wrath, a temporal and political power which has been directed against his party in Florence, and which had succeeded in effecting Dante's banishment from his beloved city and his consequent life of exile.

Boniface VIII was the Pope whom Dante believed had finally usurped the Papacy and thus emptied it of spiritual authority, the very Pope who had opposed imperial claims of sovereignty with his own doctrine of the universal supremacy of the Pope in Christian society, and who is his last letter or bull, *Unam Sanctum* (1302), had claimed that the political and legal authority of the Church is higher than that of the State, and that every Christian should be subject to the apostolic authority of the Pope. This is the Pope who was Dante's deepest political enemy, and not surprisingly his is the dominant papal presence in the *Commedia*, and although Dante can liken the final defeat of Boniface VIII to the Crucifixion (*Purgatorio* XX, 90), Boniface VIII is nonetheless a truly demonic figure in the *Commedia*, and one who profoundly affects Dante's whole understanding of the Papacy. For in Dante's judgment Boniface VIII's claim to ultimate worldly power was the greatest of all public evils, a full inversion of the true nature of the Church. Thereby the Church becomes, at least in its public or civil reality, the very opposite of its original and apostolic identity. Only once is the name of Boniface pronounced in the *Commedia*; this is when it is uttered by his predecessor Nicholas III who is awaiting Boniface in Hell, and who ironically mistakes Dante for Boniface (*Inferno* XIX, 53). Then Dante speaks perhaps his harshest words in the *Commedia*, which culminate with this ultimate condemnation:

> "You, shepherds, the Evangelist had noticed when he saw her who sits upon the waters and realized she fornicates with kings, she who was born with seven heads and had the power and support of the ten horns, as long as virtue was her husband's pleasure.
>
> You've made yourselves a god of gold and silver; how are you different from idolaters, save that they worship one and you a hundred?
>
> Ah, Constantine, what wickedness was born — and not from your conversion — from the dower that you bestowed upon the first rich father!" (Mandelbaum translation)

This is nothing less than an identification of the Papacy with the Antichrist, an identification that will soon be reborn in Wycliffe and Hus, and then be fully realized in the Protestant Reformation.

It is in the concluding cantos of the *Inferno* that violence makes its deepest penetration thus far into Western poetry, and most particularly so in cantos XXXII and XXXIII, whose evocation of both the earthly and the eternal identity of treachery make violence fully and finally incarnate. Nowhere is Dante's poetry more realistic, and nowhere does it have a more immediate power, for treachery now becomes manifest as the full opposite of love, and its overwhelming immediacy in the demonic depths of Hell is fully parallel to its angelic opposite in the heights of Heaven. Finally, we must recognize that the dark and demonic realism of the *Inferno* is absolutely necessary to ground and sustain the anagogic vision of the *Paradiso*. Only in the *Inferno*, and to a lesser extent in the *Purgatorio*, is the vision of the *Commedia* fully rooted in an earthly and historical reality, a reality that is never fully real in the *Paradiso's* celebration of the Holy Roman Empire, and that cannot be real in a visionary world which transcends and leaves behind all earthly and bodily reality. But the echo and horizon of that reality is nevertheless present in the *Paradiso*: apart from that presence the *Paradiso* could be little more than fantasy, the very fantasy that initially comes to an end in Western literature with the creation of the *Commedia*. Thus the *Inferno* is necessary to the *Paradiso*, just as the *Purgatorio* is necessary to each as their mediator, but so likewise is the *Paradiso* necessary to the *Inferno*. For not one of these parts of the *Commedia* can stand or be real alone, each is an integral part of an organic unity, and each must perish in its intended meaning if it stands in isolation.

Once we come to understand the integral and organic unity of the *Commedia*, a unity which is also present in Gothic architecture, sculpture, and painting, then we can be prepared to resolve a paradox that otherwise is inexplicable. How could Dante be so ecstatically inspired by a real Beatrice whom he scarcely knew? And how could a political realist such as Dante so ardently believe in Henry VII as the promised Messiah, a weak emperor who reigned less than four years, and who failed in all his political efforts in Italy? The very organic form of the *Commedia* brings light to these questions, for even as the truly new organic form of Gothic architecture embodied a new perception of light, so likewise the new epic form of the *Commedia* embodies a new individual consciousness, a full and actual form of self-consciousness that realizes itself in the full and actual reality of the world. Never previously in history can we discover a form or mode of self-consciousness which is simultaneously open to nature, society, and transcendence, just as there is no previous record or sign of an individual quest or destiny which moves from and through the full actuality of the world to an exalted and infinite transcendence. If the dazzling splendor of Dante's Heaven is poetically and humanly insep-arable from the violent horror of his Hell, then the new transcendence that is present in the *Commedia* is indissolubly grounded in the full earthly actuality of time and the world.

This is an actuality which is present in Beatrice Portinari, a human being who is herself and no other, and whom Dante in a transfiguring moment saw as perhaps no individual human being had ever been seen before. So likewise if Henry VII was the first reigning monarch who had been seen and recognized by a great visionary as the one true Messiah, this cannot be unrelated to the fact that only in the late Gothic world does such a mode of vision first become historically actual. For this is the first time in history that a full conjunction and union between time and eternity first becomes manifest as such. Never before had a form of consciousness been present and real which could know and experience the real and actual coming together of history and transcendence, so that never before did there exist the human and historical possibility of experiencing and knowing an historical and unique individual as an instrument and embodiment of an eternal destiny and will. The very fact that in a thousand years of history the unique and individual Jesus of history had never been actually present as such in the Christian consciousness of the eternal Son of God — a historical metamorphosis which does not fully occur until the Gothic world, and then most gloriously so in Giotto and St. Francis — should establish a perspective whereby it is possible for us to see that a truly new messianic consciousness now becomes possible, and one that for the first time can know a full historical actuality that "even now" is passing into eternity.

The *Commedia* is the first Christian and apocalyptic epic. Therein it most decisively differs from its ground in *The Aeneid*, and therein and thereby it incorporates the new apocalyptic consciousness of the Gothic world, a consciousness that in a Joachim of Fiore could know both a new Church and a new history as the third *status* or age of the Spirit, a *status* that in the *Commedia* is realized as a new organic unity of time and eternity. If Beatrice and Henry VII are themselves present in the *Commedia* only in Heaven, this is a presence which is realized by their presence on earth, an earthly presence which is known by this apocalyptic visionary as an apocalyptic presence, a presence realizing a new union of time and eternity. Here, nothing is more important than the actual presences of Henry VII and Beatrice on earth, for even if only Dante alone knew their presence as an apocalyptic presence, this was a real and actual act of knowledge and vision, an act which is overwhelmingly real in the new poetry of the *Commedia*. Dante no less than Giotto was a revolutionary artist, and each gave birth to a new and revolutionary art, an art that continues beyond them far into the future, and thus an art realizing a truly new world.

If Augustine could know a Church which "even now" is the kingdom of God, Dante and the Gothic world could know a new creation and a new history which even now is eternity, and it was the very advent of this new world which made possible a radical spiritualization of the Church. That spiritualization is fully present in the *Commedia*, and it accompanies and is essentially related to a new and revolutionary sense of the ultimate order of history and the world, an order which is personified in the new Gothic identity of "Fortune." When Dante asks Virgil who is this Fortune, Virgil declares:

> Who made the heavens and who gave them guides was he whose wisdom transcends everything; that every part may shine unto the other,
> He had the light apportioned equally; similarly, for worldly splen-dors, He ordained a general minister and guide to shift, from time to time, those empty goods from nation to nation, clan to clan, in ways that human reason can't prevent; just so, one people rules, one languishes, obeying the decision she has given, which, like a serpent in the grass, is hidden.
> Your knowledge cannot stand against her force; for she foresees and judges and maintains her kingdom as the other gods do theirs.
> (*Inferno*, VII, 73–87, Mandelbaum translation)

While fortune is a primal deity glorying in her bliss, she is nevertheless ordained by God, and is, indeed, simply the pagan identity of the Queen of Heaven. That Queen is the ruler of history, and hers is a redemptive rule, and a redemptive rule of love, a love which even now is transforming time into eternity.

In the Gothic world as a whole, only the Mother of God is immanently and intimately present. Even St. Francis employed the feminine symbolic *figura* of Lady Poverty when speaking of that ultimate love for which Christ renounced Heaven and became incarnate. But as opposed to all ancient forms and epiphanies of the Goddess, this is a goddess who is now known to be present not only at the center of space but also at the center of time and history, and thus a Goddess who is truly the Bride of the Incarnate Christ. This is why the *Song of Songs* was known even to Thomas Aquinas as the most sacred of all texts, for the Bride of God is the Mother of God, a Mother who is both mother and daughter of her Son, and therefore a Mother who is the immediate presence of incarnate love. Dante was fully representative of the Gothic world in envisioning the Mother of God as the full embodiment and temporal presence of her son, a presence which alone releases the full anagogical union of time and eternity, and which also is actually present on earth, and so present for Dante in Beatrice. But great poet that he is, Dante is often a poet in spite of himself, and nowhere more fully so than in his portrait of Francesca, who so clearly and so unquestionably genuinely loves, and whose love is so decisively realized in a single and eternal act. Indeed, Francesca is actual and real in the *Commedia* as Beatrice never is, and, upon reflection, we realize that the damned in the *Inferno* are more real or realistic than are the redeemed in the *Paradiso.* Even if the redeemed are redeemed only as a consequence of their life on earth, it is nonetheless true that they are little more than shadows when compared with their counterparts in Hell, and if that is not true of St. Peter, that is because Peter alone among the redeemed embodies passion in Heaven, even if it is the passion of wrath. Thus if the *Inferno* and the *Paradiso* are integrally related and necessary to each other, they are also in opposition to each other, and nowhere more so than in the one's giving an actual taste of damnation as opposed to the other's ideal vision of salvation.

Already in the *Commedia* the roots are fully present of that explosion which will soon disrupt and dissolve the Gothic world, an explosion in which reason and revelation, nature and grace, and time and eternity will all lose their integral and harmonious relationship to each other. At the very moment when the Gothic style became universal in Europe in the fourteenth century, it passed into its full contrary, and the Gothic world came to an end. That end lies beneath the surface of the *Commedia*, and is perhaps related to that immediate apocalyptic expectation which Dante even now will not abandon (*Purgatorio* XXXIII), but the violent polarities released by that end are partially present in this apocalyptic epic, and most clearly so in Dante's anguished response to the destiny of both Fortune and Heaven. Although Dante virtually invented the category of the Neutrals who are neither damned nor redeemed, and created a Limbo going far beyond its counterparts in the Christian tradition, nothing in his world made possible a redemption apart from the Church, and thus no pagan as pagan can ever be saved. This despite the fact that Virgil is the primary source of wisdom in the *Commedia*, just as the Classical world was the primary source of knowledge in the medieval world, and even as Virgil himself is Dante's prime poetic inspiration. Perhaps even more disturbing is the fact that here the Roman Empire is the source and ground of the new Christian Empire, and the Roman Empire is not simply the providential instrument of God, but also the gracious embodiment of the law and justice of God, so that even the Crucifixion was executed according to God's justice (*Paradiso*, VII, 40–50).

If Dante alone could believe that the Crucifixion was a fully just and legal act, this is but one sign of that absolute sanction which the *Commedia* bestows upon the Roman Empire. That absolute sanction is necessary to Dante's understanding and vision of providence or salvation history, a history which both proceeds out of and is finally directed to eternity. There is a circle whose center is everywhere in the *Commedia*, and that center is everywhere in the new and comprehensive identity of history which was born in the Gothic world, but its periphery is somewhere, and that somewhere is an eternal and unchanging Heaven and Hell. Inevitably, the conjunction of the totality of a fully dynamic history and a static and eternal Heaven and Hell must explode, and explode it does in the history following the *Commedia*. But prior to that explosion, history and eternity fully come together in this apocalyptic epic, just as they do so in the Gothic world. For a time, the *novitas mundi* could shine forth simultaneously in Aquinas' *ipsum esse* and in

Eckhart's "nothingness" of the creation, in the "central nothing" of the Franciscan Spirituals and the dazzling splendor of Gothic art, in the Spiritual Church of the third *status* and the new vision of a Christian Empire. But the glory of that historical moment was inevitably and necessarily a precarious and evanescent glory, or was so in its original form, for it was destined to be renewed again and again in the future. Never again will that glory be embodied in a unitary and organic world. Yet having been once, though only once, having been once on earth, can it ever be cancelled?

Chapter Seven

Milton and the English Revolution

Although the transition form the medieval to the modern world occurred over a period of four centuries, it was not decisively realized until the seventeenth century which embodied not only the birth of modern science but also the advent of political revolution, for these were the revolutionary forces which most openly turned the world upside down. England was the primary site of both of these forces, and it was in England that the transition from the medieval to the modern world first fully occurred, a transition which eventually and finally brought an end to the ancient world. It was between 1560 and 1640, or even between 1580 and 1620, that a social transformation occurred in England that both eroded the ground of the medieval world and established the dominant social forces of early modernity. Then it was that the state in England first fully established its authority; that the British Isles, England, Wales, Scotland, and Ireland were first effectively united; that a full and radical Protestantism elevated the individual conscience over all authority of traditional obedience; that the first ingegration of private men into the political order occurred; that the House of Commons first emerged as the dominant legislative power, a House of Commons which in 1640 was the best educated in English history before or since; that a new intelligentsia first became a full branch of the propertied classes; that a capitalistic ethics, population growth, and monetary inflation undermined the management and traditional ownership of land; that modern communications and modern publications such as the public newspaper were born; and that higher education first became widely disseminated among both the higher and the middle classes. In short, a new gentry came into power as the dominant social, economic, and political force in England.

It has often been remarked that a man like Richard Cromwell, who was born under Charles I and lived into the eighteenth century, had seen the end of the Christian Middle Ages and the full advent of the modern world, and between his birth and death the educated person's conception of both man and nature had undergone a radical transformation. So likewise was the English nation transformed, and not only internally, for England at the accession of James I in 1603 was a second-class world power, whereas Great Britain at the accession of George I in 1714 was the greatest power in the world. Innumerable ironies and paradoxes accompanied this process of radical transformation. For if the period between 1580 and 1620 was a time of unprecedented economic mobility among the middle landowning groups, a mobility making possible the victory of a new gentry, social stratification was apparently not affected ty this process, for the new wealthy class was effectively absorbed into the ranks of the landed gentry. Nevertheless, this was a time which witnessed a crisis of the aristocracy, a crisis powerfully eroding both its wealth and its prestige, and a crisis embodying a universal weakening of the hierarchical order of upper class society in the early seventeenth century. So it is that although the new gentry was initially absorbed into the traditional hierarchical order of England, it was this same gentry which brought the foundation of that order to an end in the English Revolution, even if this gentry was itself divided during the Civil War. But perhaps most paradoxical of all, anticlericalism was both more passionate and more universal in early seventeenth century England than it has ever been elsewhere in history. Yet it was a radical religious passion and faith, a passion conjoining an overwhelming sense of sin with a burning apocalyptic expectation, that was the dominant driving energy of the English Revolution.

The English Revolution was itself the most paradoxical political revolution in history, for if it was the first revolution to bring an end to the political and legal ground of a history going back to the very dawn of civilization, and this occurred with the trial and execution of Charles I, it also resulted in a seemingly total political failure within a single generation, a failure wherein all of the newly established political, legal and religious institutions were restored, and restored after they had apparently come to a final and irrevocable end. Yet the English Revolution inaugurated a comprehensive revolutionary process of transformation which has still not spent its force. Within the realms of language and thinking it is perhaps the most successful revolution in history, for if it had little direct or immediate effect upon English or European institutional history, it nevertheless transformed language and consciousness, and did so as has no other event in history. The revolution itself was enacted by only a small minority of the nation, for the rural masses were totally passive and politically neutral, as were the vast majority of the wage-earners in cities and towns. Indeed, during this period at least half of England's four million inhabitants needed food and clothing above all else, for a doubling of the population which had begun about 1520 was accompanied by a serious decline in the purchasing power of wages, so that the new wealth of the middle classes went hand in hand with a new poverty of the majority. But just as a new poverty was a potent factor in the French and Russian Revolutions, so a new poverty contributed to a weakening of law and order in England, a weakening making possible a sudden vacuum that was filled by the English Revolution. And even if there is no clear reason or reasons as to why this vacuum should have occurred, occur it did, and its occurrence unloosened the deepest foundations of authority.

Charles I, himself, could respond to parliamentary opposition to his rule in 1642 with the warning that if such opposition continued: "at last the common people . . . will set up for themselves, call parity and independence liberty, . . . destroy all rights and properties, all distinctions of families and merit, so that eventually government would end in a dark, equal chaos of confusion, and the long line of our many noble ancestors in a Jack Cade or a Wat Tyler." Nevertheless, opposition did continue, for the propertied classes themselves were alienated from the royal government, and not least because of the profound unsettlement now advancing upon England with such fury. This was certainly not because England was then ruled by a tyrannical government, or because Charles I was a lesser or more unjust ruler than his predecessors, or because the propertied classes faced an economic crisis or even a decline in income. The disequilibrium and unsettlement was far deeper than any of these currents, a disequilibrium breeding a profound insecurity and unease. This discord was probably only openly manifest in poetic language, for English poetry had just undergone as radical a poetic revolution as has ever occurred in any language, a revolution unveiling and embodying a profound turbulence at the very center of self-consciousness.

Yet a real political transformation did occur in the short period between 1640 and 1642, a transformation which led to the dissolution of government, which in turn brought on civil war. And political transformation continued to occur, for in 1642 there were few republicans and few who supported religious toleration, but in 1649 England was a republic and wide religious toleration had been achieved. At no point is this transformation of England more manifest than in the proliferation of publications which occurred after 1640, when censorship broke down and the church courts collapsed. Milton, in *Areopagitica*, argued that public controversy is a fundamental foundation of liberty and truth, and it is England that is now the mansion house of liberty, for: "The people, or the greater part, more than at other times, wholly taken up with the study of highest and most important matters to be reformed, . . . disputing, reasoning, reading, inventing, discovering . . . things not before discovered or written of. . . . All the Lord's people are become prophets." The very number of published pamphlets increased from 22 to 1,966 between 1640 and 1642, and there was a huge increase in the number of newspapers and books, and this deeply disquieted Protestant and Parliamentary leaders, hence the necessity of *Areopagitica*. If the English people as a whole did not become prophets, they surely became sectarian in one form or another, and Milton himself could declare in *Eikonoklastes* (the Image-Breaker) that "I never knew that time in England when men of truest Religion were not called Sectaries."

For it was in England that the radical Reformation first triumphed, a reformation to be distinguished from the magisterial Reformation of Luther and Calvin, and a reformation which is a primal source of modern revolutionary history. The radical Reformation was first communally realized in Switzerland in 1524 among the Zwinglian Radicals, who were the first Anabaptists. The Anabaptists believed that Christianity had not actually or truly existed for almost fifteen years; this was the significance of their repudiation of the sacrament of baptism, and they were dedicated to the restitution of the primitive or New Testament Church. Anabaptists were present in England prior to 1536, and in the sixteenth century a distinctive feature of the radical movement in England was the close interrelationship of Libertinism, anti-Trinitarianism, Anabaptism, and Spiritualism. One may also speak of an underlying catholicity in the radical Reformation as a whole, one revolving about an imminent expectation of the Kingdom of God and a sense of both the universality of the work of the Spirit and the full and historical actuality of the New Covenant, a covenant ending all traditional order and authority. While the magisterial Reformation knew the inner through the outward, or the Spirit through the letter, the radical Reformation ascribed salvation to the inner Word or Spirit alone. Thereby it not only sharply distinguished the Old and New Testaments, but also the old and new societies, and their progressive acceptance of a universal lay apostolate went far beyond the Lutheran doctrine of the priesthood of all believers in the direction of what gradually was to become a modern social revolution.

Milton's call in *Areopagitica* to the reforming of Reformation was certainly not confined to Milton, or even to a small group. For it deeply motivated the most decisive years of Cromwell's political leadership, and for many years was the most powerful force in the revolutionary army. Indeed, it could be said that it was only in England between 1642 and 1649 that the radical Reformation was fully embodied in history, an embodiment that may well have been the deepest energy and power in the English Revolution and whose reversal in 1649 was followed four years later with the victory of political and religious conservatism in the establishment of the Protectorate. Moreover, it was only in England during the early years of the revolution that the language of radical Protestantism fully passed into a real and actual political language. Only here has radical Protestantism had a full and open impact upon history and society, an impact that may be clearly observed in both the language and the action of most of the major revolutionary political actors during this period, and not least in Oliver Cromwell, to say nothing of Cromwell's Latin Secretary, John Milton. Certainly one of the most fascinating and deeply moving presences in the English Revolution is that of the radical Protestant sects, ranging from the Levelers, who had a real political impact; to the Ranters, who had none but who were nevertheless as pure and total a spiritual sect as ever existed in history; to the Fifth Monarchists, who at least terrified established society; to the Diggers, whose leader, Gerrard Winstanley, was the greatest of the leaders of the poor, and who was perhaps the first communistic political thinker in history, and Winstanley insisted that to give the land to the poor "is the work of the true Savior to doe, who is the true & faithful Leveler even the Spirit & power of universal love" (*A New*–yeers Gift for the Parliament & Armie).

Now it is true that the radical sects had little lasting effect upon the course of the English Revolution. Nevertheless it was individuals from these groups who first wrote with clarity and passion of full political freedom, a political freedom which was the expression of a new religious freedom, and one which for the first time was effectively communicated to everyone who could read. The Levelers were the first political group to insist upon a drastic extension of the franchise and upon a constitutional guarantee of those personal liberties which would much later appear in the American Bill of Rights, thus making them the first democratic political movement in modern history, and even if they repudiated the Diggers by refusing an economic leveling, they nevertheless demanded the genuine answerability of parliaments to the people as a whole. For a time the Levelers appeared to be the dominant voice in the revolutionary army. Certainly the debates at Putney are one of the great moments in democratic history, they were perhaps the first time that a political elite actually heard the voices of the people, and heard them with a deep attention and response, as witness the account of Cromwell's response in the Clarke Manuscripts. For it is in the Putney and the Whitehall debates of 1647 and 1648, and in the radical pamphlets published between 1645 and 1649, that common speech is born as political speech and a common language for the first time in history becomes a major political actor and force. This very occurrence was an ultimate political event, and one which gradually was to have an overwhelming impact upon world history. For this is the first real political recognition of the common man in history, and it marks the initial point at which the actual language and consciousness of humanity becomes a real and realized political and social power.

Paradise Lost is the epic celebration of this new language and consciousness. Thereby it is the grounding epic of the modern world, for it is our only epic that both embodies and reflects a pure and total energy and light, an energy that is total only by being internally turned and directed against itself. We know more about Milton than about any earlier writer, and he has given us more didactic and polemical writing than any other major poet, and even left us in his 735 page manuscript, *De Doctrina Christiana*, a full systematic theology, a theology that was probably completed before the composition of *Paradise Lost*, and that is perhaps the most fully Biblical theology that has ever been written. Yet the real author or creator of *Paradise Lost* remains unknown to us. In one of his most intimate autobiographical confessions, contained in *The Second Defense of the People of England*, 1654, Milton remarks that: "My eyes are the only dissembling part of me, but they dissemble against my will." These are the eyes that will be nearly blinded when he creates *Paradise Lost*, the very eyes that here are a source of the most glorious visual poetic imagery in any language, eyes that cannot only see a "darkness visible," but can see into depths that go far beyond anything that is visible either to the naked eye or to the purely rational mind. Milton's dissembling eyes, which dissemble against his will, might well be taken as emblematic of the creator of *Paradise Lost*, a creator who alone among our poets believed himself to be possessed by Moses, and who exercised his loyalty to Moses by re-creating Genesis and Exodus, and re-creating them so as to make them one.

There is now common critical agreement that *De Doctrina Christiana* is a fundamental key to *Paradise Lost*, and although much has been done to correlate the *Doctrina* and *Paradise Lost*, there is as yet little understanding of the theological identity of the *Doctrina*. Here, Milton initially remarks that it is only to the individual faith of each that God has opened the way of salvation, and that God requires that he who would be saved should have "a personal belief of his own," so that Milton resolves not to repose on the faith or judgment of others, but rather, having taken the grounds of his faith from divine revelation alone, to seek to ascertain for himself his own religious belief by the most careful study and meditation of the Holy Scriptures themselves. Individual faith and *Scriptura sola* were, of course, hallmarks of the Reformation as a whole. But not until *De Doctrina Christiana* do these primal Protestant motifs fully pass into writing, for not until then are we given both a fully Biblical and a fully individual theology, and a theology that is individual and Biblical at once. At both of these points a distance is thereby established between Milton's *Doctrina* and Calvin's *Institutes of the Christian Religion*. For the *Institutes* never realize either a fully individual belief nor a fully Biblical argument; and cannot do so if only because of Calvin's bondage to Patristic theology, and above all so to Augustine, a bondage locating the *Institutes* on a borderline between the medieval and the modern worlds.

Milton refers to his *Doctrina* as his best and richest possession, and yet it appears to contain very little of himself, for it goes beyond all theological works either before or since by being an "original treatise" derived solely from the Bible itself, and in such a manner that it is executed with all possible fidelity without any imposition of Milton himself. The great bulk of these manuscript pages consist of quotations from Scripture: "so that as little space as possible might be left for my own words, even when they arise from the context of revelation itself." Nevertheless, this is truly Milton's Christian doctrine, *His Christian Doctrine*, even if it is finally primarily a passageway to *Paradise Lost*. But in being that passageway it is our first fully modern theology just as it is our only genuine theology grounded in revelation alone, even if that revelation did not become openly manifest or actually real until the dawning of the modern world. For Milton's *Christian Doctrine* is very much an expression of the radical Reformation, indeed, its greatest purely theological expression. Only here and in *Paradise Lost* do we find a Spirit that transcends the letter of Scripture even while fully speaking through the Scriptural text, and that does so in such a way that its own text is simultaneously letter and Spirit at once. This is a text which is not truly realized until *Paradise Lost*, but the *Doctrina* made possible that realization by embodying the purest Scriptural theology which thus far had been written and conceived, even while being a theology which was and is uniquely Milton's alone.

The argument of the *Doctrina* opens by identifying Christian doctrine as that divine revelation disclosed in various ages by Christ, for under the name of Christ are here comprehended both Moses and the Old Testament prophets, so that no distinction of the letter remains between the Old and New Testaments. Later we are instructed that Christ himself teaches us nothing in the gospels respecting God that the Law had not taught before (I, v), for Milton even as Calvin repudiates the Lutheran dichotomy between Law and Gospel. Now even if it is impossible for us to know God as He really is, God has lowered Himself to our level in condescending to accommodate Himself to our capacities, thereby showing us what He desires that we should understand him to be. This occurs in revelation, and it occurs through Christ and the Holy Spirit, both of whom are agents or instruments of God, and also creations of God, who is the sole source of everything whatsoever. Nothing is more distinctive of the *Doctrina* than its understanding of God, and of God the Father and Creator: only becoming Father through the generation of Christ, and necessarily being the Creator because nothing which exists can have any cause or origin other than God Himself. Therefore creation is not out of nothing, it is out of God alone. Nor is it by or with the Son, or by the Word and Spirit; it is by the Father alone, and only through the Word and Spirit. For the Father is not only the primary cause of creation, He comprehends all lesser causes, including the Son and the Spirit, and is Himself both the primal and efficient or actual cause of all things whatsoever. Needless to say, Milton here and elsewhere in the *Doctrina* speaks through the text of Scripture, a text or texts which leads him to conclude that creation is out of matter (I, vii). If Scripture, even as reason, demonstrates that creation cannot be out of nothing, and God is the sole and absolute cause of all, therefore He is the material as well as the final cause of the world, and is so by virtue of an "original matter" within Him, a "matter" intrinsically good, and the "chief productive stock" of every subsequent good.

Now if it may be very difficult for even his most trusting reader to regard this doctrine as solely inspired by Scripture, it can be understood to follow from a uniquely Miltonic understanding of the absolute sovereignty of God, and that understanding can be seen as having a Scriptural warrant. Here Milton is also more Augustinian than Augustine himself, for matter itself is not originally imperfect, but rather "proceeded" (*prodiit*) incorruptible from God, and even since the Fall it remains incorruptible in its essence. Thus, even if matter was originally confused and formless, it is embellished through the acquisition of forms, and such embellishment enlarges but does not transform its original state. Indeed, there is some bodily power in the very substance of God (Colossians 2:9: "in Him dwelleth all the fullness of the Godhead bodily"), a power which is the ground of spirit and soul, and also a ground of salvation, as witness the resurrection of the body. Thus there can be no intrinsic or essential distinction between body and soul or spirit and nature. Just as the whole man is the soul, "nature cannot possibly mean anything but the mysterious power and efficacy of that divine voice which went forth in the beginning, and to which, as to a perpetual command, all things have since paid obedience" (I, viii). That is paid obedience until the Fall.

Milton's understanding of providence is no less radical than his understanding of creation, and both have the same ground, the absolute sovereignty of God. In an earlier section of the *Doctrina* (I, iii) Milton distinguishes between the general and the special decrees of God, the one decreed from all eternity and the other occurring in time, the one absolute and the other contingent. The absolute decree is independent of the power of free agents, whereas the contingent or special decree is realized through the actuality of human or angelic liberty. Now in his discussion of providence (I, viii), Milton distinguishes between God's general and His special government of the universe, the one dealing with the whole of creation, and the other dealing with angels and men alone. All too significantly it is the former that is decisive. Here we are made intimately acquainted with God's impelling sinners to the commission of sin, His hardening of their hearts, and His blinding of their understandings. All of this is straightforwardly discussed and we learn that God never makes evil that which before was good, but only affects the sinner so that the sinner alone effects evil, and does so out of its own wickedness alone. For even as God creates light out of darkness, He always brings forth good out of evil. By this means He "proves the inmost intentions," for in calling forth the evil within us, He makes us deeply aware of our sinful state, and thereby we either repent or lapse into a wickedness that will eternally consume us. So it is that God eventually converts every evil deed into an instrument of good, even if that good is the good of damnation. So likewise just as God's instigating the sinner does not make God the author of sin, so neither does his hardening the heart nor blinding the understanding involve that consequence, for these, too, are intended only for a good effect. God deceives us only to beguile us into our own punishment. While God certainly tempts us, He does not do so to entice or persuade us to sin, but rather to prove us, as in the case of Job, and this is a good temptation which is to be desired.

For Milton as for Augustine everything that happens is both good and just, and everything happens or occurs through the will of God, just as the wisdom of God perfectly foreknows from the beginning everything that will occur in the future (I, iii). In the *Doctrina*, if apparently not in *Paradise Lost*, Milton affirms the doctrine of predestination. Thus he understands predestination as a consequence of God's pity in foreseeing the Fall, a pity effecting the special decree of predestination, which is necessary to salvation, and was decreed before the creation (I, iv). Nevertheless, Milton, unlike Augustine and Calvin, does not include reprobation or damnation within predestination. For predestination is election to salvation alone, and it is only a general predestination or election, for those whom God foreknew to become believers He predestinated, and called them that they might believe. So it is that God gives grace to all and rejects only the disobedient and the unbelieving. Or, in other words, all are elected to grace save those who refuse it, but the refusal of grace is nevertheless the refusal of a gift received. This is so even when God out of his foreknowledge of our refusal impels us to sin, and does so by way of His infinitely wise and just governance of the universe, a governance or providence whereby and wherein even the most destructive and terrible evils are all instruments of God's beneficence, and therefore gifts of his grace. Furthermore, we sin only out of our own free will and act, no matter how fully assisted by the providence of God. For even if everything we do falls under and within God's absolute governance of the world, our evil acts are ours alone and proceed from our refusal of God's authority and Law, including that eternal law of nature that is written within us all. Reprobation or damnation is confined to the obstinate alone, for even if that includes the vast majority of men, it always proceeds out of a refusal of grace, the refusal of a grace offered to all, and therefore present to all, even if only present as the occasion and ground of our disobedience.

If the doctrine of predestination is alien to the contemporary mind, it was at the very core of the thinking of the Reformation, just as it was central to the mature Augustine, and accepted and affirmed by all of the classical Christian theologians, including Dante. But in the English Revolution it gained a radical identity that was new. So it is that the Anglican theologian, Mathew Brooks, could insist to Archbishop Abbott in 1630: "This doctrine of predestination is the root of puritanism, and puritanism is the root of all rebellions and disobedient untractableness in Parliament, etc., and of all schisms and sauciness in the country, nay, in the church itself." For predestination is not only a divine decree, it is decreed by God before the creation of the world, and thus is independent not only of the order and structure of the world, but also of all that order and authority which has evolved in history. The Anabaptists were dedicated to the restitution of the primitive Church, but Milton was dedicated to the restitution of an ultimately primordial order and authority, an order prior to the creation itself, and thus an absolutely primordial order. But it is also an absolutely sovereign order, an order totally transcending all forms of historical order and authority, and yet an order which is absolutely sovereign over all such forms. Thus the special decree of predestination is simultaneously realized through the "liberty" of all thinking beings even while being a consequence of the wisdom, will, and pity of an absolutely omniscient and omnipotent God.

And predestination is a grace offered to all, here Milton deeply differed from Augustine, Luther, and Calvin. Thus it is absolute grace and power at once, a grace making possible salvation itself, and making it possible to all, a major motif of the radical Reformation, but it is not possible for all, but only for those whom God foreknew would turn and repent. But those who have turned and repented, and know in their hearts the call and the presence of Christ, can now know themselves to be instruments of absolute grace and power, and thereby recipients of a grace wholly transcending the creation, and yet a grace which is absolute power itself. Then they can dare and defy all, and do so by their very obedience to God, an obedience wholly lifting them outside all worldly power and authority, and yet wholly directing them to the triumph of an absolutely sovereign grace. Not insignificantly predestination and intense apocalyptic expectation go hand in hand in the English Revolution, for the very assurance of being the chosen instrument of an absolutely primordial power brings with it the certainty that the Apocalypse is inevitably and immediately at hand. Yet it is at hand in the fullness of reality itself, a reality that even now makes manifest to the elect the absolute triumph of God, and a triumph not in Heaven but rather in the fullness and the actuality of the totality of existence itself.

Not only is predestination a special decree of God in the *Doctrina*, but so likewise is the generation of the Son of God, for this generation is not and cannot be an eternal generation. Milton insists that there is no Scriptural warrant for this dogma, and that it contradicts all rational principles as well. But most of all Milton rejects the eternal generation of the Son because it would make the deity of the Son equal to that of the Father, and this to Milton, an absolutely God-obsessed man, could only be an ultimate blasphemy and defiance. A younger Milton accepted the dogma of the Trinity, but the mature Milton consistently and passionately refused it, and at that point he was one with the main body of the radical Reformation. Why should the doctrine of the Trinity have then been the subject of much theological controversy, and above all so to passionate believers in Christ, believers who often acted as though this were the ultimate apostasy of the ancient and traditional Church? Again, it is well to note that the magisterial Reformation never questioned this or any other Patristic dogma. Yet, in the chaos that appeared to be the radical Reformation, anti-Trinitarianism abounds, and in England if not on the Continent anti-Trinitarianism went hand in hand with the other major motifs of the radical Reformation.

Calvin, in his primary presentation of the Trinity in the *Institutes* (I, xiii), maintains that while the essence of God is simple and individual, the Father expresses Himself wholly in the Son, just as He does in the Holy Spirit, and thus there are three "hypostases" or "persons" in God. While freely employing Scriptural texts, it is clear that Calvin's primary authority here is Patristic theology, and this impels him to insist that the name "God" in Scripture does not refer to the Father alone, and that the Son is to be comprehended under the unparticularized name "God." This is precisely the kind of theological thinking that Milton attacks in the *Doctrina*, and attacks because it subordinates Scripture to tradition, and he goes so far as to insist that we are forbidden to pay any regard whatsoever to human traditions (I, xxx). By confining himself to Scripture alone, Milton demonstrates that in Scripture itself the Son is clearly subordinate to the Father, and thus there is no Scriptural warrant for the doctrine of the Trinity. This truth was to be rediscovered two hundred years later by England's one other great theologian, John Henry Newman, and it subsequently became commonly accepted in Biblical scholarship. But Milton was the first theologian to face the full consequences of this realization, even if this becomes fully manifest only in *Paradise Lost*.

The generation of the Son, in the *Doctrina*, along with creation and providence, is an "external efficiency" of God, whereby God effects by "external agency" whatever decrees He has willed within Himself. For it was in God's power not to have begotten the Son, else God would not be God. So it is that the generation of the Son proceeded from the Father's own free will. Thus the Son was begotten within the limits of time, for the decree must have been anterior to its execution, and God only imparted to the Son as much as He pleased of the divine nature and substance, and could not have given the Son the whole essence of Himself without ceasing to be God (I, v). Milton is even persuaded that the principle that the Father alone is a "Self-existent God" is so self-evident as to require no explanation. But a careful reading of Scripture makes clear that the Father and the Son are certainly not one in essence. For the Father and Son are one only insofar as they speak with unanimity, and this is so in the same manner as we are one with the Father, that is, in love, spirit, and glory. Whatever divinity is in the Son has been communicated to the Son by the Father, but since the essence of the Father is infinite, this cannot be communicated to another. Thus Christ received his fullness from the Father even as we have received our fullness from Christ. Then he emptied himself of that which he had received, an emptying that would have been impossible for the essence of deity itself.

This kenotic movement or self-emptying of the Son is of vital importance to Milton, as it was to Luther if not to Calvin, and it rapidly became a dominant motif of the radical Reformation. Accordingly, Milton, in discussing the Son's ministry of redemption (I, xvi), places a primary emphasis upon the humiliation of Christ, a humiliation in both his life and death. But it was in his death above all that he fully and freely accepted the divine wrath that necessarily fell upon him, and became wholly God-forsaken for us. Christ truly became the sacrificial lamb, the lamb slain for us, and he must be considered as slain in the whole of his nature. Self-evident as this point may now appear to be, it was once revolutionary, and Milton was the first systematic theologian to accept the full death of Christ. Here, for the first time in systematic theology, although the ground had fully been prepared by Luther, the resurrection of Christ is truly a resurrection from the dead. Only as a consequence of that exaltation is Christ restored to his originally immortal state. Here, too, lies a primary ground for Milton's Mortalism, for we are fully condemned to death as a consequence of sin. Immortality can now only be a consequence of the resurrection from the dead, a resurrection which first occurs in Christ.

Not until Milton is death taken with total seriousness in the Christian theological tradition, and it is not until Milton that theology liberates itself from pagan ideas of immortality. Such ideas had crept into the New Testament itself, even if not into the Old, and had until Milton lain at the very center of Christian theological thinking. Now it becomes fully manifest that eternal life is possible for us only through the justification effected by Christ's death, a death in which he paid the ransom for our sins, which he freely took upon himself, and thus of his own accord and merit (I, xxi). But this "merit" of Christ cannot become manifest until it is known or understood that he truly died. So long as Christ was not thought to have fully died upon the cross, there could be no real understanding of that merit, and hence no real understanding of the source of our justification. Consequently, Milton enables us to see that it is our clinging to the illusion of immortality — an illusion that should be possible for no one who is aware of the real nature of sin — that is a deep source of our inability to accept the free offering of Christ, a truly sacrificial offering that is fully and finally real only in Christ's free and individual acceptance of death.

Yet here we also see another deep ground of Milton's anti-Trinitarianism. For Christ's acceptance of death was freely and individually his own, in no sense was it or could it have been an act of the Father, nor could it possibly have been real for an eternal Son of God. It is only real as an acceptance and willing of real death, a death that is clearly impossible for an eternal Godhead, an impossible as well for a divine humanity that is inseparable from that Godhead. We could even say that anti-Trinitarianism is an inevitable consequence of a full acceptance of the death of Christ, just as it is a necessary consequence of a full and interior acceptance of the ultimate reality of sin. Such an acceptance does not comprehensively occur until the birth of the modern world, but then it progressively unfolds with such force as to shatter all grounds for assurance and peace. For once sin can no longer interiorly be known as nothingness, but rather is actual and manifest as being absolutely and totally real, there can be no hope in a redeemer or mediator who does not actually and fully die, and this because such a redeemer could never affect or even come in contact with the brute reality of sin. It was Luther, of course, who first fully realized this all too modern theological truth, but he was never able to formulate it in a systematic theological form, and this because he would not or could not break away from the authority of the creeds and confessions of the Patristic Church.

Milton is the first systematic theologian who decisively makes that break. He makes it most clearly and most forcefully in his understanding of the Son of God, for the Son is the redeemer who has freely and fully died, and therefore the Son, for Milton, cannot be the fullness of Godhead, cannot be the God who is only God. Yet unlike the radical Protestant theologians who were Milton's predecessors, here the Son is fully the redeemer, and the redemptive act of the Son in dying for us was an act of "merit." No such act had been possible for humanity since the Fall, nor before the Fall since death was then actually unreal.

Now that act occurs, and occurs as an ultimate event. But its occurrence is a free and individual act, and therefore it can be "communicated" to its recipients, recipients who become free and individual as a consequence of this act. Just as the Catholic mass is a repetition of the death of Christ, an *anamnesis* or re-presentation of the source of redemption, Milton understands Christ's "merit" as an act and an actuality that can be repeated and renewed in Christian freedom. This is a freedom, it is true, made possible only by Christ's act of redemption, but nevertheless a freedom which can be humanly realized in the fullness of a new life. And it can be realized in us because Christ in his person and essence is not wholly other than us. He is the New Adam who has justified us by "satisfying" the absolute justice of the Father; and thereby and therein imputed to us his own "merit," a "merit" which is gratuitously given us in faith, and a faith which lives in us only in our acts (I, xxii).

In his chapter on adoption, Milton affirms that the Father adopts those who are justified through faith, true liberty comes from that adoption, and thereby we ourselves become "sons" of God by a new generation or rebirth (I, xxiii). So it is that we thereby become one with the Father in the same manner as the Son is one with the Father, that is, not in essence, but in love, communion, and spirit (I, v). Thus we can understand and enact ourselves as truly reborn only if we know and are united with a Son who is not eternally generated by the Father, but is rather generated in time rather than in eternity, and thus can actually be a model and source for our new generation and adoption by the Father. If nothing else, Milton's radical understanding of human freedom is a full expression of that new freedom which was realized in the English Revolution, a freedom inaugurating the full advent of the modern world. But it is also a freedom which occurs and is realized in a truly turbulent world, a world wherein centuries and even millennia of history and tradition are breaking down and coming to an end. For the modern world was born in a fully apocalyptic situation and crisis, and a crisis that nowhere was more fully present than in the English Revolution.

Nothing in Milton's poetry and prose is more baffling theologically than the role and identity of Satan in *Paradise Lost*. There is seemingly nothing in the *Doctrina* preparing the way for such an epiphany, except for a yawning chasm potentially present between an absolutely sovereign God and that real and actual freedom which He temporally or newly generates in His Son and "sons." At no point is *Paradise Lost* further from its ground in the *Commedia*, for the Satan who appears at the conclusion of the *Inferno* is a silent and impotent figure who is encrusted in ice, the very embodiment of an Augustinian and scholastic understanding of the nothingness of evil. But the Satan of *Paradise Lost*, if not the Satan of *Paradise Regained*, is a glorious and majestic figure who is the primal actor and speaker in the epic as a whole. Little or nothing in the Christian and Western tradition prepares the way for such a Satan, except for late-medieval painting, which itself in part reflects the dark sensibility of the waning Middle Ages, a sensibility which is perhaps most powerfully present in Luther himself. And out of that tradition there arose a mystical thinker who directly or indirectly exercised a profound impact upon modernity, Jakob Böhme.

While there is good evidence that Milton may have been influenced by Böhme's new and radical vision of the dark or negative potency in the Godhead, there is no direct evidence of such an influence in his work, and Milton's understanding of the Father as the totality of the Godhead would appear to be at an infinite distance from Böhme's theosophical speculations. Nevertheless, Milton thought and wrote in an historical world in which Böhme was a significant figure, as witness the number of English translations of his work that appeared in this period, to say nothing of the beliefs and visions of the Ranters that so fully paralleled Böhme's visions, and the Ranters numbered many thousands in the London of Milton's day. Moreover, both Böhme and the Ranters were reborn in England in William Blake in the following century, and Milton was the poet and seer with whom Blake most deeply struggled throughout his life. But most important of all, the Satan of *Paradise Lost* seems to demand a ground in a cosmic and ultimate negative potency or power. At the very least, this Mitonic Satan embodies an ultimate illusion of sin that is grounded in an infinitely darker interior ground and source than anything present in Dante's horizon and world. Indeed, Milton's most original vision of Satan, in both *Paradise Lost* and *Paradise Regained*, is of Satan as the full and actual opposite of Christ. This surely parallels Böhme's visions of the dark and light or good and evil potencies in the Godhead.

But an anomaly here confronts us — and one of extraordinary significance for a poet such as Milton who takes language with total seriousness — and that is that while the name of Christ occurs innumerable times in his prose, in the whole of his poetical works Milton employs it only in the title of *The Nativity Ode* and in the sonnet protesting against forcing consciences "that Christ set free." Thus the actual name of Christ never appears in either *Paradise Lost* or *Paradise Regained*, despite the fact that Christ is the primary actor and speaker in the latter, or is so with Satan, and that he is both the literal and the spiritual center and ground of *Paradise Lost*. When one recognizes the new and primal role the name of Christ assumed in early Protestantism, and that such a large portion of the *Doctrina* is devoted to Christology, this problem is magnified all the more, and most particularly so since Milton's Christology is uniquely his own even while being a primary and truly original epic and dramatic ground of both *Paradise Lost* and *Paradise Regained*. Apparently Milton the poet could not pronounce the name of Christ, speaking instead of Son, Son of God, or Messiah. Yet this same poet pronounces the name of Satan as it has never been pronounced either before or since. For without any question it is Satan who is the dramatic and linguistic center of *Paradise Lost*, as the very name of Satan is here realized as the primary portal to this new epic world.

Paradise Lost opens with a lamentation of the death and woe brought into the world by man's first disobedience, till "one greater Man" restore us, and it does so by invoking that heavenly muse who inspired Moses, the very Moses who is reborn in the creation of this epic. For *Paradise Lost* is all too clearly a renewal and re-creation of the Biblical epic.

Almost at once, Satan enters the epic as the source of the Fall, a Satan who "trusted to have equalled the most high," then raised war in heaven against the throne and monarchy of God, only to be hurled down to bottomless perdition. A doomed and tormented Satan now appears, viewing with pride and hate his horrible dungeon, a dungeon enclosed by flames which give forth no light but only "darkness visible," an utter darkness confining torture without end, the very Hell which "eternal justice" had prepared for these rebellious angels. Satan in his initial speech embodies his original pride. Refusing to change or repent, he insists that:

> All is not lost; the unconquerable will,
> And study of revenge, immortal hate
> And courage never to submit or yield:
> And what else is not to be overcome?
> That glory never shall his wrath or might
> extort from me. To bow and sue for grace
> With suppliant knee, and deify his power.
> Who from the terror of this arm so late
> Doubted his empire, that were low indeed,
> That were an ignominy and shame beneath
> This downfall, since by fate the strength of gods
> And this empyreal substance cannot fail,
> Since through experience of this great event
> In arms not worse, in foresight much advanced,
> We may with more successful hope resolve
> To wage by force or guile eternal war
> Irreconcilable to our grand foe,
> Who now triumphs, and in the excess of joy
> Sole reigning holds the tyranny of heaven. (I, 106–124)

So it is that at the very beginning of the epic we are confronted with that absolute defiance which is the motivating power of its dramatic movement, a defiance that in fact will triumph in the epic, so that Satan will finally rejoice that the Creator has given up both his beloved man and all this world to sin, death, and Himself (X, 488).

While this seemingly infinite resolution of Satan proceeds from despair, it has the high permission of all-ruling heaven, and all his malice ultimately serves but to bring forth infinite goodness grace, and mercy on man, even if only triple confusion, wrath, and vengeance poured on Satan. The Miltonic Satan knows full well that providence seeks to bring good out of his evil, but his is a labor seeking to pervert that end, so that out of good ways may be found to evil, an evil that is the fallen angels' sole delight (I, 160–165). Despair itself uplifts Satan high beyond hope, an exaltation realized by "merit," and in that exaltation Satan looks forward to celestial "virtues" gloriously and dreadfully arising from his very descent and fall (II, 5–16). Yet even now the fallen angels reverence Satan as a god, extol him as equal to the highest in Heaven, so that Hell's dread emperor reigns in imitation of God, and transcendent glory raises him above his fellows with monarchical pride. In short, Satan rules in Hell even as the Son now rules in Heaven, and even as the Son will abandon that rule to sacrifice himself for fallen man, so Satan now abandons his sovereignty in Hell to embark upon a solitary voyage to discover unfallen man: "and one for all my self-expose, with lonely steps to tread the unfounded deep, and through the void immense to search with wandering quest a place foretold" (II, 827–830).

All too clearly Satan's lonely voyage through the immense void between Hell and earth fully parallels and anticipates the reverse movement of the Incarnation. Each is a purely solitary movement through either darkness or light, each is the consequence of a free and solitary decision, each entails a voluntary abandonment of sovereignty, and each is a sacrifice or self-exposure for others. But in *Paradise Lost*, Satan's kenotic movement occurs before the Son's, and it can even be understood as a response to the Son. For it was the Father's exaltation and crowning of the Son that occasioned Satan's rebellion against God, a rebellion leading to his fall and damnation, and thus to the necessity of a voyage intending to reverse that fall. At this point we enter one of the thorniest problems of Miltonic scholarship. Is Milton's understanding of the exaltation of Christ uniquely his own or did it organically proceed out of the Christian tradition? One thing is clear: there is no such account of the Son's exaltation in the *Doctrina*, despite the fact that so much analysis is given to the generation of the Son. But it is controversial as to whether or not the exaltation of the Son in *Paradise Lost* is also his generation, as would appear to be the case in the words of the omnipotent Father effecting that exaltation:

> Hear all ye angels, progeny of light,
> Thrones, dominations, princedoms, virtues, powers,
> Hear my decree, which unrevoked shall stand.
> This day I have begot whom I declare
> My only Son, and on this holy hill
> Him have anointed, whom ye now behold
> At my right hand; your head I him appoint;
> And by my self have sworn to him shall bow
> All knees in heaven, and shall confess him Lord:
> Under his great vicegerent reign abide
> United as one individual soul;
> For ever happy: him who disobeys
> Me disobeys, breaks union, and that day
> Cast out from God and blessed vision, falls
> Into utter darkness, deep engulfed, his place
> Ordained without redemption, without end. (V, 600–615)

Only one line speaks here of the generation of the Son, and it does seem incredible that this could have occurred after the creation of the angels. But it is difficult to avoid the impression that the exaltation of the Son plays the same role in *Paradise Lost* that the generation of the Son plays in the *Doctrina*, and each embodies Milton's most original Christology.

Certainly it is the exaltation of the Son which initiates the dramatic movement of *Paradise Lost*, for this and this alone provokes the rebellion of Satan, a rebellion against the Father, which Satan says is provoked by His "new laws" (V, 679). These new laws give all but God's power to another, thereby eclipsing the angels under an anointed king, and replacing an original equality or harmony of the heavenly beings with an absolute monarchic and everlasting power. Now if we assume that the exaltation is not the generation of the Son, we are then left with the problem of the identity of the Son before the exaltation, for presumably he could not then have been the anointed monarch of Heaven. Does the Son only gain "power" through the exaltation? And is this the power that is forsaken when the Son offers himself as a sacrifice for humanity, but a power apart from which there could be no genuine movement of humiliation? In offering himself as a sacrifice, the Son says that he will leave the bosom of the Father and freely put off his glory so as to die for humanity. To this the Father can respond:

> Nor shalt thou by descending to assume
> Man's nature, lessen or degrade thine own.
> Because thou hast, though throned in highest bliss
> Equal to God, and equally enjoying
> Godlike fruition, quitted all to save
> A world from utter loss, and hast been found
> By merit more than birthright Son of God,
> Found worthiest to be so by being good,
> Far more than great or high; because in thee
> Love hath abounded more than glory abounds,
> Therefore thy humiliation shall exalt
> With thee thy manhood also to this throne,
> Here shalt thou sit incarnate, here shalt reign
> Both God and man, Son both of God and man,
> Anointed universal king, all power
> I give thee, reign for ever, and assume
> Thy merits; . . . (III, 303–319)

But here lies an apparent confusion. For the descent of the Son does not lessen or degrade the nature of the Son, yet it effects an exaltation of the Son to his original monarchic glory, even if now the anointed is both God and man. And is the only difference between this glory of Christ and his original glory that he now reigns as both God and man? If so, what can that mean?

Can it mean a higher glory, a glory possible only through humiliation, and a humiliation realized by a "merit" transcending the divinely generated origin of the Son? If so, it is a "merit" that is only possible because of the rebellion of Satan, and the consequent entrance of sin and death into humanity, an entrance which is possible only because of Satan's kenotic voyage. Nothing is more baffling or more fundamental in *Paradise Lost* than the identity of "merit." This is a "merit" that is only actual and realized in Satan and the Son, then it is the source both of Satan's rebellion and of the Son's sacrifice. In each case it is their "merit" rather than their "birthright" which is the origin of their deepest and most original identity and acts. Moreover, the "merit" of each is integrally and necessarily related to the "merit" of the other. For the Son fully realizes "merit" only by submitting himself to and opposing Satanic power, just as Satan realizes "merit" only by opposing the authority and the majesty of the Son. That authority and majesty is finally and apocalyptically real only as a consequence of the incarnate and atoning movement of the Son, a movement which itself is possible only because of the rebellion and subsequent victory of Satan. Now both *Paradise Lost* and the Christian tradition as a whole are grounded in the paradox of the fortunate fall, the paradox that fall itself makes redemption possible, a final redemption transcending an original and primordial state of bliss. Yet *Paradise Lost* goes beyond the Christian tradition which it inherited by envisioning both the redeemer and his opposite, Satan, as being mutually and dialectically grounded in the downward and chaotic movement of fall.

Indeed, it is the downward and self-destructive or self-emptying movement of fall which actualizes the "merit" of both Satan and the Son, a "merit" which would be unactualized and therefore unreal apart from that movement. This is that "merit" which is most integral and individual to both the identities of the Son as Son and Satan as Satan. It only arises or comes into existence when each realizes an identity transcending his given or original identity, and this is an identity that both for and within each is integrally and necessarily related to the identity of the other. But it is also true that each realizes his "merit" only by inverting and reversing the "merit" of the other. So that Satan reverses the crowning and exaltation of the Son by rebelling against the Father and thence being thrown down into Hell, and the Son reverses the proud rebellion of Satan by radically humiliating and emptying himself even unto death. Now not only does each of these downward movements culminate in death, the rebellion of Satan culminating in his eternal death in Hell, and the sacrifice of the Son culminating in the atoning death of Crucifixion, but each of these movements fully coincides with the other. For each reverses the identity of the other in realizing a "merit" which is uniquely his own, a reversal realizing that unique redemption which is the paradoxical consequence of fall. Consequently, "merit" is real and realized only through fall and death. Moreover, it is realized only in a wholly paradoxical and dialectical manner and mode, and a mode in which the opposite identities and energies of Satan and the Son are fully essential and necessary to each other.

Not until *Paradise Lost* does Satan become a majestic and glorious figure in the Christian tradition. But not until then are sin and death fully envisioned as having a primordial ground or is Christ envisioned as fully undergoing the kenotic or self-emptying movement of sacrifice and death. While it is true that post-Gothic painting does envision the full and actual death of Christ, that death does not enter dramatic and poetic language until *Paradise Lost*, and then it is a death which is human, cosmic, and divine at ònce, a death both finally realizing the "merit" of the Son, and a death making possible the anointment and exaltation of one who now reigns as both God and man. But that exaltation is inseparable form the triple damnation of Satan, who is the inverse Trinity of Sin, Death, and Satan. This is that Satan whose fierce energy and pride inverts the passion of Christ, an inversion releasing the "merit" of Satan, and therefore releasing a Satanic majesty and power that dominates the dramatic action of the poem. So it is that in *Paradise Lost* a radically new Satanic majesty and energy is an inversion of the self-emptying and humiliation of the Son. Never before had these polar opposites been envisioned and actualized as full and total opposites. And never before had these opposites realized a dramatic and dialectical relationship to each other, a fully integral and mutual relationship in which each is truly himself only through his relationship to the other.

Satan and the Son are polar and dialectical twins in *Paradise Lost.* They embody an energy and a power which are truly new in poetry, a dramatic energy which is a dialectical power and force, a new force proceeding out of a self-division or self-alienation at the very source of energy and life. This is a force which surely lies at the origin of modernity, a force which is alien to the integral and comprehensive unity pervading the *Commedia,* and yet a force evolving out of an inversion of an original totality, the very totality celebrated in the *Commedia.* Dante and Milton are the Christian poets who are most deeply grounded in Classical poetry, the *Commedia* is clearly a rebirth and renewal of *The Aeneid,* and so likewise *Paradise Lost* is a renewal of the epic poetry of both Homer and Virgil. But these Christian epics are also rebirths of the Bible, and rebirths of the Bible in truly new worlds, worlds which are resurrections of the Classical world, but also worlds which are Christian worlds, and Christian worlds which are Classical and Christian at once. If the *Commedia* realizes a comprehensive unity and totality which was never present in either the Classical or Biblical worlds, *Paradise Lost* embodies a comprehensive dramatic energy and power which was never fully present and actual until the dawn of modernity, a modernity which brought the ancient world to an end. That ending is most fully realized in the very advent of a purely negative energy and force, an energy and passion that is divided and polarized in its very center, thus making possible a new naming and a new realization of both Satan and the Son.

We need not be surprised that the deeply Christian and Protestant Milton refused to employ the name of Christ in either *Paradise Lost* or *Paradise Regained.* For the Son is a new Christ in each of these poems, a Christ who is at once a fully Biblical and yet fully modern Christ, and above all so in *Paradise Lost.* Nothing is more distinctive of the Son of *Paradise Lost* than his simultaneous ground in the New Testament and the Old, and while this clearly proceeds from the theological analysis of the *Doctrina,* it is nevertheless a unique fusion of Old Testament and New Testament imagery and language, and so much so that here those testaments become one. But clearly the Son of *Paradise Lost* is not simply a Biblical Christ; he cannot be so if only because of his integral if dialectical union with Satan, a union which is nowhere present in the Bible, nor in any Christian imaginative tradition prior to Milton. Yet Christ had not been a fully dramatic figure in that tradition, this does not fully occur in Christian art until Rembrandt, and it is noteworthy that the Son of God of the *Paradiso* is as silent and immoble as is the Satan of the *Inferno.* For not until the seventeenth century does a Christ become real in the Christian imagination who is capable of a deep and primal conflict with an opposing power, and not only a cosmic and mythological conflict, but also a deep and profound conflict within.

Critics of *Paradise Lost* have observed that its soliloquies always occur either in Hell or under the direct influence of Satan, and if only for this reason Satan is the dramatic center of the poem. For *Paradise Lost* is an interior as well as a cosmic epic, and its dramatic action is cosmic and interior at once. But it is all too significant that here interior conflict and dialogue occur only in Satan's domain, for this is above all the domain of the purely negative consciousness, a consciousness whose very activity and life is a negative movement and energy, and negative above all in its pure negation of itself. Thus it is the essence of Satanic energy, as Milton envisioned it, that it can act and be real only by acting against itself. Book IV opens with an evocation of the warning voice of the Book of Revelation, a voice that cried in Heaven when Satan fell. For that fall is an eternal fall, as Hell eternally deepens itself in Satan:

> horror and doubt distract
> His troubled thoughts, and from the bottom stir
> The Hell within him, for within him Hell
> He brings, and round about him, nor from Hell
> One step no more than from himself can fly
> By change of place: now conscience wakes despair

That slumbered, wakes the bitter memory
Of what he was, what is, and what must be
Worse; of worse deeds worse sufferings must ensue. (18–26)

Therefore Satan can turn the very love of God into Hell, as witness this soliloquy:

Hadst thou the same free will and power to stand?
Thou hadst: whom has thou then or what to accuse,
But heaven's free love dealt equally to all?
Be then his love accursed, since love or hate,
To me alike, it deals eternal woe.
Nay the cursed be thou; since against his thy will
Chose freely what it now so justly rues.
Me miserable! Which way shall I fly
Infinite wrath, and infinite despair?
Which way I fly is Hell; my self am Hell;
And in the lowest deep a lower deep
Still threatening to devour me opens wide,
To which the Hell I suffer seems a Heaven. (IV, 66–78)

Accordingly, Satan's very will to evil — "Evil be thou my good" (IV, 110) — is Hell itself, and not a static and unchanging Hell, but rather a Hell that eternally deepens itself.

This purely negative identity and will of Satan is reversed in the Son's free and individual acceptance of humiliation and atoning death. But whereas Satan's rebellion destines him eternally to Hell, the Son's sacrifice is made with the assurance that his death will be followed by His resurrection and final victory over Satan (III, 245–265). So it is that the providence of God brings forth infinite goodness, grace, and mercy from the infinite malice of Satan. Nevertheless the fact remains that the poetry that celebrates this paradoxical and providential triumph dramatically centers upon the evil will, whether in Satan and the fallen angels or in Eve and Adam. Nowhere in our literature can we find such a full and dramatic portrait of a spontaneous and yet fully free choice of evil as we do in Milton's portrait of the temptation and fall of Eve, and it is made all the more compelling by the uniquely Miltonic account of the original glory of Eden, a glory comprehending even sensuous and sexual ecstacy. Satan's temptation of Eve is the dramatic center of *Paradise Lost*, and it brings to a full dramatic resolution Satan's purely negative will and movement, a movement culminating in his kenotic incarnation in the serpent. All too clearly that negative incarnation parallels the positive incarnation of the Son, and it releases the deepest and most ecstatic self-consciousness of Eve, a negative self-consciousness which parallels if it does not embody the negative selfhood of Satan.

At only one point in *Paradise Lost* does the Son have a comparable effect upon self-consciousness, and that is in Lucifer's response to the original anointment and exaltation of the Son, when Lucifer — "affecting all equality with God, in imitation of that mount whereon Messiah was declared in sight of Heaven" (V, 764) — undergoes a metamorphosis into Satan. For the truth is that all epiphanies of self-consciousness in *Paradise Lost* are negative epiphanies, epiphanies realizing a negative identity and a negative will. Thus the driving energy of this all too modern epic is a negative energy. The one epiphany of the Son to Adam and Eve is a negative epiphany as their judge, for the Father transfers all judgment to the Son (X, 56). So it is that the forward and redemptive movement of the *Commedia* is fully and comprehensively reversed in the negative movement of *Paradise Lost*, and that reversal realizes a new embodiment of self-consciousness. Indeed, it actualizes for the first time in epic poetry a truly isolated and solitary self-consciousness, and a self-consciousness that can will and be real only by willing against itself. It is small wonder that the person of the Son is here virtually eclipsed by the person of Satan, or that the movement of the Son enters the dramatic movement of the poem only when the Son as warrior and head of the loyal angelic host defeats Satan and the rebellious angels. For the sacrifice of the Son, unlike the rebellion of Satan, is not and cannot be given a genuinely dramatic expression in this epic, or to the extent that it is a dramatic movement it is a foil and a counterpart to the dramatic movement of the epic as a whole.

It is not surprising that *Paradise Regained* is so overshadowed and eclipsed by *Paradise Lost*, or that the last two books of *Paradise Lost*, with their major theme of redemption, are so much weaker poetically than are all of the previous books. What is truly surprising about *Paradise Lost* is its power over us, and even as *The Aeneid* and the *Commedia* it was almost immediately accepted by its audience as a great epic poem, and this despite the fact that Milton then lived in political defeat and disgrace. Twenty years after the publication of *Paradise Lost*, Newton gave the world his *Principia*, and the *Principia* along with *Paradise Lost* is a grounding center of modernity, and a center realizing a new totality proceeding out of the very disintegration of the old. The *Principia* is the fullest embodiment of the scientific revolution of the seventeenth century, a revolution which destroyed a transcendent celestial world by an ontological and mathematical realization of an infinite universe, and did so with an apocalyptic finality. And both *Paradise Lost* and the *Principia* bring a definitive end to the heavens of the ancient and medieval worlds. For even if *Paradise Lost* preserves the absolute sovereignty of the heavenly Lord, it does so only by way of realizing a wholly new meaning and identity of that sovereignty, for now the sovereignty of God is exercised over a wholly fallen world. Thus as a consequence of the Fall the universe itself loses the ideal order of its prelapsarian state, and its original symmetrical simplicity passes into a new order that transcends all imaginative vision and understanding.

It is important to recognize that in *Paradise Lost* only the prefallen universe embodies an integral and harmonious order, for even if this is the universe which is celebrated in the great body of the poem, it is a lost universe, lost as a consequence of the universal movement of fall. Spring is perpetual on the earth of our original universe, for then there were neither solstices nor seasons, and the heavenly bodies moved in a simple and coincident order. Then nature is both "wild above rule or art" and "enormous bliss" (V, 297). Accordingly, Raphael can inform an unfallen Adam:

O Adam, one almighty is, from whom
All things proceed, and up to him return
If not depraved from good, created all
Such to perfection, one first matter all,
Indued with various forms, various degrees
Of substance, and in things that live, of life;
But more refined, more spirituous, and pure,
As nearer to him placed or nearer tending
Each in their several active spheres assigned,
Till body up to spirit work, in bounds
Proportioned to each kind. (V, 469–479)

Here we see the classical paradigm of the Great Chain of Being, but the chain breaks asunder with the victory of Satanic energy; "one first matter all" disintegrates or disappears from view, and body can now return to spirit only as a consequence of a future apocalyptic transformation.

Now even if Milton could believe that nature itself can be identified with the power and efficacy of the divine voice (*Docrina*, I, viii), and that matter and form are substantially within the Godhead (*Doctrina*, I, vii), this is a nature and a matter and form which are no longer humanly visible or knowable. For the Fall inverts the original order of the universe itself, and a new cosmic system and order, which resists and transcends all imaginative meaning and identity, then becomes real and universal. This was the very system that was discovered in the seventeenth century, and discovered by Milton as well as by Newton. If Newton himself could know space as the boundless and uniform *Sensorium* of God, that knowledge never truly entered his or any other modern scientific system, for a virginal nature came to an end with the full advent of the modern world. That ending is epically present in *Paradise Lost*. Here it is an apocalyptic ending, so that even Raphael's account of the creation in Book VII conjoins the creation itself with the original fall of Satan and the rebellious angels, a creation that the Father declares will "repair" the detriment done by that rebellion. Then the Creator declares His intention to create:

Another world, out of one man a race
Of men innumerable, there to dwell,
Not here, till by degrees of merit raised
They open to themselves at length the way
Up hither, under long obedience tried,
And earth be changed to heaven, and heaven to earth,
One kingdom, joy and union without end. (155–161)

Here, and for the first time in the Christian tradition, alpha and omega, creation and apocalypse, are merged and become one. Now the creation of the world is inseparable from the apocalyptic transformation of the world, and not in the Neoplatonic sense of the circular emanation of the One, as the words of the Creator go on to declare:

And thou my Word, begotten Son, by thee
This I perform, speak thou, and be it done:
My overshadowing spirit and might with thee
I send along, ride forth, and bid the deep
Within appointed bounds be heaven and earth,
Boundless the deep, because I am who fill
Infinitude, nor vacuous the space.
Though I uncircumscribed by my self retire,
And put not forth my goodness, which is free
To act or not, necessity and change
Approach not me, and what I will is fate. (163–173)

Thus the very necessity, and absolute necessity, of the retirement of the Father in the act of creation, a necessity which is the absolute freedom and sovereignty of God, necessitates that the creation be "by" the Word or the generated Son. This is a formula refused by the Milton of the *Doctrina*, but employed by the Milton of *Paradise Lost*, and employed if only to preserve the absolute sovereignty of God, a sovereignty which, while filling all infinitude and space, cannot be present as God in the new act of creation. For the Creator can be present in the creation only through the Son, that Son who is the "radiant image of His glory" (III, 63), and a glory which becomes most glorious when the Son freely accepts and wills the atoning act of self-sacrifice. For then "in his face Divine compassion visibly appeared, love without end, and without measure grace" (III, 140). Whether or not the Miltonic Son freely and individually acts as the Creator's agent and instrument of creation, he certainly so acts when he wills the self-negation of his glory in accepting an atoning death for a fallen humanity, and thereby and thereby alone be becomes not only "most glorious" but also most fully himself, and most fully himself because then "love hath abounded more than glory abounds" (III, 312).

This is a love which at the very least is potentially present in the Son when he acts as the instrument of the Father in the creation. But it is a love which cannot be realized apart from the Fall, and thus not realized apart from the victory of Satan. Thus it is that the Father not only foresees and foreknows the fall both of Satan and of Eve and Adam, but that fall is necessary and essential to the goal or end of the creation itself. Therefore creation itself is a response to rebellion in Heaven, and is consummated as creation in that "one kingdom" when earth will be transformed into Heaven and Heaven transformed into earth. *Paradise Lost* is the first imaginative vision of the ultimate union of the original act of creation with the movements and acts of fall, atonement, and apocalypse. Now these acts and movements become not only inseparable, but also deeply and comprehensively grounded in the dialectical and paradoxical union of Satan and the Son. This is an apocalyptic union which embodies both a new and radical energy and a new providential order, a dialectical order in which good is realized through evil, even if that good is invisible in a now darkened cosmos. Yet darkness becomes visible through grace, and then darkness can be manifest as light. For even if the glorious light of *Paradise Lost* is the reflection of an original but now fallen cosmos, it is light nonetheless, and in the perspective of a fallen world that light can be known not only to make manifest but also to embody an apocalyptic destiny. This is the destiny that is known by the elect, and while the elect now live in darkness, they can nevertheless know that darkness as light, and thus can act in that darkness with a radical and ultimate freedom and power.

Just as no scientific work has realized and created a greater and more comprehensive system and order than Newton's *Principia*, no work of art realizes and creates a greater and more powerful order than does *Paradise Lost*. In each case these new visions and embodiments of order proceed out of the disintegration of ancient systems and embodiments of order, systems which come to an end with the birth of the modern world. With that ending a new and total energy is released in the world, an energy expressing and realizing itself in all the modes and realms of consciousness and society, as an ancient world and cosmos is truly turned upside down. While this concretely occurs in the trial and execution of the English monarch, the first such event in history, it gradually but ever more comprehensively occurs throughout all the spheres and structures of society and consciousness, but most immediately and decisively so in the *Principia* and *Paradise Lost*. If the trial and execution of Charles I in 1649 is a founding and paradigmatic event in our history, then so likewise is the creation of *Paradise Lost*. And just as the public judgment and execution of the king brought an initial end to the sacred and primal ground of all ancient political and legal order, so *Paradise Lost* brings an end to all imaginative and mythical orders and structures of the cosmos, and does so by realizing all such order and structure as a paradise lost.

Never again will a work of art even attempt to realize and embody an integral and harmonious order and structure of the cosmos. *Paradise Lost* is the last imaginative creation realizing a total world order. Here that order is the order of a world that is lost, so that *Paradise Lost* is itself a "wake" for a cosmic corpse, for a universe that has finally disappeared. But modern revolution was born out of the disappearance of that universe, only then does an ultimate void and chaos appear and become real which can make possible a total and comprehensive revolution, and that chaos can only imaginatively and mythically be named as Satan. So it is that Satan does not become a full and total figure in the imagination until the birth of the modern world. If Bosch was the first artist to realize this epiphany, and Böhme the first mystical and mythical seer to record the birth of an ultimate and divine darkness, it is only Milton in *Paradise Lost* who created a total imaginative order and system both making possible and actually embodying the new and revolutionary primacy of Satanic energy and power, a revolutionary and purely negative power that is finally and inversely directed to a total redemptive and apocalyptic goal and end. And only with the realization and embodiment of a finally redemptive Satanic power and energy do the powers and modes of redemption pass into an apocalyptic and organic unity, so that creation, providence, incarnation, atonement, and apocalypse now for the first time become united in imaginative vision. Only the absolute sovereignty of God now stands outside of this redemptive process. Even if that sovereignty can here be known to direct and sustain all cosmic and human events, it is also now known, and so known for the first time, as a wholly isolated and absolutely solitary sovereignty. This sovereignty can no longer either be interiorly or cosmically present and manifest as itself, but only so present through the glory and the grace which it freely bestows upon the Son.

But the work and role of that Son is inseparable from the role and work of Satan, a Satan embodying the "high permission of all-ruling Heaven" (I, 212), and a Satan whose pure evil finally realizes infinite grace. Therefore the role of Satan is ultimately a redemptive role. While Satan is truly the dark opposite of the Son, it is only through an actual embodiment of that dark and total opposition that a redemption can become manifest which is both total and apocalyptic. But it can be so realized only by and through a new form and mode of self-consciousness, a newly and fully isolated and solitary self-consciousness, but precisely thereby an autonomous and individual self-consciousness whose freedom is newly and only its own. This is that freedom which is the fierce and driving energy of modern revolution, a revolution which is not only total and comprehensive in its power and effect, but which is integrally and finally directed to an apocalyptic goal, a goal ultimately directed to realizing that "one kingdom" which is Heaven and earth at once. Only the final loss of an ancient and original Heaven and heavens can make possible this new interior and apocalyptic resolution, for only the final loss of an original paradise can free all life and energy from an attachment and bondage to the sacrality and ultimacy of the primordial and the past. The very loss of that ultimacy is the grounding center of a new and revolutionary freedom that for the first time can finally and totally embrace a future and apocalyptic goal.

Chapter Eight

Blake and the French Revolution

Nothing is more problematic today than is the French Revolution, and this despite the fact that almost since its occurrence the French Revolution has become established as the primal ground and center of modern history, a center and ground apart from which modern history loses both its coherence and identity. For we have known the French Revolution not only as that primal event that finally ended the ancient and premodern world, but also as the first universal historical event, the first historical event which was destined to transform world history, and to transform world history by realizing it as a universal history. Above all it is the Marxist understanding of the French Revolution, an understanding made possible by Hegel, that established the normative identity of the French Revolution, an identity wherein the French Revolution is the triumph of the bourgeoisie over feudalism, a triumph which is simultaneously the final ending of the ancient world and the irreversible beginning of a universal modernity. So it is that the revolutionary calendar which was created in 1793, a calendar wherein the world began anew with the proclamation of a republic in France, became a fundamental ground of the modern consciousness itself. Now it has become apparent that this is a mythical understanding of the French Revolution, and even if it is as strong as ever in French historiography, it is elsewhere collapsing as a critical and historical interpretation, and most clearly so because it is now manifest that feudalism ended in Western Europe long before the French Revolution.

It has long since been critically established that feudalism ceased to be a historically truly essential characteristic of the political systems or social structures of Western Europe after the thirteenth century. By the eighteenth century, the medieval social and economic institution of feudalism had virtually ceased to exist in Western Europe, even if the word *feudalism* was very much at the center of social and political struggle. But this was a feudalism that was very different from its medieval forebear. Now the tenant was the true proprietor of the land, the ownership both of land and of *seigneuries* or seignorial rights had long since become separable from *noblesse* as a personal quality, for the conquest of land by nonnobles had already begun in the medieval world, and now vast tracts of land and their accompanying seignorial rights and dues were owned both by bourgeous townsmen and by peasants themselves. Indeed, after the Constituent Assembly "abolished feudalism" in 1789, it subsequently proved impossible to distinguish dues that were feudal in origin from those payments or services accruing from economic rent. Nor was this "abolition of feudalism" by the Constituent Assembly a consequence of bourgeous leadership. It was rather a defensive response to the peasant revolts of 1789, revolts which terrified established society, and the peasants followed these revolts by simply refusing to pay their dues, a refusal which after the event was sanctioned by successive Assemblies.

It has also long since become clear that the French Revolution began as an aristocratic revolt against a severely weakening or even collapsing absolute monarchy, a revolt that was then occurring throughout Western Europe, for there was a general resurgence of aristocratic power in the eighteenth century. Moreover, the aristocracy itself was largely becoming a bourgeois institution, and particularly so in France, where the *noblesse de robe*, recruited in earlier centuries from the bourgeoisie, had by the eighteenth century realized a wealth and influence that rivaled all but the greatest families of the *noblesse de l'épée*. At the time of the French Revolution the bourgeoisie in France was so diverse that it did not constitute a homogeneous class, but we do know that the revolutionary bourgeoisie were primarily drawn from an economically declining class of *officiers*, lawyers, and other professionals, with few representatives from the world of commerce and industry. While there was a new economic growth and prosperity in France after 1720, this growth was halted and then reversed by the French Revolution, and the industrial revolution did not occur in France until the mid-nineteenth century. Socially and economically, the Revolution was not the triumph of a new business and industrial bourgeoisie, but rather the triumph of a conservative and landowning bourgeoisie and peasantry, a triumph consolidated and fulfilled in Napoleonic France, and one which would politically and socially dominate France for one hundred and fifty years.

Thus the French Revolution was not a modern victory over medieval feudalism, nor the victory of an economically and socially modernizing class of the bourgeoisie, even if it did finally and ultimately issue in an end both of the aristocracy and of premodern Europe. But this ending was accomplished far more fundamentally by the industrial revolution, a revolution that began in England and was resisted by France, and most resisted by the powers that triumphed in the French Revolution. What the French Revolution most clearly accomplished was an ideological revolution. Even if the ideas of the Enlightenment played very little role in the genesis of the French Revolution, they played an enormous role in the impact of the French Revolution upon the world, and it is due to that impact alone that we may speak of the French Revolution as a dividing line in world history. This is surely the primary difference between the American and the French Revolutions, for whereas the American Revolution had little major impact beyond its own shores, the French Revolution had a revolutionary influence, and not only upon Europe, but gradually upon the world as a whole. If the greatest positive social effect of the French Revolution upon France was its radical and comprehensive reformation of the French legal and administrative systems, this was made possible by the new thinking of the Enlightenment, and implemented by disciples of the *philosophes*, and most forcefully so by Robespierre. Now even if Rousseau was both embodied in and ignored or betrayed by the French Revolution, it is impossible to dissociate the French Revolution from the new and radical idea of national sovereignty, an idea that is at once the embodiment of the transformation of royal sovereignty into popular sovereignty, and of the transformation of the sovereignty of God into the sovereignty of the people. This cannot be dissociated from Rousseau's "General Will" (*la volonté générale*), a will which is simultaneously a universal and an individual will, and a will which is the source of all legal and political legitimacy and authority.

At no point did the French Revolution have a clearer and a greater impact, at first upon France and later upon Europe as a whole, than in its dissolution of the established grounds of Christendom. In the course of a century this dissolution brought an end to Christian Europe. Of course, Christianity was already weak by the eighteenth century, perhaps mortally weakened. But France was then a conformist, Catholic country, and religious practises were never more general in France than between 1650 and 1789. Jansenism, a movement which was centered in the primacy and ultimacy of original sin, was perhaps as passionate a movement as France has ever known, and yet it was soon followed by the French Enlightenment, a movement whose very essence was the rejection and reversal of the idea of original sin. The Catholic Church in France was then as corrupt as any religious institution has ever been. All of its bishops were aristocrats, most of whom were worldly and many of whom were unbelievers, and so much so that Louis XVI seriously declared that the Archbishop of Paris should at least believe in God. Yet the majority of the second estate, including one-fifth of the bishops, voted to join the third estate in 1789, thereby decisively inaugurating the French Revolution. Within less than five months the Constituent Assembly voted by 510 to 346 that all Church property was "at the disposal of the nation," which would be responsible for paying the clergy and caring for the poor. This was followed eight months later in July, 1790, by the Civil Constitution of the Clergy, and political revolution in France, which had previously been supported by the vast majority of the population, was transformed into civil war.

Now that it is clear that the declaration and implementation of the Civil Constitution of the Clergy was the most disruptive event that occurred in France during the Revolution, it is odd that so little attention has been paid to the religious dimension of the French Revolution, at least by its defenders. France had long been the most populous state in Europe, and the vast majority of the French were peasants, for in 1789 while there were perhaps two-and-a-half million people in urban centers, there were between twenty-two and twenty-four million in rural areas. Moreover, between 1715 and 1789 the French population had increased by possibly eight million people, and this clearly led to rural overpopulation, which occasioned intense suffering. So it is that the majority of the peasants were very poor and one-fifth of the French population as a whole was indigent. These were the very people who commonly were deeply attached to the Church, and if the peasants were largely ignored during the French Revolution, it is also true that the Revolutionary leaders had little sense of the realities of rural and peasant life. Otherwise it is difficult to imagine how they could have embarked upon a violent campaign of de-Christianization, a campaign passionately resisted by Robespierre, but at the very center of the revolutionary passion of the *sans-culottes*.

The new revolutionary calendar itself declared France to be a post-Christian country, and it is manifest that for the majority of the revolutionary leaders, even including those outside of Paris, the Revolution itself was inseparable from a dissolution of Christianity. This, of course, did not mean a dissolution of religion, which at that time was virtually inconceivable, with the result that much energy was given to the creation of a secular and revolutionary religion, and above all so by Robespierre. The new religion revolved about the worship of a "Supreme Being" and was grounded in the apocalyptic advent of a new world. Thus Deism became the established religion of revolutionary France, a Deism very different from its English counterpart, for it was dedicated to the revolutionary transformation of the world. Needless to say, this revolutionary Deism meant little to the great majority of the nation, but insofar as the newly constituted State church rapidly withered away, the inevitable result was that the great body of the nation had a vastly diminished possibility of practicing any form of religion. Certainly this was a revolutionary situation, and one not unrelated to the fury and the labor that was given to de-Christianization. De-Christianization was most responsible initially for the spread of revolutionary "terror," and de-Christianization resulted in the Church's becoming the major victim of the French Revolution.

If there was a "materialistic core" at the heart of the French Revolution, this was surely the auction of the vast body of Church property, an auction which had an enormous effect, for the buyers of Church property were the mainstay of the new order. Although we still lack an economic history of revolutionary France, there is good reason to believe that this auction played a major role in creating a new land-owning and conservative French class, one that came to full power in the nineteenth century, thereby making France the most conservative modern nation in the world. And a decisive effect of this process was the alienation of the higher or purer expressions of French thinking and culture from all pragmatic realities. Such alienation was unknown before the French Revolution, and for that matter unknown in any previous historical era. This is assuredly one of the most profound effects upon France of the French Revolution, and it is inseparable from the ideological revolution that was then given birth, and above all so in the new revolutionary ideal of "equality." It is fascinating that throughout the French Revolution the ultimate sanctity of private property went virtually unquestioned. Little effort was made to relieve the suffering of the majority of the nation, and even if this was largely due to the nation's being at war, it is also true that with the war came a far greater power to the central government than had existed in France since Louis XIV.

It is important to note that class consciousness in the modern sense was not born until after the French Revolution. It played no role in the Revolution itself, and only one of the great *journées*, or popular insurrections and demonstrations in Paris, was motivated by economic grievances going beyond the price of bread. The truth is that the revolutionary ideal of "equality" had no economic foundation, or, rather it was an ideal that simply took for granted the economic or material condition of the third estate, despite the fact that the third estate constituted less than a tenth of the nation. Nothing makes this so clear as does what modern historians have discovered about the *sans-culottes*. Now we know that this vitally important revolutionary body consisted neither of criminals nor of the poor. These were rather men who commonly thought of themselves as artisans and who are often revealed by their tax returns as being affluent contractors or comfortable *rentiers*, and, who, while declaring themselves to be the elite of the revolutionary movement, deeply believed in the sanctity of family and work. They were the "moral majority" in the France of their day, and their deepest preoccupation was with a complete break with the past. Yet this led them to no economic program at all. Even the *enragés*, a name given them by their enemies, were less than a dozen all told, and they had no political effect.

If it is true that in the perspective of world history the significant originality of the French Revolution was in its emphasis upon equal rights, this was an emphasis upon political and legal equality which at that time had little effect upon the majority of the nation, and even the elections during the revolutionary era were participated in by only a small minority. Soon the revolutionary dictatorship transcended even this minority, and although it ruled in the name of the "social contract" and national sovereignty, Robespierre clearly grasped the teaching of the *Contrat social* on the impossibility of legally and politically representing the "General Will." True, Robespierre could not and would not abandon what he thought was the true Rousseauist principle of the identification of the "General Will" with the direct action of the people. For the direct action of the people is the ultimate sanction of authority, even if in his view the people resorted to direct action only for the purpose of protecting the principles of the Revolution by intimidating its enemies. In the conditions of national and civil war, a war or wars to preserve the Revolution, this could only mean that the direct action of the people is terrorism. Robespierre's argument was that in peace the people rule by virtue, but in time of revolution virtue must be supplemented by terror, which as an application of justice is an emanation of virtue. Hence the Reign of Terror, a "terror," it is true extraordinarily mild by the standards of the twentieth century. Its executed victims during a year and a half under conditions of war were perhaps less than those who perished during the week that followed the defeat of the Paris Commune in 1871. Nevertheless, the "terror" of the French Revolution has continued both to fascinate and to horrify the world, for like the victims of Stalinism and Maoism its victims were executed in the name of virtue and justice.

It is not insignificant that Robespierre was the high priest or pope of the French Revolution, and sophisticated and sympathetic scholars have often identified him as a second Calvin, for there is little reason to doubt his deeply moral and even religious integrity. Shortly before the end, Robespierre destroyed the professional de-Christianizers who were so offending the peasantry and the world, and then transformed the cult of Reason into the cult of the *Être Suprême*, the creed of which became the Deistic one of the existence of God and the immortality of the soul. Then he and David created the festival of a now personified Supreme Being, Robespierre led the procession and presided over the festival, and the Convention decreed the observance of this festival throughout France. Less than two months later, on July 28, 1794, Robespierre himself was executed, and that date (Thermidor 10; An II) subsequently became established as the end of the French Revolution, for the death of Robespierre was the death of the French Revolution. It was Napoleon who five years later seized the mantle of Robespierre, a Napoleon who in the Concordat of 1802 was actually to effect religiously what Robespierre only intended. Although Napoleon himself was bereft of religion, he did believe that society cannot exist without inequality of wealth, and inequality of wealth cannot exist without religion.

Marx believed that the English and the French Revolutions were essentially and inextricably related to one another, for the revolutions of 1648 and 1789 were not simply English or French revolutions, but

rather European revolutions.Nor were they only the triumph of a particular class of society over the old political order. They were rather
the proclamation of the political order for a new European society.
While the bourgeoisie won that victory, this victory of the bourgeoisie
was then the victory of a new order of society — the victory of bourgeois over feudal property, of nationalism over provincialism, of compe-
tition over guilds, of equality of inheritance over primogeniture, of
the domination of the owners of land over the rule through landowners,
of enlightenment over superstition, of family over family name, of
industriousness over gentlemanly slothfulness, of civic rights over
medieval privileges. These revolutions were also primal embodiments
of a forward-moving and cumulative historical process, so that the
Revolution of 1648 was the triumph of the seventeenth century over
the sixteenth, and the Revolution of 1789 was the victory of the eighteenth century over the seventeenth. So it is that even the Manifesto
of the Communist Party identifies the bourgeoisie as a revolutionary
force in history, going so far as to claim that the bourgeoisie cannot
exist without constantly revolutionizing the instruments of production, and thereby the relations of production, and with them the whole
relations of society. All fixed and frozen relations are now swept away,
and all newly formed ones become antiquated before they can ossify:
"All that is solid melts into air, all that is holy is profaned, and man
is at last compelled to face with sober senses his real conditions of
life, and his relations with his kind."

Certainly one of the decisive achievements the English and French
Revolutions share in common is a profound transformation of
language. Each gave birth not only to a new political and social
language, but also to a new imaginative language that continues to
record and embody the deeper currents of our revolutionary history.
In the early years of the French Revolution, revolutionary journalists
forged a new, postaristocratic form of French that was rich in
neologisms and hailed as *la langue universelle de la République*. This
language was forced on the dialect-rich provinces as a means of
establishing a new national unity, and for the first time after 1792 the

public documents of the national government were no longer even translated into the provincial dialects. Moreover, this new language was derived from the living speech of the revolution itself, a speech incorporating a new and earthy rhetoric directed at the masses. For even though the revolutionary leaders observed correct speech, they discovered in their own way that homiletic power that was born in the Protestant Reformation, and that was so supremely present in the English Revolution. Many of our fundamental political words, at least in their modern meaning, derive from the French Revolution. Not until then is the word *democracy* employed in a positive and fully pragmatic political meaning. The two nouns, *democrat* and *aristocrat* were coinages of the period, unknown before the 1780s. Neither word was current in English before 1789, and, in France, *aristocrate* appears for the first time in the reign of Louis XVI, *démocrate* not until 1789. These new words record new realities, for just as the *ancien régime* did not become *ancien* until the triumph of the Revolution, the aristocrat could not be named as an *aristocrate* until he had lost his social sanction, and the democrat could not be named as a *démocrate* until a political democracy actually appeared in France.

Now even if romanticism is a consequence of the French Revolution, French romantic literature is not clearly or manifestly an expression of the French Revolution. Rather it is in England, the greatest enemy of the French Revolution, that an imaginative language first appears that fully and openly embodies the French Revolution. This most deeply and most comprehensively occurs in Blake's prophetic and epic poetry, for Blake is the poet par excellence of the French Revolution, and of the French Revolution as a universal and apocalyptic event, an event embodying the actual historical and political advent of humanity as a whole. Blake's first full prophetic poem, *America*, which was engraved in 1793, is Blake's response to the American Revolution, which he envisions as the dawning of an apocalyptic transformation of the world. It records the first modern vision of the death of God, whom the seer names as Urizen:

Over the hills, the vales, the cities, rage the red flames fierce;
The Heavens melted from north to south; and Urizen who sat
Above all heavens in thunders wrap'd, emerg'd his leprous head
From out his holy shrine, his tears in deluge piteous
Falling into the deep sublime! flag'd with grey-brow'd snows
And thunderous visages, his jealous wings wav'd over the deep;
Weeping in dismal howling woe he dark descended howling
Around the Smitten bands, clothed in tears & trembling
    shudd'ring cold.
His stored snows he poured forth, and his icy magazines
He open'd on the deep, and on the Atlantic sea white shiv'ring.
Leprous his limbs, all over white, and hoary was his visage.
Weeping in dismal howlings before the stern Americans
Hiding the demon red with clouds & cold mists from the earth;
Till Angels & weak men twelve years should govern o'er the strong:
And then their end should come, when France received the
Demons light.

                                  (16:1–15)

Blake was the first seer to grasp and envision the unity of the American and French Revolutions, a unity marking the advent of a truly new world, indeed, an apocalyptic world, for this advent is inseparable from the end of all previous history. Nothing is more primal and universal in Blake's prophetic and epic poetry than its realization of this end, for here a historical and eschatological ending becomes a poetic and imaginative ending. If this issues in *Milton* and *Jerasulem* in a truly new genre of apocalyptic poetry, it also brings to an end the integral and organic coherence of the Western epic tradition. *Jerusalem*, in its dark chaos, transcends and leaves behind all manifest traces of a forward-moving and unilinear plot. Indeed, it reverses the epic movement which it inherits, so that the only detectable movement in its turbulent and violent language is a universal and comprehensive movement of fall, even if that fall culminates in Apocalypse. So it is that Christian epic poetry in Blake culminates in a fully apocalyptic poetry. But that poetry is released and made possible by an apocalyptic vision of the death of God, an ultimate death that is here inseparable from Apocalypse. This apocalyptic vision both embodies and realizes the end of history, an ending which shatters and reverses every ground of a previously established consciousness and reality, and it is this primal and final shattering of all given identity which this prophetic and apocalyptic seer unveils as the true identity of modern revolution. Thus it is that Blake envisions the death of God as the deepest ground of the French Revolution, an eschatological death that dawns in the American Revolution and is decisively realized in the French Revolution. With the death of God there everywhere breaks forth a profound disruption of every center and source of meaning and identity, a disruption that is nowhere more fully present at this time than it is in Blake's prophetic and apocalyptic poetry.

Blake's relationship to the French Revolution was both deeply ambivalent and profoundly dialectical. No artist or thinker then or later was more distant from the ideology of the Enlightenment than is Blake, none has been more deeply, more consistently, and more comprehensively hostile toward "Reason," "Nature," and "Natural Virtue" than our greatest modern apocalyptic poet. Yet none of our modern artists and visionaries has created an imaginative and linguistic world that so fully and so purely embodies and carries forward the deeper and more radical currents of modern revolution than does the work and vision of William Blake. There is now good reason to believe that Blake was not the isolated prophet that he appears to be. On the contrary, he is the original yet authentic voice of a long tradition of English radicalism, one certainly going back to the seventeenth century sects if not far earlier, and a tradition that continued into the nineteenth century with the birth of the English working class. For the industrial revolution in England transformed the eighteenth century mob into the new collective self-consciousness of the working class. "Radical London" was the center of this revolutionary transformation, and the very period of Blake's creative work was also the period of the formation of the English working class. Yet this was also the period of intense counterrevolution in England. Not only was England the primary political enemy of revolutionary France, but it was only in England that a spontaneous conservative movement arose in Europe, and nowhere else did radical poets, who had initially embraced the French Revolution, so fully despair over its historical consequences, a despair commonly leading to a reversal or transformation of their poetic vision. Blake himself came to believe in his final years that the American and French Revolutions had failed politically: "since the French Revolution Englishmen are all Intermeasurable One by Another." Certainly the transformation of his early prophetic poetry into his mature apocalyptic poetry was decisively affected by this deep political disappointment.

Nevertheless, Blake from beginning to end was a radical political poet. In the perspective of subsequent history we can now see that so far from reversing his early political radicalism, his gradual development into a full epic and apocalyptic poet and artist profoundly deepened his earlier radicalism. At no point is this truth so apparent as it is in Blake's progressive and deepening assaults upon all forms of authority. An early assault upon royal authority becomes an assault upon all forms of political and legal authority, and an early attack upon established morality and religion becomes a revolutionary and apocalyptic war upon all religion and morality. Moreover, this assault upon authority ever more progressively and comprehensively becomes a universal assault, so that an attack upon external legal and political authority spontaneously if gradually passes into an attack upon rational and logical authority, and the names of Newton and Locke come to symbolize a demonic otherness that is just as destructive and self-lacerating as is the repressive authority of king and priest. For as "Vala" or "The Four Zoas" passes into *Milton* and *Jerusalem* (1795–1820), every alien "other" undergoes a transformation into a universal "otherness." Now every manifest identity and power, precisely insofar as it is manifest and real in itself as an identity and power, becomes unveiled as a dark and fallen otherness, indeed, a darkening and falling otherness, an otherness that even now is undergoing a universal transformation into its apocalyptic opposite.

On the frontispiece to *Europe* (1794), there is a portrait of the almighty Creator, a portrait realizing a Miltonic image of the absolute Creator, and a Creator who creates in absolute solitude. All too significantly *Europe* culminates in the apocalyptic advent of the French Revolution, but this is preceded by an eschatological announcement of the last doom:

A mighty Spirit leap'd from the land of Albion,
Nam'd Newton; he seiz'd the Trump, & blow'd the enormous blast!
(13:4)

For it is Newton who first unveils a totally fallen "Nature," a nature as isolated and apart as is the almighty Creator. But nature realizes its totally fallen and isolated form only on the very eve of apocalyptic transfiguration, and it is the full and final appearance of an infinitely distant "Nature" which is a decisive sign and signal of Apocalypse. So likewise it is the full and final appearance of an infinitely distant and absolutely solitary God which is also such an apocalyptic sign, as a Miltonic unveiling of the absolute sovereignty of God is now unveiled as an apocalyptic sign of the imminent end of the world. In *The Book of Urizen* (1794), that absolutely sovereign and solitary God is now manifest as the Lawgiver and Revealer, a Revealer who reveals "The Net of Religion":

Laws of peace, of love, of unity:
Of pity, compassion, forgiveness.
Let each chuse one habitation:
His ancient infinite mansion:
One command, one joy, one desire,
One curse, one weight, one measure
One King, one God, one Law. (4:35–40)

Only at the end of history is God revealed as being only "one God," that one God whose one Law and one Monarchy confines a single joy and desire under a single command and curse, and that curse consumes all life under a single weight and measure. Deism is the ideology that celebrates this curse as freedom, the very Deism which became the established religion of the French Revolution, and the very "Reason" which was infinitely exalted by that Revolution now becomes unveiled as Satan's mantle. Not even Burke so passionately attacked the ideology of the French Revolution as did Blake, and finally, in *Jerusalem*, he reached the judgment that all the destruction in Christian Europe has arisen from Deism or "Natural Religion":

> You O Deists profess yourselves the Enemies of Christianity: and you are so: you are also the Enemies of the Human Race & of Universal Nature. Man is born a Spectre or Satan & is altogether an Evil, & requires a New Selfhood continually & must continually be changed into his direct Contrary. (52)

But only in the apocalyptic situation of the end of the world does either the possibility or the necessity of our continual transformation and transfiguration into our direct contrary become manifest and real. Although this possibility and necessity was first apprehended and named by Paul, just as it was Paul who created both the idea and the symbol of original sin, so it is that it is our apocalyptic situation that draws forth Blake's vision of regeneration, an apocalyptic regeneration that is inseparable from our deep ground in original sin. Thus it is that it is the very Blake who was the first modern seer to envision the death of God that is the Blake who rediscovered and reenvisioned the original apocalyptic ground of Christianity. This occurs at least half a century before its occurrence in historical scholarship, and with it occurs the deepest and darkest vision of the totality of the Fall. This vision, it is true, is in full continuity with Milton's vision, but nevertheless it radicalizes and totalizes its Miltonic source by apprehending the Fall as being all in all.

Blake, even as Milton, was a God-obsessed man and seer, and as that obsession deepened, so, too, deepened his apprehension and naming of the totality of the Fall, but a totality which most immediately and forcefully appears in the naming of God as Satan. This most deeply occurs in *Milton* and *Jerusalem* and in the illustrations to The Book of Job, but it is already present in *The Marriage of Heaven and Hell* and in the earlier prophetic poetry, although in this earlier form it is muted by Blake's initial identification of Satan as the agent and fire of political and moral revolution. Once that identification is deepened into a realization of the pure negativity and universality of Satanic power, there is an accompanying realization of the dark emptiness and vacuity of that power, a realization that reverses all poetic naming and issues in the dissolution or self-dissolution of every center and source of all given or manifest identity. Thus the modern vision of the death of God is by necessity an eschatological vision of the end of the world. It is precisely the vision of the death of God that makes possible and realizes modern apocalyptic vision, a vision wherein and whereby every source and center of identity collapses, and collapses so as to embody a total chaos as the primal ground of all vision and experience. Many responsible literary critics and scholars have long looked upon Blake's apocalyptic epics as the product of madness, a madness seemingly become total in *Jerusalem*, for its chaos is most total just when it is most poetic and most creative, even if these very points are also most prophetic of a post-modern history and consciousness.

Blake's contemporary, Hegel, created the philosophy of history, or an all too modern philosophical theology of history, a theology grounded in the apocalyptic certainty that our world is the last stage of history, a stage inaugurated by the French Revolution. The French Revolution, for Hegel, is a world-historical event, and it issues in a new world in which secular life or history is the positive and definite embodiment of the Kingdom of God. Accordingly, this is a glorious mental dawn, all thinking beings shared in the jubilation of this epoch, for a new spiritual enthusiasm thrilled the whole world, as if the final reconciliation between God and the world was now first accomplished. Now Spirit realizes itself as absolute freedom, for now self-consciousness realizes that its certainty of itself is the very essence of the real world, and the world for it is simply its own will, and this is a "general will" (*Phenomenology of Spirit*, 584). This will is the will of all individuals as such, so that now the self-conscious essence of each and every individual is undivided from the whole. What appears to be done by the whole is at bottom the direct and conscious deed of each individual, and each individual consciousness is universal consciousness and will. But the greatest antithesis to this universal freedom released by the French Revolution is the freedom and individuality of actual self-consciousness itself, for universal freedom is a cold and abstract universality, a universality bringing with it a new "self-willed atomism" of actual self-consciousness. And this new and modern atomism of the existing individual is inseparable form this new universal freedom. Indeed, it is its consequence, for an abstract universality gives itself to the destruction of all human and historical traditions, thereby reducing the individual to a bare integer of existence.

Now that it has completed the destruction of the actual organization of the world, and exists now just for itself, this is its sole object, an object that no longer has any content, possession, existence, or outer extension, but is merely this knowledge of itself as an absolutely pure and individual self. All that remains of the object by which it can be laid hold of is solely its *abstract* existence as such. . . . The sole work and deed of universal freedom is therefore *death*, a death too which has no inner significance or filling, for what is negated is the empty point of the absolutely free self. It is thus the coldest and meanest of all deaths, with no more significance than cutting off a head of cabbage or swallowing a mouthful of water. (*Phenomenology of Spirit*, 590, Miller translation)

Since universal freedom is wholly an abstract freedom, and its ground and object a wholly abstract existence, it can never realize an act or deed of an actual universal self-consciousness. There is left for it only negative action, for universal freedom is actually merely the fury of destruction. Thus absolute freedom becomes explicitly objective to itself in the cold, matter-of-fact annihilation of the existent self, and therein self-consciousness learns what absolute freedom in effect is. For, in itself, absolute freedom is just this purely abstract self-consciousness, a self-consciousness which effaces all distinction and all continuance of distinction with it. It is as such that it is objective to itself: "the *terror* of death is the vision of this negative nature of itself" (592). Therefore this absolutely free self-consciousness is an absolutely empty self-consciousness, and absolute freedom as the pure self-identity of the universal will can realize itself only in a pure negativity, a negativity which is the ultimate abstraction of the universal will, but a negativity which also here and now becomes all in all. Here lies the historical origin of that primal Hegelian category of pure negativity, a negativity that is only actually and universally realized in the modern world, that very world which is the final and eschatological epoch of history. Ours is truly the Joachimite *status* or age of the Spirit, but it is actually so only in the universal realization of pure negativity. This pure negativity is released only by the advent of a pure and total abstract universality, which is itself the very opposite of Spirit.

It is vitally important to realize that the advent of a full abstract universality is itself an eschatological event. Only now does God become manifest and real as a vacuous *Être Suprême* (586), and only now does an absolute contradiction become fully real and realized in history and consciousness, a contradiciton which by an ultimate dialectical certainty must explode into Apocalypse. What Blake named as Urizen, as Selfhood, as Spectre, and as Satan, is conceived by Hegel as abstract Spirit or the "Bad Infinite" or the God who alone is God. And the total universality of Satan which is finally realized in Blake's imaginative vision or "System" is simultaneously conceptually realized in Hegel's philosophical system, a philosophical system which is every bit as apocalyptic as is Blake's *Jerusalem*, and is so above all in its very apprehension of a purely negative Totality. And unlike the negative Totality of Mahayana Buddhism, which is negative and positive at once, the negative Totality of Hegelian Spirit is wholly actual and real in consciousness and self-consciousness as a purely negative actuality, an actuality which is itself the consequence of the real and historical advent of a final and total abstract universality. No philosophical system has ever had a firmer or more real historical ground than does Hegel's, but that ground here becomes a universal ground only by way of its negative epiphany and its negative actualization in consciousness and self-consciousness. This self-consciousness finally becomes an empty consciousness, and not in the positive sense of Buddhism, but rather in the negative sense of an absolute self-alienation, self-estrangement, and self-negation.

Nothing is or could be more Hegelian than is Blake's vision of "Self-Annihilation," a "Self-Annihilation" which is a pure negation of negation, and a negation which can be real or realized only through the final advent of a purely Satanic world and totality. Underlying the Hegelian dialectic is the primal and negative movement of Spirit's becoming its own "other," an "other" which is the intricate opposite of the original identity of Spirit, and an "other" which is realized in the actuality of history and consciousness. It is this negative "labor" or movement of Spirit which is the source of all activity and life. Thereby and therein Spirit becomes alienated and other from itself, but this is the process of Spirit's own becoming, a process without which Spirit would be lifeless and alone. Thus it is that Hegel can conclude the *Phenomenology of Spirit* with the affirmation that this process is the "inwardizing" and the Calvary of absolute Spirit. It is the actuality, truth, and certainty of its throne, for the throne or kingdom of Spirit is the kenotic or self-emptying and self-alienating process of Spirit's actually and truly becoming its own other. Yet this process is only fully realized and actualized with the birth of modernity, a birth that becomes fully and finally actual in the French Revolution, and that is precisely the time and world in which Spirit is first manifest and real in its full and final opposition to and alienation and estrangement from itself.

So it is that the French Revolution is the historical point at which a universal consciousness first fully and finally becomes actual and real. It is real most clearly and most decisively in the antithesis that now arises between universal freedom and the individuality and freedom of actual self-consciousness itself, an antithesis which is itself the source of a new and universal energy and will. For the full advent of an abstract and objective consciousness is inseparable from the birth of a new subjective and interior consciousness, an "I" or self-

consciousness which is only itself. It is only itself by virtue of its antithetical relationship to an objective and universal consciousness that
is the intrinsic and necessary otherness of itself. Moreover, the interior
depths of this new subjective consciousness are inseparable from their
ground in the universality and totality of a new objective consciousness,
for a universal consciousness can realize itself objectively and actually
only by negating its own subjective ground or pole. Now, for the first
time, death is objectively meaningless and insignificant. But it is
subjectively more real than ever before, and thus death itself becomes
the one and only portal to a full and final subjective and interior resolution and fulfillment. Hegel's term for that form of consciousness that
realizes itself by losing all the essence and substance of itself is the
Unhappy Consciousness, a consciousness which realizes itself by
interiorly relizing that *God Himself is dead.*

> This hard saying is the expression of innermost simple self-knowledge,
> the return of consciousness into the depths of the night in which "I"
> = "I", a night which no longer distinguishes or knows anything out-
> side of it. This feeling is, in fact, the loss of substance and of its
> appearance over against consciousness; but it is at the same time the
> pure *subjectivity* of substance, or the pure certainty of itself which it lacked
> when it was object, or the immediate, or pure essence. This Knowing
> is the inbreathing of the Spirit, whereby Substance becomes Subject,
> by which its abstraction and lifelessness have died, and Substance has
> therefore become *actual* and simple and universal Self-consciousness.
> (*Phenomenology of Spirit*, 785, Miller translation)

If Spirit alone, for Hegel, is actual and real, that is because world
or "Substance" fully becomes and realizes itself as "Subject." This does
not fully or actually occur until the birth of the modern world. Then
it subjectively or interiorly occurs in the realization that God is dead,
a realization that inaugurates a new universal self-consciousness, which
is the center and ground of an apocalyptic explosion and transformation of the world. Thus both Hegel and Blake correlate and integrate
the death of God and Apocalypse. Both understand and envision the
French Revolution as the historical advent and embodiment of an

apocalyptic death of God, and both envision the death of God as the death of a wholly abstract and alien form or manifestation of God, an epiphany or realization of God which does not occur or become real until the birth of the modern world. Blake and Hegel also envision the death of God as the act of Spirit itself. The death of God becomes possible and actually real only when Spirit has realized itself in its most negative mode and epiphany. For only when Spirit exists wholly and fully in self-alienation and self-estrangement can it undergo an ultimate movement of self-negation, a movement in which a real end or death occurs of a wholly alienated and estranged form and mode of Spirit. Thus it is dialectically and apocalyptically necessary that Spirit become wholly estranged and alienated from itself before it can realize and embody its own self-negation. For it is precisely the wholly alien and abstract God who dies in the birth of universal self-consciousness, the very God or *Être Suprême* who was worshipped in the cult of the French Revolution and who is the ground of a modern and universal objective consciousness. This is, of course, the God whom Blake named as Satan, but this is the only God who can be named and envisioned in modernity as God alone, the only God who can be manifest and real in our consciousness as the God who alone is God, the God who is an infinitely transcendent mystery.

Blake is the only poet or artist who created a whole mythology. Although in the beginning this was realized with some consistency and coherence, this initial systematic order was broken and disrupted when Blake's "System" became most fundamentally and truly his own, a movement occurring after his turn against the French Revolution in 1795 and decisively recorded in his long and disorderly revisions of his manuscript epic, "Vala" or "The Four Zoas." It is not insignificant that Blake kept rearranging his *Songs of Innocence and Experience* and the plates of *Urizen* and *Milton* and *Jerusalem* until the very end. His mythical system became a "System" only by transcending all logical systematic order, just as his prophetic poetry fully passed into an apocalyptic epic only by bringing to an end the linear movement and order of the Western epic tradition. As Blake's epic vision gradually but decisively became ever more circular and fluid, characters and images move within and without his range in a baffling and perplexing manner, even as these images and figures not only undergo multiple transformations in terms of their own integral identities but also insofar as they come ever more progressively to pass into one another. This is most deeply true of Blake's most original mythical creations, Urizen, Vala, and Luvah. Whereas Blake derived the majority of his mythical figures and symbols from various historical traditions, these symbolic figures are uniquely his own, and their multiple and discordant movements and epiphanies embody Blake's most revolutionary epic and prophetic breakthroughs.

It is also true that as his vision unfolded its symbolic figures underwent ever more universal epiphanies, so that they enter and embody increasingly multiple realms, which are cosmic, historical, and interior, and psychological, political, and transcendent as well. Intially, Urizen or Nobodaddy is a silent and invisible God of jealousy, the author of the tyrannically harsh but obscure laws of revelation, and the transcendent enemy of all liberty and joy. But Urizen ever more progressively expands into a multiple totality, not simply as the Zoa who symbolizes Reason ("Your Reason"), but also as the Creator, who is Satan and also the Revealer of Law and Religion. This Creator becomes ensnared in his own Web or Net of Religion, a primary source of that repression and violence which is the dominant power in a fallen world. Vala is the Goddess Nature, but she does not appear until "The Four Zoas," which originally was to be entitled "Vala." Nevertheless, she is a far more dominant and fundamental figure in *Jerusalem* than in "The Four Zoas." There her movements and epiphanies are so complex and contradictory as to defy all rational and logical analysis. For hers is a demonic and negative energy that is present throughout all the modes and dimensions of a wholly fallen world and totality and that is itself both a source and an embodiment of both cosmic and interior repression.

There is no figure in the whole range of Blake's mythology that has created more confusion and controversy than Luvah — and for good reason, for Luvah is the least consistent figure in Blake's vision. Never at any point does he appear with full clarity. Rather, Luvah is that figure through whom Blake most frequently expressed his own imaginative breakthroughs, and he embodies all the ambivalence of an initial stroke of vision. Although Luvah is first mentioned in *The Book of Thel* (1789), he does not reappear until "The Four Zoas," but here he is a truly major dramatic and symbolic figure. He is an extraordinarily complex one as well, being the center and ground of a universal and eternal process of fall as well as the center of those "Wine presses" which are love and death and war and redemption at once. Luvah is both the point of our departure from Eden and the goal of our return. At the summit he is Christ, and at the nadir he is Satan. For Luvah is an apocalyptic and dialectical *coincidentia oppositorum*, because he is the primal mythical embodiment of that Fall which is a fortunate Fall, a Fall which is simultaneously totally fallen and totally redemptive and thus a redemptive fallenness which is embodied in history and the cosmos as a whole. The Lamb of God descends to redeem when clothed in Luvah's robes of blood. Thus the daughters of humanity greet the Lamb:

> "We now behold . . .
> Where death Eternal is put off Eternally
> Assume the dark Satanic body in the Virgin's womb,
> O Lamb Divine! it cannot thee annoy. O pitying one,
> Thy pity is from the foundation of the World, & thy Redemption
> Begun already in Eternity. Come, then, O Lamb of God,
> Come, Lord Jesus, come quickly."
>
> ("The Four Zoas" 104:11–17)

Not only does this apocalyptic prayer have an exact historical parallel in the earliest Christian prayer, but this passage shows that Blake finally united the Miltonic Son and the Miltonic Satan. For this Lamb cannot be fully incarnate until he assumes the dark "Satanic body," where eternal death is put off eternally.

Consequently, Luvah is a deeply ambivalent and dialectical figure: (1) he symbolically embodies the sacrificial movement of energy or

passion from its original fall to its ultimate self-sacrifice in Christ, and
thence to the repetition of that sacrifice in the suffering of humanity;
and (2) he also embodies the dark or evil forces of passion and must
himself become Satan if he is actually to accomplish his work.

> "Satan is the State of Death & not a Human existence:
> But Luvah is named Satan, because he has enter'd that State.
> A World where Man is by Nature the Enemy of Man
> Because the Evil is Created into a State that Men
> May be deliver'd time after time evermore. Amen."
> *(Jerusalem* 49.67–71)

But not only does Luvah enter the State of Satan, so likewise does
Albion or the "Eternal Man."

> "Albion goes to Eternal Death: In Me all Eternity.
> Must pass tho' condemnation, and awake beyond the Grave!
> . . . .
> Albion hath enter'd the State Satan! Be permanent O State!
> And be thou forever accursed! that Albion may arise again:
> And be thou created into a State! I go forth to Create
> States: to deliver Individuals evermore! Amen."
> *(Jerusalem* 31.9–16)

States are cosmic and interior modes of fallenness. Although they
exist in every man, they must not be confused with the "Minute
Particular" or the concrete individual.

> "Distinguish therefore States from Individuals in those States.
> States Change: but Individual Identities never change nor cease:
> You cannot go to Eternal Death in that which can never Die."
> *(Milton* 32.22–24)

So it is that even though States are forms and degrees of fallenness,
they exist as negative and sacrificial modes of existence that make
possible the reversal of that fallenness for all those individuals who
actually pass through these States.

Blake's Luvah or "Energy" is yet another imaginative and symbolic form of a Hegelian absolute or pure negativity. Therefore it passes between the opposite forms of Christ and Satan and for that very reason can pass in or through any form or mode of existence whatsoever. Nevertheless, at bottom, Luvah is always a violent and sacrificial passion. Its movement is ever a movement to death, but a death which is an eternal, and therefore a redemptive death, reversing the energy it incarnates. Blake, even as Hegel, ultimately came to see the whole of history as a redemptive totality. For even though the actuality of history is a world of violence and horror, and is so for both Hegel and Blake, nonetheless that horror is finally a redemptive horror. It is a redemptive horror because it is a total horror drawing "all Eternity" into itself. Not only do "The Ruins of Time build Mansions in Eternity" (letter to Hayley, May 6, 1800), "But Jesus, breaking thro' the Central Zones of Death & Hell, Opens Eternity in Time & Space, triumphant in Mercy" (*Jerusalem* 75.21). Luvah, who is the violence and horror of history, is also the atoning Lamb of God because he has entered the State of Satan and Death, a state which is universal in our fallen history but which must be passed through if Spirit or "The Eternal Great Humanity Divine" is to be and to become itself. When Blake, in his Laocoön engraving of 1820, declared that "God is Jesus," he provided us with his simplest formula for his mature vision, a vision in which the Divine Body of God himself and the Eternal Body of man are that "One Man," Jesus.

Just as Blake most fully inherited Milton's prophetic and political role, so, too, it was Blake who most decisively reenacted and recreated *Paradise Lost*. He did so by creating a purely apocalyptic epic directed wholly to establishing and realizing the final apocalyptic triumph of the New Jerusalem and made possible by the full and final union of the Miltonic Satan and the Miltonic Son. *Milton* and *Jerusalem* are the joint expressions of that epic, the one embodying Milton's or Satan's apocalyptic and interior movement into damnation or "Self-Annihilation," and the other recording and embodying the cosmic and historical fall of Christ and Adam into Satan, until that fall finally reverses itself by realizing the apocalyptic totality of the New Jerusalem. In *Milton*, the "Human Imagination" is identified with the "Divine Body of the Lord Jesus" (3.3). This imagination in a reborn Milton now begins its final journey, a journey grounded in the passage of Jesus into a curse, a sacrificial offering, and an atonement (2.13). This journey finally realizes its culmination when Milton stands in Satan's bosom and beholds its desolations, the desolations not only of a Miltonic Hell but also of the "ruin'd building of God" (38.16). Then Milton addresses Satan:

> "Satan! my Spectre! I know my power thee to annihilate
> And be a greater in thy place, & be thy Tabernacle
> A covering for thee to do thy will, till one greater comes
> And smites me as I smote thee & becomes my covering.
> Such are the Laws of thy false Heavens! but Laws of Eternity
> Are not such: know thou: I come to Self Annihilation
> Such are the Laws of Eternity that each shall mutually Annihilate
> himself for others good, as I for thee."
>
> (38.29–36)

Now Milton's purpose is to explore "Satans Seat" and to put off in "Self Annihilation" all that is not of God alone: "To put off Self & all that I have ever & ever Amen" (49). Satan heard, and coming in a cloud, with trumpets and flaming fire:

> Saying, "I am God the judge of all, the living & the dead
> Fall therefore down & worship me. Submit thy supreme
> Dictate, to my eternal Will & to my dictate bow
> I hold the Balences of Right & Just & mine the Sword
> Seven Angels bear my Name & in those Seven I appear
> But I alone am God & I alone in Heaven & Earth
> Of all that live dare utter this, others tremble and bow
> Till All Things become One Great Satan, in Holiness
> Oppos'd to Mercy, and the Divine Delusion Jesus be no more."
>
> (38.51–39.2)

Thus, in *Milton*, Satan does not undergo a full and final epiphany into God alone until confronted with the Crucifixion of the Son, a

crucifixion whose full meaning and reality is not unveiled until the
Apocalypse, a self-annihilation annihilating all selfhood, but most
fundamentally annihilating that selfhood which is the "I alone" of God.
All things only become "One Great Satan" in response to the "Self-
Annihilation" of God, which empties the divine and transcendent
realms of all life and energy, thereby making manifest and real that
God who only now is Satan, a final and apocalyptic Satan who is a
consequence of the Calvary of absolute Spirit. Blake's primary biblical
source for his apocalyptic vision is, of course, the Book of Revelation.
It is from that book that he derived the image of the seven eyes of
God. But in Blake's vision these eyes become biblical names and forms
of an alien and transcendent God ever struggling to become incarnate,
until He comes and freely dies in Jesus. Accordingly, the Crucifixion
is the culmination and fulfillment of a long revelatory and incarnate
movement of God. For Jesus dies the death that has always been God's
destiny, a death apocalyptically transforming and reversing the innermost identity of God, but it is precisely that death that is the source
of Apocalypse. This is surely primarily why "Jesus only" is the motto
of *Jerusalem* and why a fully mature Blake can affirm that "God is Jesus."
But God is Jesus only after God has died as God, thereby annihilating
His own selfhood, which now passes into the Spectre, the Shadow,
and the Selfhood of Satan.

So it is that Satan is manifest and real as Satan only as a consequence of the self-negation or the "Self-Annihilation" of God. This
is that ultimate negation of negation which releases the Apocalypse,
thereby revealing that "One Man" who is all in all:

> Mutual in one anothers love and wrath all renewing
> We live as One Man; for contracting our infinite senses
> We behold multitude; or expanding: we behold as one,
> As One Man all in the Universal Family; and that One Man
> We call Jesus the Christ; and he in us, and we in him,
> Live in perfect harmony in Eden the land of life,
> Giving, receiving, and forgiving each others trespasses.
> He is the Good shepherd, he is the Lord and master:

> He is the Shepherd of Albion, he is all in all,
> In Eden: in the garden of God: and in heavenly Jerusalem.
>   (*Jerusalem* 34.16–25)

It is a universal Selfhood which isolates man from man and man from God, a selfhood which is identical with sin, death, and Satan, but which fully becomes or makes manifest itself only with the embodiment and realization of an eternal death, a death which is the forgiveness and finally the abolition of sin. At the end of *Jerusalem*, an ending which is epic and apocalyptic at once, there occurs an apocalyptic *coincidentia oppositorum* of Jesus and Satan, an apocalyptic Jesus who is Jerusalem and an apocalyptic Satan who is God the Creator and Redeemer, or that Selfhood who is apprehended and known as Redeemer and Creator.

On the ninety-sixth plate of *Jerusalem*, there is a deeply disconcerting and seemingly discordant illustration of two majestic figures rising together while drawing closer together in an ecstatic embrace. The figure on the left can only be the divine Creator and Judge, and the figure on the right is a beautiful and naked woman who must be Jerusalem. Satan-Urizen ("The Ancient of Days") looks to the right while baring his right foot, both of which symbolize a spiritual ascent, whereas Jerusalem, who unlike her divine counterpart is facing us, rises on her left foot and looks to her right and our left. This is manifestly a vision of the universal and apocalyptic process of Crucifixion or Self-Annihilation, if only because Satan and Jerusalem are engaged in a mutual negation of that Selfhood which isolates each from the other: Satan reverses his destructive Selfhood so as to become Spirit, and Jerusalem reverses her spiritual movement so as to become "flesh" (that is, *sarx*, in the Pauline sense of existence outside of or apart from Spirit). For Self-Annihilation is the dialectical process of negating the negations created by the birth of Selfhood. Therefore it is the negative process of reversing the Fall, of transposing the contraries evolved by the contraction of the "Human Form Divine." The text on this plate is saturated with apocalyptic imagery. It opens with a vision of the sun and moon leading forward the "Visions of Heaven & Earth," which is immediately followed by an apocalyptic epiphany of Jesus as the Son of Man:

> Then Jesus appeared standing by Albion as the Good Shepherd
> By the lost Sheep that he hath found & Albion knew that it
> Was the Lord the Universal Humanity, & Albion saw his Form
> A Man. & they conversed as Man with Man, in Ages of Eternity
> And the Divine Appearance was the likeness & similitude of Los.
>
> (96.3–7)

Los is the temporal and historical form and expression of the "Human Imagination," an Imagination which is Jesus or the universal process of Self-Annihilation. Here, Jesus is Jerusalem, a Jerusalem who is embracing Satan, who now has his back turned toward us. In the lines facing His awesome buttocks, Albion laments his own cruel and deceitful Selfhood, finally recognizing that the biblical God has ensnared him in a deadly sleep of six thousand years: "I know it is my Self, O my Divine Creator & Redeemer." Thus Albion can recognize his own selfhood only as the deadly Selfhood of Satan at the very time when he can address Jesus as his divine Redeemer and Creator. This is certainly an apocalyptic *coincidentia oppositorum*, and one released by a divine and eternal passage through death. Accordingly, Jesus responds to Albion's terror of his own Selfhood with these words: "Fear not Albion: unless I die thou canst not live; but if I die I shall rise again & thou with me. . . . "

> So Jesus spoke: the Covering Cherub coming on in darkness
> Overshadow'd them, & Jesus said: "Thus do Men in Eternity
> One for another to put off by forgiveness, every sin."
>
> (96.14–19)

But the Satan whose darkness engulfs Jesus and Albion is the Satan who undergoes a cosmic reversal by dying in Jesus's death:

> Jesus said: "Wouldest thou love one who never dies
> For thee, or ever die for one who had not died for thee.
> And if God dieth not for Man & giveth not himself
> Eternally for Man Man could not exist; for Man is Love:
> As God is Love: every kindness to another is a little Death
> In the Divine Image nor can Man exist but by Brotherhood."
>   (96.23–28)

Thus, in this ultimate apocalyptic vision, the Satan who is a consequence of the eternal death of God is a Satan who is united with Jesus, and united by His union with Jerusalem, a final Jerusalem whose apocalyptic movement and actuality is released and made possible by God Himself dying eternally for "Man." The "Divine Image" dies in Jesus so as to abolish the solitary and transcendent God who is the source of judgment and bring about an apocalyptic union that is a full coming together of God and Man.

Almost the whole of the penultimate plate of *Jerusalem* is given to a magnificent illustration of this final apocalyptic union. This is obviously a portrait of the consummation of the initial union between Satan and Jerusalem, and for the most part it lies below the final words of the epic, "The End of the Song of Jerusalem." Now Satan has clearly and fully assumed the face and visage of God, so much so that this is the face of the Father and Son at once, as the white hair of the Father stands beneath the cruciform halo of Christ. In the latest of the four extant copies of *Jerusalem*, and the only one printed in color (on paper dated 1820), the final epiphany of God as Satan is simultaneously an epiphany of God as Christ. But this is that God who now enters into a final apocalyptic union with Jerusalem, whose rising body accompanies flames which are also rising, flames which are dark currents of passion or energy ascending toward the left so as to curve back and down upon the ecstatic body of God. This circular movement of energy unites all the estranged contraries which had become wholly divided and estranged in the course of the epic and who are now united in this conclusion by way of the ecstatic union of Satan and Jerusalem, a union in which Jerusalem and Satan pass into each other with a final vibrant and ecstatic energy. Against a circular background of blue, the heads of God and Jerusalem merge into an icon of Christ, as Jerusalem's upward glance fulfills the motion of her buttocks by enclosing the originally white and sepulchral face of God in the human and triangular space created by her outstretched arms, a space embodying that "One Man" who is now all in all.

"One Man," or an actual and universal self-consciousness, is realized and finally real only as a consequence of a universal and eternal movement through death, a real and actual death which brings a final end to every previous ground and mode of consciousness. This is that end which is historically manifest and real in the French Revolution. But not only is the French Revolution a universal historical event gradually but inevitably bringing an end to all ancient worlds, it is also an apocalyptic and universal actuality realizing and embodying itself in all identity whatsoever. Initially, this new and apocalyptic actuality appears and occurs in a profound distruption of consciousness and society assaulting and shattering every previosuly established symbolic sanction and authority. This occurs not only in economic, political, and social realms, but in interior and cosmic realms as well. Thereby an earlier disruption and transformation of consciousness, one fully present in the triumphs of modern science, philosophy, poetry, and art, undergoes a universal expression and embodiment. Not only does this lead to an economic and demographic explosion, but it also leads to the public and historical advent of humanity at large. Yet a universal humanity appears and is real only as a consequence of a dissolution of the center and ground of self-consciousness.

Blake's prophetic and apocalyptic epics are embodiments of this dissolution and reversal of the ground and center of a Western and interior self-consciousness. Even as they evolve so as to transpose history and cosmos into each other, they not only progressively reverse their original poetic and imaginative ground, but that reversal passes into poetic voice and language itself, so that poetic language ever more fully ceases to be the voice of an interior self-consciousness. Now a fully interior selfhood and self-consciousness can speak and be real only in and as the voice of Satan, who is a purely transcendent Selfhood and therefore the intrinsic otherness of all energy and life. And this Satan is a universal Satan. It is present in a new universal logic and reason, a new sovereign and ubiquitous nature, a new objective consciousness and society, and a new autonomy of subjective consciousness. Although the seeds and grounds of these new forms of universality were centuries in the making, it is only after the French Revolution that they coalesce and become one, so that it is only then that all becomes "One Great Satan" who is both the voice and the center of all actual meaning and identity. No poet grasped this new actuality more fully and more comprehensively than did Blake. If this led to a disruption and shattering of Blake's own epic, that is a decisive sign of its genuinely epic status, for it records and embodies a world and humanity that is passing through a cataclysmic crisis and transformation.

While Blake believed that individual identities never change nor cease to be, he also came to believe that since the French Revolution concrete individuals are all intermeasurable one by another. For all humanity has now become enslaved to Selfhood, and that human form that once could be called divine is now but a "Worm seventy inches long" (*Jerusalem* 29.5). At the end of *Milton* there is a cryptic passage declaring that "the Starry Eight became One Man, Jesus the Saviour, wonderful! (42.10). Not until the fifth-fifth plate of *Jerusalem* does the symbol of the "Starry Eight" appear again, and there it is identified as the final embodiment of the incarnate and redemptive movement of God:

> And they Elected Seven, call'd the Seven Eyes of God;
> Lucifer, Molech, Elohim, Shaddai, Pahad, Jehovah, Jesus.
> They nam'd the Eighth. he came not, he hid in Albions Forests.
>   (55.31–33)

If the eighth Eye of God is now hidden in Albion's forests — buried in the "Minute Particulars" — there can be no question of the presence now of a concrete individual who is wholly and simply human, just as there also is no possibility of the presence of a resurrected Lord or Life who is recognizable as "One Man." That "One Man," who is an actual and universal self-consciousness, is invisible as such, for the only actual signs of this apocalyptic presence are the final withering away of all the given and identifiable modes of human consciousness and experience.

But it is precisely a final dissolution of all human presence which is a decisive sign of an apocalyptic presence. It is the death of God that actualizes and ushers in that presence, a death that is inwardly present in the loss of all the essence and substance of selfhood and that is outwardly or historically present in the advent of an abstract and objective universality that dissolves and consumes every subjective and individual presence and identity. And so far from being a repetition or rebirth of a prehistorical and primordial universality, our objective universality is fully present as such in mathematical, scientific, and technological expressions, and also ever increasingly in social, political, and cultural expressions, all of which effect an erasure of concrete and interior individuality, so that an inward self-consciousness can now only actually and objectively be realized in an abstract and universal voice and language, the very language and voice of Blake's Satan. If Satan has, indeed, been apocalyptically united with Jerusalem, there is no way by which this can be said or expressed in any manifest language without profound discord and discoherence. Unlike the chaos of an actual primordial mythology, the chaos released by this discordance embodies in itself a certitude of its own actuality. Once it has been heard, it can never be forgotten, and once it has been fully heard, no pure harmony is ever hearable again.

Chapter Nine

Joyce and the End of History

Nothing is more baffling in epic language than its intrinsic authority, an authority immediately confronting its hearer or reader, and nowhere is this power more fully manifest than in the language of *Ulysses*. Joyce, even as Virgil, Dante, and Milton, had established his power as a poet and artist well before the publication of his first epic in 1922, and like his predecessors he had undergone a long initiation into his role as an epic poet. But unlike Dante and Milton, although reenacting Blake, Joyce initiated himself into Christian rather than Classical epic poetry; and despite appearances to the contrary, Homer and Virgil are only indirect presences in Joyce's work. His brother, Stanislaus, remembered deeply that, as a youth, Joyce's gods were Blake and Dante. Not only did this linguistic genius never learn Greek, but he chose the theme of Ulysses in large measure because of a persuasion that the Homeric epic has Semitic or Biblical roots. It is Dante above all who is Joyce's primary archetypal model or source, and while he declared that his intention in *Ulysses* "is to transpose the myth *sub specie temporis nostri*" (letter 9/21/20), the myth that he thereby and thereafter transposes is far more deeply a Christian rather than a Classical myth. Now even if Joyce knew more profoundly than anyone that Catholicism is the "Old Religion" reborn, and thus is inseparable from its archaic ground, that archaic ritual and myth is recreated by Joyce in a fully Christian form and mode. Thus it is all too natural that Joyce is so commonly considered to be our modern Dante.

Perhaps most startling of all, Joyce's epics, even as Dante's, Milton's, and Blake's, fully conjoin and unite mythology and history, so that the historical actuality of our own time and world is not simply present but is spoken in the epic language of *Ulysses* and *Finnegans Wake*, and respoken so that it is history and myth at once. At no other point is the authority and power of epic language more manifestly present, for not only does myth hereby pass into "our time," but our time and history thereby realize a full ritual and mythical identity, and so much so that once this has occurred our history can never again be dissociated from myth. Surely this has always been a primary function of the epic bard, but no previous epic poet confronted such a radically demythologized history as did Joyce. If this was less true in Ireland than in the rest of Western Europe, it is no less true that no other epic poet, with the possible exception of Homer, so violently wrenched himself away from his original mythical or religious roots as did Joyce. For Joyce, no less than Dante, Milton, and Blake, is a passionately religious poet, and even if he is so only by being religious and irreligious simultaneously, this itself was made possible only by a deep turn against the mythical and historical identity which he initially was given or received.

Hypocrisy was always for Joyce the unforgivable sin, and nowhere could hypocrisy have been more fully present than in a European country or province intending to be Christian in the late nineteenth century. Thereby hypocrisy becomes virtually indistinguishable from its religious ground, and the Joyce who believed that he had never met anyone as religious as himself, may well have been the only twentieth century *homo religiosus* who fully freed himself from the deepest grounds of religious hypocrisy. This is the situation necessitating blasphemy as the major mode of religious speech. Like its archaic and prophetic counterparts, Joyce's blasphemy is directed against the primal center and ground of its own world, even if the Ireland Joyce knew and re-created was then the most religious nation in Western Europe. Certainly the Ireland of *Ulysses* and *Finnegans Wake* is infinitely more religious than is any modern nation, but this is not simply because of the epic form of these works, but also because the Ireland Joyce created is Dante's Catholic Church and Christian Empire reborn, and reborn so as to be a total and all too modern history and world.

If no previous epic poet had fully or decisively confronted a profane or demythologized history, it is also true that no earlier bard had so continually and so passionately demanded of himself such an exactitude of historical and factual detail. Indeed, it is only with Joyce, or perhaps somewhat earlier in Chekhov, that a uniquely modern realism if fully born in imaginative literature, a realism revolving about not only an earthly but an all too exact and empirical world. Joyce, even as Picasso, was a realist before he was a visionary, and as in Picasso's painting that realism was deepened rather than transcended in his full visionary work, for even *Finnegans Wake* never abandons a depth and universality of linguistic exactness that is met in no other literary work. As opposed to all the epic poets who preceded him, there are no purely imaginative creations in Joyce's epics. For even as poetry and prose become one in *Ulysses* and *Finnegans Wake*, then so likewise myth and history here become one, and do so while each fully remains and wholly realizes itself. It is fantasy in all of its forms which finally ends in *Ulysses*, for even the Circe episode is the epiphany of an all too real unconscious language. But this is an unconscious language proceeding naturally and spontaneously from the first epic hero who is everyman, and an everyman who is a totally concrete and actual individual.

Both in *Stephen Hero* and in *A Portrait of the Artist as a Young Man*, Joyce advances a theory of the three forms of art that is truly his own, even if it is not unrelated to the esthetic theories of Schiller, Schelling, and Hegel. These forms are the lyrical, the epical, and the dramatic, forms in which art necessarily divides itself as it progresses from one to the next. Each of these is a form in which the artist presents his own image: presenting it in immediate relation to himself in lyric, in mediate relation to himself and others in epic, and in immediate relation to others in drama. Now these three forms correspond to Joyce's three major works, and they give witness to a progressive movement of an artist who is first in immediate relation to himself, then in mediate relation to himself and others, and finally in immediate relation not only to others but to all others whatsoever. Therein and thereby the artist is not only transformed, but is necessarily and progressively transformed by the very evolution of his art; and transformed so that an original individual immediacy is finally consummated in a universal immediacy with all and everyone. Although something very like this occurs in the beatification of the poet in the *Paradiso*, and in Blake's vision of his own "Self-Annihilation" in the first book of *Milton*, never before does the artist as a full and concrete human being undergo such a transformation, and never before, although this transformation is fully foreshadowed in the *Commedia*, does an artist's work undergo such a necessary, such a progressive, and such a comprehensive transformation.

Just as there is a far greater distance between *Finnegans Wake* and *A Portrait* than there is between the late and the early quartets of Beethoven, or even between the mature and the early painting of Picasso, so there is a greater distance between the creator of the *Wake* and the creator of the *Portrait* than we may find elsewhere in the world of art. But that distance does correspond to the radical transformation of self-consciousness that occurred between 1908 and 1938, or between the turn of the century and the Second World War. This transformation is comprehensively present in the art of the twentieth century, but nowhere is it more fully present than in *Ulysses* and *Finnegans Wake*. These epics might even be treated as a clinical record of that transformation, and they are certainly far more detailed and "factual" than are the case histories of psychoananlysis, to say nothing of the fact that transformation is here truly self-transformtion, and that it occurs in language and in texts which are themselves a primary source and ground of a post-modern consciousness.

It is seldom remarked that the conversion of Stephen in *A Portrait* outshines all the conversion confessions presented in William James' *Varieties of Religious Experience*, and does so even in its veracity. For although this is not an autobiographical account, it nevertheless is extraordinarily real, and not least both in the solidity of its theological ideas and in its images of damnation. Here, Joyce is manifestly a son of Dante, although a Dante and an Aquinas mediated through a neo-Scholastic and post-Tridentine Catholicism, which is to say a non-Gothic and nonhistorical Dante. Nowhere else may we see so fully the religious and mythical world against which Joyce rebelled, for despite its homiletic and liturgical power, this is a dark and Irish-Jansenist world that crushes all life and energy and directs its repressive power most forefully and most immediately against libido or the very source of life. Accordingly, we can see that from the beginning Joyce associated Christianity with a death instinct, perhaps with the death instinct. Above all the Christian Creator and Judge is now an embodiment of death, a God who would not be God if He were not a God of total and eternal judgment. It is significant that even the postconversion Stephen of *A Portrait* is persuaded that Jesus is more like a son of God than a son of Mary (513), whereas in *Stephen Hero* he claims that he has made Jesus into a common noun (141). The truth is that Jesus never openly appears as Jesus in Joyce's epics, and never either as Jesus or as Christ, for both Jesus and Christ were absent from the Catholicism that Joyce knew, as is so clearly indicated in this statement of Stephen's in *Ulysses*:

> Fatherhood, in the sense of conscious begetting, is unknown to man. It is a mystical estate, an apostolic succession, from only begetter to only begotten. On that mystery and not on the madonna which the cunning Italian intellect flung to the mob of Europe the church is founded and founded irremovably because founded, like the world, macro- and microcosm, upon the void. Upon incertitude, upon unlikelihood. (207)

It would be difficult to discover a theological statement that so voids both the son of God and the son of man. It is almost as though Joyce realized the final Miltonic consequences of the dogma of the eternal generation of the Son, a generation which finally unveils itself as a generation from nothingness or the void.

Certainly a primal symbol of the void dominates Joyce's work from its beginning to its end. That symbol undergoes a necessary and progressive metamorphosis in the evolution of that work, a metamorphosis wherein and whereby voidness or emptiness ever more fully and more finally becomes all in all. Already in *Stephen Hero*, the artist anticipates this destiny.

> Stephen did not attach himself to art in any spirit of youthful dillettantism but strove to pierce to the significant heart of everything. He doubled backwards into the past of humanity and caught glimpses of emergent art as one might have a vision of the pleisiosauros emerging from the ocean of slime. He seemed almost to hear the simple cries of fear and joy and wonder which are antecedent to all song, the savage rhythms of men pulling at the oar, to see the rude scrawls and the portable gods of men whose legacy Leonardo and Michelangelo inherit. And over all this chaos of history and legend, of fact and supposition, he strove to draw out a line or order, to reduce the abysses of the past to order by a diagram. (33)

The abysses of the past do not cease to be abysses when they are recovered in Joyce's epics. On the contrary, the progressive and necessary order of those epics ever enlarges and universalizes a primal and primordial abyss, and so much so that finally both history and consciousness are indistinguishable from that abyss.

Critical analysis has now fully established the incredibly intricate and organic structure of *Ulysses*, a structure whose only real historical precedent is the *Commedia*, but nevertheless a structure whose very form and mode conjoins and unites cosmos and chaos, so that this epical realization of a fully modern cosmic order is simultaneously and necessarily an apocalyptic epiphany of a long hidden but original primordial abyss. Now that abyss fully passes into language and text, and does so more fully and more finally than ever previously in the West, even if this all too modern epic is in full continuity with the Western Christian epic from Dante through Blake. But never before had epic so fully passed into writing or text, for never before had the Christian epic so fully absorbed and consumed its scriptural source.

Only now at the end of that epic tradition do Scripture and epic finally and fully become indistinguishable from each other. Therein and thereby a truly new language is born, a language it is true in full continuity with its past, as is so marvellously manifest in episode 14, which reenacts the history of English prose from its beginnings to modern slang. Yet that very history irrefutably demonstrates the newness of the language which now is present, a language in which exterior and interior are indistinguishable from one another, in which subject as subject is everywhere and everyone, and in which object is totally exterior and factually at hand even while being indistinguishable from a speaker or subject.

If a uniquely modern language is a language of chaos, or a language in which cosmos and chaos become one, it is thereby a language recovering a primal rite or ritual which had been dissolved or erased by the very evolution of language in the West. At no point is Joyce more deeply Catholic than in the power and immediacy with which he recovers and re-creates a pure ritual language, a language which had been largely lost or forgotten in the Catholic Church itself, as witness the assaults upon the postpatristic Church in the modern liturgical movement, assaults which were sanctioned by the Church itself in the Second Vatican Council. Significantly enough, however, a truly modern liturgical theology is simply absent and unknown, apparently not even being upon the agenda of modern Catholic theology. Perhaps one reason for this is that it is only in *Ulysses* and in *Finnegans Wake* that there lies present and manifest to all a fully modern or postmodern liturgical language, and a language which is here inseparable from a violently anti-Catholic assault. Indeed, it is precisely by way of a comprehensive and polemical assault upon the Catholic Church that a primal ritual language is here recovered and renewed, and renewed so that ritual language is now indistinguishable from cosmic and historical language, for herewith dawns or returns a ritual language that is indistinguishable from language itself.

Sacrifice, and an original and primordial sacrifice, is the primary center and ground of all full or fully enacted ritual, and most particularly so in the Western or Latin rite. Just as a fundamental difference between Eastern and Western Christianity is the dominant role of atonement and reconciliation in the latter, so likewise the Western liturgy is distinctive in its centering upon the institution of the Eucharist as itself a sacrificial act, indeed, as the ultimate sacrificial act, an act unreal apart from the death and blood of the Crucifixion. Thus the body and blood or the bread and the wine that are consumed in the mass are the sacrificial body of Christ the Victim, and a victim who is crucified and resurrected in every repetition or reenactment of the mass. Every mass is a requiem mass that not only remembers but far more fully re-presents or reenacts (*anamnesis*) that original sacrifice which is the sole source of redemption and life. But unlike Protestant commemoration or remembrance, the Catholic mass is not simply an interior but also and simultaneously an exterior act, an act that is enacted both by word and gesture, and that is unreal apart from the community or world in which it occurs, and likewise unreal apart from the physical elements of bread and wine or their necessary substitutes.

Both the priest and the congregation reenact the role of Christ the Victim in the action of the mass, but nevertheless the priest acts and speaks in the name of the congregation, and therein his own individual and distinct identity is voided and erased. Liturgical vestments are primarily employed to set forth and make manifest this role of the priest, who therein reenacts the sacrificial action of Christ, an act which is joined by the community as a whole in their participation in the liturgy. The truth is that the gestures, acts, and even many of the words of the mass go back to the very beginnings of human history. At no other point is the Catholic Church so fully and so actually an archaic community or world, and at no other point does the Church embody a greater power and authority in its communal life. This authority and power not only profoundly shaped the life and identity of the young Joyce, it also so shaped the life of Western culture and society for over a thousand years, and beyond that perhaps a million years of sacrificial rites and celebrations have formed and molded not only our innermost identity but also many of our external gestures and acts. Tradition is never so overwhelming in the Roman Church as it is in its ritual and liturgy, and above all so in its Eucharistic liturgy, which itself is centered in Holy Week, and centered therein not in Easter as is the Eastern Christian rite but rather upon Good Friday.

One of the ironies in Joyce's employment of *The Odyssey* as the apparent source and ground of *Ulysses* is that the Homeric epics so profoundly demythologized and deritualized their archaic ground, whereas *Ulysses* recovers and resurrects that ground as does no other work of literature in the Western tradition before *Finnegans Wake*. This irony is not unrelated to the historical fact that the Homeric epics are the initial and germinating embodiment of the advent of a full individual consciousness and world in the West, whereas Joyce's epics have played such a decisive role in reversing and transforming that Homeric embodiment. If an archaic ritual comes to an end in the Homeric epics, or is so muted or transformed as to be all but invisible as such apart from archeological and historical analysis, it is already reborn in Greek tragedy, a rebirth which itself was affected by the earlier rebirth of archaic ritual in the Greek mystery cults. Now even if the Christian liturgy originated in the Jewish liturgy, it was also decisively affected by Hellenistic rituals, so that the Christian Eucharist is far more openly and manifestly an archaic ritual than is any Jewish rite, and most particularly so when after the destruction of the second Temple sacrifice ceased to be cultically practiced in Judaism.

The archaic ritual act of sacrifice is far more fully or more openly present in the Christian Eucharist than it is in any other instrument or expression of Western culture and society. Just as we may presume that an archaic sacrificial rite or rites was a grounding center of society and consciousness for hundreds of thousands of years, so it is that its new presence in the Catholic mass was a grounding center of Europe for a thousand years and more, a center which is present once again in Joyce's epics if not elsewhere in our world. But in these epics that center becomes conjoined with an everyday, a prosaic, and an empirical world. While it is true that a synthesis of this order is present in the Gothic world, as witness the *Commedia*, and that it is perhaps reborn in Elizabethan drama, it never before is such a fully ritual synthesis as it is in *Ulysses* and *Finnegans Wake*. Never before Joyce is a pure and archaic ritual conjoined with a radically secular and demythologized world. One might well believe that it is the end of Christian Europe which makes possible this epic rebirth of ritual, just as it is the dissolution or transformation of a uniquely Western self-consciousness which is the arena of its epical enactment.

At the conclusion of the Proteus episode of *Ulysses*, which fully initiates Stephen hero into his new epic role, an initiation ritually occurs by way of a passage through death, although this is a "seadeath," the mildest of all deaths known to man, but a death which makes manifest a cosmic incarnation, an incarnation in which "God becomes man becomes fish . . ." That fish is Christ as a purely ritual victim, and as such a victim wholly dissociated from any mythical form of Christ, a victim who is pure victim as such and no more, and hence by necessity a nameless or anonymous Christ.

> Come. I thirst. Clouding over. No black clouds anywhere, are there? Thunderstorm. Allbright he falls, proud lightning of the intellect, *Lucifer, dico, qui nescit occasum*. No. My cockle hat and staff and his my sandal shoon. Where? To evening lands. Evening will find itself (50).

Christ here and now becomes indistinguishable from that Lucifer who falls and yet knows no fall. Joyce's Latin phrase is borrowed from a phrase in the Roman Catholic service for Holy Saturday, the Easter Vigil, a vigil that his brother, Stanislaus, reports, Joyce never failed to attend until quite late in life, rising for the occasion about five in the morning, even though he was habitually a very late riser.

The Son of God appears mythically or dogmatically in *Ulysses* only in a heretical form, most clearly so in Sabellian Trinitarianism: "Sabellius, the African, the subtlest heresiarch of all the beasts of the field, held that the Father was Himself His Own Son" (208). This is the Father who thereby is invisible as father, but this invisibility creates the mystery upon which the Catholic Church is founded, a mystery that is manifestly present only in the Latin liturgy. But now that mystery is wholly dissociated from Catholic theology, thereby rite itself is dissociated from myth, and a primal rite stands forth which is mythically anonymous or nameless. Accordingly, the Catholic God is now only a noise or voice in the street (186, 34), even if He is thereby a "hangman God" who is doubtless all in all in all of us (213). This does make possible a new or perhaps renewed prayer to: "Our father who art not in heaven" (227). And this is the very prayer which is prayed to prepare the way for the coming of Elijah, or the apocalyptic end of the world, an end which the night language of Circe names as the "new Bloomusalem" (484). For if there is a human and individual presence of Christ in *Ulysses*, it openly or manifestly occurs only in Leopold Bloom, that perfectly ordinary man who is extraordinary only in his ordinariness, but who is factually and bodily present in the language and text of *Ulysses* as had been no imaginative presence ever before.

Joyce delighted in the crudest excesses of modern Gnosticism, and above all so in the writings of Madame Blavatsky, again and again both alluding to and ironically rewriting her writing in the profane text of *Ulysses*. Such an atmosphere is the perfect foil for Leopold Bloom, that all too worldly and prosaic one before whom even the darkest mysteries pass into the prose of an ordinary day. But that ordinary day is "Bloomsday," and it is an exact day, June 16, 1904, the very day that Joyce fell in love with his Molly. This is a day that passes into night in the course of the epic movement of *Ulysses*, and thereby its day language passes into dream or night language, that ultimately apocalyptic language which is fully and finally born in *Finnegans Wake*. The saturnalia that is the Circe episode certainly effects a literal reversal of Bloom's language and identity, but Bloom nevertheless emerges from this ritual and linguistic orgy as the Bloom whom he was at the beginning of the epic, a Bloom who is the literal opposite of any possible ritual or mythical identity. Or, rather, this textual and linguistic actualization of a primordial abyss and chaos finally issues in an inversion and reversal of a primal ritual act. For all the finality and primordial power of an original rite is now present in Bloom, or in Bloom and Molly. Nothing could be more overwhelming than Molly's sheer bodily and factual presence in the final episode, a profane and final presence which has all the power of a total primordial presence.

Now that it has been well established that it is the final monologue of Molly and the dream language and action of the Circe episode that opened the way to the night language of *Finnegans Wake*, it is necessary to inquire into the ritual identity of Joyce's final and ultimate language. For that language is not and cannot be simply and only a mythical language, if only because of the sheer immediacy of its power and effect. Certainly one source of the power of this language is its ritual effect upon its reader, an effect that is present even in a reading in which little meaning is conveyed, for here language has a power transcending all manifest or apparent meaning. This is the very kind of power present in a ritual word or act, even if that presence is real only in the actual enactment of the rite, for the power of ritual language is inseparable from its own enactment. But something like this sort of power is reenacted when we read *Finnegans Wake*, and even more forcefully so when we hear an oral reading of its text. For as Joyce himself makes clear in his reading of the Anna Livia Plurabelle passages of chapter 8, the voice of Anna is a primal and sacred voice, and its cadenced intonations immediately evoke the rhythm and the majesty of a liturgical chant. Such a liturgical ground is directly or indirectly present in the text of *Finnegans Wake* as a whole, and it is not the least source of the difficulties this text presents to the silent and individual reader.

While *Finnegans Wake* intends to embody mythical and sacred traditions from the world as a whole, it would appear that its ritual ground derives largely or wholly from the Latin liturgy, except insofar as it repeatedly evokes that original divine sacrifice which is the mythical origin of the world. Certainly the liturgical allusions in *Ulysses* are all to the Roman rite, but it is fascinating to observe how multiform and virtually innumerable these are, for Bloomsday is enacted not only in our historical world but also and simultaneously by way of the liturgy of the Roman Catholic Church. *Ulysses* is our fullest Catholic novel, and while Catholic doctrine is here present only in an ironical or heretical form, Catholic ritual pervades both the language and the action of this epic novel, for not since the *Commedia* has the Catholic Church been so fully present in a work of literature. Doubtless Joyce is a priest of the imagination, but he is a Catholic priest of the imagination, and perhaps most forcefully so when he enacts the role of the antipriest or the anti-Christ. Unquestionably the blasphemy of *Finnegans Wake* is a holy or sacred blasphemy, and is so even when it is most ribald and scatological, for it is a blasphemy which is inseparable from a sacred or primal ground. While the blasphemy in *Ulysses* is never so pure, and often as in Buck Mulligan is simply profane, its range is incredible broad, evolving all the way from the cosmic blasphemy of the Circe episode to Bloom's worldly response to the mass in episode 5. Nevertheless, there is no blasphemy at all in Molly's final monologue, and its very absence here, where we might most expect it, bespeaks a fundamental difference between *Ulysses* and *Finnegans Wake*. For in *Finnegans Wake* all life and energy is said and resaid in blasphemous acts and language, whereas in *Ulysses* pure eros or body transcends a blasphemous identity, just as Bloom's innermost consciousness even as his everyday acts are free of either a sacred or an antisacred ground.

Not the least irony of *Ulysses* is that Bloom is the least Catholic figure within it, and not simply because of his Jewish origin and loyalty, but far more deeply because of his fully and finally profane identity and character. Just as Bloom is the most factually actual character in all literature, his words and acts are invariably without the least apparent religious intonation, except when they are literally inverted in the Circe episode. But that literal inversion finally succeeds in deepening his profane or secular identity, so that Bloom can then initiate Stephen into a fully earthly or historical world, thus preparing the way for Molly's final Yes-saying to body and earth. If Bloom is a Christ figure in *Ulysses*, he is so wholly without any Catholic theological or mythological identity, and only insofar as he is a ritual victim acting and speaking at the very center of this epic action. While it is only in the Circe episode that Bloom is manifestly and purely or totally a ritual victim, he is nevertheless a foil for the meaningless speech and action surrounding him throughout the novel, and it is precisely in the context of his sanity and probity that this Catholic and Christian world stands forth as being meaningless or mad. Here, the Christians assume precisely the role that is given the Jews in the Gospel of John, a role wherein their own fullness becomes manifest as emptiness, their own faith as faithlessness, and their own virtue as hypocrisy.

Yet any such resolution is never straightforwardly presented in *Ulysses*, it is only ironically present, although it is always present when Bloom is in the presence of others. But this is the very kind of presence which is present in the parabolic Jesus of the synoptic gospels, and it is a presence which is fully present in the sacrificial Christ of the Holy Week liturgy of the Roman rite, the very liturgy which is a primal background and even an epical mode of *Ulysses*. So it is that ritual imagery and language is essential to the action of *Ulysses*, and to its epical action, an action wherein and whereby the Christian world as a whole is quite literally voided. But that voiding is the resurrection of a primordial abyss, a resurrection finally issuing in ecstatic joy. If Molly's final Yes-saying is manifestly a primal and even a sacred presence, it is a presence arising out of a void or abyss. This very abyss has finally been realized in the language and action of this epic, and it is an abyss that is the consequence of Bloom's and Molly's fully and totally profane presence, a presence whose very actuality, and full historical and factual actuality, is the center of an epic action which finally and fully negates or reverses itself. *Ulysses* culminates in closing time, the closing time of the Christian world, but this is a closing time necessarily issuing in the resurrection of *Finnegans Wake*.

One of the intrinsic sources of the power of *Ulysses* is its full conjunction of a comprehensive and total structure and order, an order renewing in a new world the total order and world of the *Commedia*, with a wholly spontaneous and free movement and speech that is every bit as arbitrary and senseless as are the actual moments of our lives. Therein and thereby the conjunction and coinherence of cosmos and chaos becomes actual and real, and actually and fully present in a *coincidentia oppositorum* wherein the opposites are real and opposing opposites even as they are united in a radically new and immediate *coincidentia*. In a parallel manner, while each episode of the epic is a fully distinct and individual organism with its own individual structure and language, it is simultaneously an integral organic component and part of the novel or epic as a whole. Even as each episode of *Ulysses* is its own microcosmic center while being inseparable from a macrocosmic whole, so it is that the comprehensive and epic movement of *Ulysses* is wholly free, spontaneous, and arbitrary, and yet nevertheless totally inevitable and necessary. However, a full and necessary conjunction of individual freedom and divine predestination has always been an essential ground of the Christian epic tradition. If that tradition is renewed and reborn in *Ulysses*, it is so by way of a new union of freedom and necessity, wherein an individual freedom and self-consciousness is finally indistinguishable from a cosmic and divine necessity and order.

Just as modern physics could discover a random and arbitrary microcosmic energy and movement that nevertheless embodies a total and comprehensive order transcending any order known in the past, so likewise Joyce's epics discover and embody a fully arbitrary and random linguistic and human movement and energy that is simultaneously a cosmic and organic order. Accordingly, it is not odd to discover a ritual order and structure in *Ulysses*, even if this is realized in a fully profane, historical, and prosaic world. Indeed, it is precisely the full conjunction of the archaic and the modern which is a primary and primordial source of the authority and the power of *Ulysses*, a power which is manifestly present in its ritual movement, and a power which in this embodiment would be unreal if it were to occur in a liturgical and sacred world. But so likewise would it be unreal if it were to occur in a mythical world, or in a mythical world in manifest or apparent continuity with the world of Christendom. So it is that a primal and archaic ritual order is fully born in Christian imagination and experience only by way of a loss and disappearance of the Christian mythical world, a disappearance fully enacted in the language and movement of *Ulysses*. But that loss and disappearance is absolutely necessary to call forth and make possible a ritual movement that is actual and present for us, which is to say a ritual movement and order that is real in our world.

Finally, *Ulysses* is no more a mythical than it is a Homeric novel, for it is a novel or epic issuing forth and realizing itself in its very voiding of the Christian world, and above all so the Christian mythical or theological world, and it is out of this dissolution and disappearance that a truly new archaic and ritual world is born. But this new ritual world is a Christian world, or it presents and realizes itself through the Latin liturgy, as for the first time the Christian rite or liturgy is given a full imaginative and textual realization. Therein it has a historical power and actuality that it never had before, a power embodying it in a fully profane and everyday world, the very world that is born with the disintegration of Christendom. That disintegration is epically enacted in this text, and it is out of that enactment that this ritual movement arises, a movement embodying a cosmic Eucharist or mass but a cosmic mass revolving about a wholly profane victim or center, a victim who already is "Here Comes Everybody." Now the world itself becomes a sanctuary, the sanctuary where this epic and linguistic movement occurs, and a sanctuary making possible a new center and victim, a victim and center who is an absolutely ordinary human being.

Only such a prosaic and fully concrete and factual center and ritual victim could break down all barriers between the altar and the world, between rite and actuality, or between a ritual and a total presence. Then the Eucharist becomes not only a cosmic but also an historical mass, a mass which is enacted in our history and world, and enacted at the very center of its brute facticity and actuality. Nothing is or could be heroic about this ritual victim, or nothing heroic in the classical sense, which is to say in a mythical sense. For Leopold Bloom is the first totally prosaic hero, the first hero who could only be identified as an anti-hero from any mythical perspective. Now this is absolutely essential to his profane or fully historical identity, an identity wherein unlike any previous form of Christian mythology, the Christ who is the high priest and eternal victim is the son of man as an actual and real human being who does not simply seem or appear to be a human being but who is a real and actual human being at the very center of his identity and consciousness. Once Leopold Bloom has come, or has been epically realized and enacted, then every previous epiphany of Word or Christ in the imagination now becomes manifest as a docetic epiphany, or an epiphany in which Word is only accidentally word, or in which Christ is neither essentially nor actually either a natural or a human being.

If Dante was unable to envision Christ in any human form whatsoever, and Milton refused to enact or envision him as an eternal and divine Word, just as Blake was never able to envision the whole Christ in a singular or individual form, it is not until the twentieth century that Christian epic can envision Christ as an actual human being. And then it can do so only by dissociating this victim or center from every earlier Christian mythology or theology, even unveiling and embodying him in and as an eternal word which is an actually spoken word, and an eternal priest and victim who is present and actual in our very midst. Only in the perspective of this epic actualization can we realize that the Christian or Incarnate Christ has never been fully incarnate before, or has never been actually seen and imagined as incarnate, or celebrated as the priest and victim who is actually and finally present in our time and flesh. Now a Eucharistic presence becomes a real presence, indeed, and a presence not upon an altar or in a sanctuary but rather in the very fullness and finality of the world. This is a presence which is only gradually presented and evolved in the Christian epic tradition. But from Dante through Milton and Blake, this epic evolution ever moves forward toward the finality of history and world, finally realizing an apocalyptic finality wherein cosmos and history are the very eschatological fullness of Christ.

As this epic revolution enacts itself in its primary texts, it continually transforms and even reverses its mythical language and form, and when it reaches its termination in Joyce's epics its initial totality is reborn in an integral whole or wholes. All the historical and cosmic power and order of the *Commedia* are reborn in *Ulysses* and *Finnegans Wake*, but that original mythical order and structure has reversed itself in a new purgatorial order and movement that moves from Eternity to time. Samuel Beckett could justly say that *Finnegans Wake* is purgatorial in the "absolute absence of the Absolute," but that absolute absence is present in the ritual language and movement of both *Ulysses* and *Finnegans Wake*, a movement and language in which a total emptiness becomes both actually and factually present. Nowhere in our tradition does a ritual movement have such power, or such comprehensive and total power, and it remains a ritual movement in the sheer immediacy of its actual presence, a presence transforming everything which is here enacted. That presence is inseparable from its profane and prosaic form, as all the power of a primordial sacrifice is enacted in these texts, as these texts themselves every progressively in their enactment become liturgical worlds embodying both the fullness and the finality of concrete and actual time and space.

Nevertheless, the fact remains that it is our first fully and wholly prosaic hero who is the center of the new epic language and action of *Ulysses*. The acts and language of this epic hero are not only everyday and ordinary words and acts, but they are acts and words which therein and thereby are indistinguishable from those of their audience or reader, so that this new epic hero is heroic precisely and most deeply in his antiheroic identity. So likewise if Bloom is a Christlike figure he is so only by way of a reversal of every mythical identity of Christ, and it is by that very reversal that he becomes an actual and factual presence, a presence that could be actually present only in a totally prosaic world. But Bloom is present in that world as is no other heroic or antiheroic figure in our modern imaginative traditions, and it is just such a real presence which we must understand as a Eucharistic presence, for it is a presence releasing and embodying a sheer immediacy of energy and life. Moreover, the epical presence and action of Bloom in *Ulysses* is a sacrificial presence and act. It is precisely the transmythical and the antiheroic form of this actual presence which is the source of a new and profane or prosaic life, a new worldly energy and presence which is released by the actual and factual presence of this all too secular and worldly Christ. True, it is impossible for us to imagine Bloom as Christ, but his epical presence in this text affects us even as does a ritual enactment, for both make actual a real presence which is the presence of life itself.

And that life is a sacrificial or self-negating life, a life that is itself only by being other than itself, and is a Christlike presence only by being other than every positive or majestic image or identity of Christ. Blake's "Starry Eight" or eighth eye of God is not fully born or actual until the advent of Leopold Bloom. Then that eye is fully and wholly a "minute particular," and it is as such that it is really and factually present. But the eighth eye, even as the seventh eye, is a sacrificial eye: it, too, comes and freely dies, and its death, too, ends an individual and interior presence, although now that ending is extended to all interior and individual presence. So it is that Bloom's epical and ritual presence in *Ulysses* is a comprehensive and ever impacting and transforming presence which draws forth every actual presence it meets in such a way as to end its individual and private presence. That ending is itself enacted by the reader or the audience of this epic, so that the real presence of this antihero and anti-Christ is the actual and factual presence of a full emptiness drawing everything it encounters and enacts into its own prosaic and truly universal world.

Joyce is a priest of the anti-Christ, and he is not without precursors as such, one of whom indirectly exercised an enormous impact upon Joyce, and that prophetic precursor delighted in identifying himself as an anti-Christ, Nietzsche. Nietzsche not only discovered the archaic ground of Greek tragedy, but even more deeply the archaic and primordial ground of the individuality and interiority of consciousness itself, a discovery making possible a postmodern realization that the advent of the interiority and individualiy of consciousness is a fall from an original and primordial innocence and bliss. If that bliss is reborn in Molly Bloom's final act of Yes-saying, it is also reborn in a new Zarathustra, a Zarathustra whose proclamation of Eternal Recurrence is certainly both a preparation for and a full anticipation of the epic novels of Joyce. It would be tempting to think of Joyce's relation to Nietzsche as paralleling that of Dante's to Aquinas, but there is no evidence or sign that Joyce ever read Nietzsche carefully, just as there is no evidence that he was ever immersed in any philosophical text, including those of Aquinas. But Joyce was shaped as a young artist and scholar by the world of late-nineteenth-century European literature and criticism, and that world was awakening to the power of Nietzsche, even if Nietzsche did not have a full impact upon Europe until that time when Joyce was withdrawing from every contemporary intellectual and literary influence, a withdrawal made necessary by the writing of *Finnegans Wake*.

What is far more significant is that Joyce as an artist was closer to the integral center of Nietzsche's thinking than Dante as a poet was to the center of Aquinas's theological thinking, and so much so that there is no thinker, including Vico, who offers us a fuller way into the night language of *Finnegans Wake* than does Nietzsche. Nietzsche's tragic and lifelong conflict with nihilism anticipated the coming of the language and the world of *Finnegans Wake*, as did his late identification of nihilism as the ultimate logical conclusion of our greatest values and ideals. Only this identification makes possible the Nietzschean and Joycean realization that the actual human being is much higher than an ideal humanity. Even more fundamentally, Nietzsche's discovery that the "I" both of pure thinking and of self-consciousness itself is an "it," that our deepest interior and internal identity is at bottom and inescapably also a wholly external and exterior identity, is ever more progressively orchestrated in Joyce's work, until it finally triumphs in *Finnegans Wake*. That triumph is also and thereby the triumph of the total Yes-saying of Zarathustra, but that Yes-saying is inseparable from a full realization of the totality of No-saying, a No-saying or "bad conscience" or *ressentiment* which is the source and the origin of everything which is internal and within.

As Joyce evolved as an epic artist, memory became ever more important in his creative work, and he could even declare to Frank Budgen: "Imagination is memory." Just as no previous epic poet was given to speaking and envisioning a prosaic and factual exactitude, so none before Joyce had recorded an actually spoken language, or an interiorly and individually experienced day and night. Therefore it is not until *Ulysses* and *Finnegans Wake* that memory or *anamnesis* becomes the primary vehicle of epic creation. No thinker since Plato and Augustine has understood memory as deeply as Nietzsche. In the essay on guilt and bad conscience in the *Genealogy of Morals*, Nietzsche responds in an almost Joycean manner to the question of how memory is created for the human animal:

> One can well believe that the answers and methods for solving this primeval problem were not precisely gentle; perhaps indeed there was nothing more fearful and uncanny in the whole prehistory of man than his *mnemotechnics*. "If something is to stay in the memory it must be burned in: only that which never ceases to *hurt* stays in the memory" — this is a main cause of the oldest (unhappily also the most enduring) psychology on earth. One might even say that wherever on earth solemnity, seriousness, mystery, and gloomy coloring still distinguish the life of man and a people, something of the terror that formerly attended all promises, pledges, and vows on earth is still *effective*: the past, the longest, deepest and sternest past, breathes upon us and rises up in us whenever we become "serious." (Kaufmann translation)

Not only is pain the primary vehicle and mode of memory, but forgetting or forgetfulness is an active and positive faculty of repression and control. For not only is forgetfulness a preserver of psychic order and repose, but without it there would and could be no present time or moment.

This Nietzschean insight offers us an illuminating way into *Finnegans Wake*. For nowhere else is such a pure and total memory present of language and speech, a memory here embodying itself as the full and total opposite of forgetfulness. This is a memory intending to embody all our past in the text before us, and most particularly and most forcefully so that past which is a cruel and painful past for us, a past which is the source of that which is most deeply given within us. Nietzsche's Zarathustra identifies "it was" as the will's most secret melancholy, for the deepest source of the bondage of our will is the brute fact that we cannot will backwards, and thus we are wholly powerless against everything that has occurred and has been done. Accordingly, Zarathustra offers a redemption to all those who live bound to the past by way of a re-creation of all "it was" into "thus I willed it" and "thus I shall will it" (*Zarathustra*, II, "On Redemption"). This new Dionysian redemptive way is nothing more and nothing less than the proclamation and the dance of Eternal Recurrence. Yet this is a uniquely modern or postmodern identity of eternal recurrence, for it reverses the archaic symbol of eternal return by both apprehending and creating an Eternity or "Being" which *is* the pure immanence of a present and actual moment. That pure immanence dawns only when the Eternity and the Being of our past have been wholly forgotten, only when God is dead. Then and only then is that center everywhere whereby and wherein: "Being begins in every Now" (*Zarathustra*, III, "The Convalescent"). So it is that the eternal recurrence that Nietzsche discovered is possible and real only by way of the death of the Christian God, and above all so the death or dissolution of our memory of the Christian God, a memory which is itself inseparable from our deepest and most guilty and most self-lacerating pain.

That pain is nowhere more fully present than in our language and speech, a speech and a language which is itself both a source and a ground of our self-hatred and guilt, and thus a language which is not only a source of the bondage of our will, but also a source of our bondage to the past, to the very givenness and finality of "it was." In one of the last entries in his notebook, Nietzsche confessed that: "To attain a height and bird's eye view, so one grasps how everything actually happens as it ought to happen; how every kind of 'imperfection' and the suffering to which it gives rise are part of the highest desirability" (*The Will To Power*, 1004, Kaufmann translation). No one understood more deeply than did Nietzsche that the very advent of consciousness is a fall, a sudden and irreversible fall, for it is identical with that internalization and interiorization of humanity which is the source of that bad conscience which is our deepest pain and disaster (*Genealogy of Morals*, II, 16). But the suffering to which bad conscience gives rise is desirable above all else, for it alone embodies and gives rise to the No-saying and *ressentiment* of guilt and revenge, and it is the transformation and reversal of that guilt which is the ecstatic joy of the Yes-saying of total affirmation. Thus the fall into consciousness is a fortunate fall, a *felix culpa*, that very fall which is a primal ground of the Christian epic tradition, and which is reborn so comprehensively in *Ulysses* and *Finnegans Wake*.

The origins of this modern apprehension of a total but finally fortunate fall go back at least as far as the advent of Christianity, and the advent of an apocalyptic Christianity, as fully manifest in the earliest Christian writing or scripture, the letters of Paul. There it is precisely the appearance or the actual advent of the world or cosmos as "old aeon" or "flesh" which is the decisive sign of the triumph of the new age of the Spirit. Just as Christ is the second Adam, the Crucifixion or "blood" of Christ is a renewal and reversal of original sin, and as such is the sole source of salvation. Not until Paul does Scripture or mythology in the West know a full and pure dichotomy between old and new, or flesh and Spririt, or sin and grace. And the advent of this dichotomy brings with it a wholly new identity to the "other," to darkness and evil, to fall and sin. Now even sacred or revealed language cannot dissociate light and darkness or sin and grace, or cannot name one without evoking or speaking the other. For not only is the Christian simultaneously a sinner and yet justified, but there is no way by which the Christain can know his or her justification except through the new portal of original sin or pure darkness. So it is that if the Christian Scripture is the first writing in the world fully and decisively to name Satan as Satan, this is an inevitable consequence of the naming of Christ. For the proclamation of the resurrection of Christ is a celebration of the end of evil and darkness, a celebration necessarily issuing in a new naming of the negation of negation or the death of death, a death which only now can be known so as to be fully spoken or named.

Just as nothing more manifestly distinguishes the Old Testament from the New than does the absence of Satan, or the Christian Satan, from the Old, so likewise nothing more forcefully distinguishes Christian from Classical epic than does the absence of even a shadow of Satan from Homeric and Virgilian epic. Moreover, there is an evolution of the identity and power of Satan in Christian epic poetry, evolving from the wholly frozen, impotent, and silent Satan of the *Inferno*, to the majestic and glorious Satan of *Paradise Lost*, a Satan who is now at the center rather than at the periphery of epic language and action, to the Satan of *Milton* and *Jerusalem*, who is the almighty Creator and Lord, and whose own final metamorphosis is not simply the sign but is the very center of resurrection and apocalypse. *Ulysses* and *Finnegans Wake* carry forward this evolution, but now Satan is indistinguishable as Satan, for he has undergone a final metamorphosis into the totality of cosmos and history, and thus has become that Satan who knows no fall, or whose fallenness and darkness is indistinguishable from light and resurrection. Not only does the Joycean Satan evolve out of the Blakean Satan, but the Blakean Satan evolves out of the Miltonic Satan, and even if there is no apparent precedent in Dante for Milton's Satan, the Miltonic Satan is far closer to the all too powerful and active Satan of the New Testament than is an infernal Satan who can neither move nor speak. Nevertheless, we can see Dante's presence once again in Joyce, for the Satan of the *Commedia*, who is silent and impotent, is simultaneously the final source and ground of a new evil and chaos, indeed, the greatest discord and violence which had thus far entered Western poetry or art. For Dante, Satan even now is destroying the earthly Catholic Church, by becoming virtually incarnate in its hierarchy, an incarnation ending the temporal authority and status of the Church. All of this for Joyce is simply and irrefutably given, or is so after the *Portrait*, so at this point the challenge to our final epic poet is to bring together his early gods, Blake and Dante, by conjoining the Satans of Dante and Blake, a conjunction and union wherein these Satans not only become one but therein and thereby realize and embody an ultimate Satanic identity and power.

On the very first page of *Finnegans Wake* we encounter and hear Satan's cry as he falls from paradise — "bababadalgharaghtakammin-arronnkonnbronntonnerronnuonntrovarrhounawnskawntoohoohoord-enenthurnuk!" — a cry repeating the name and thunder of every sky god, and the cry of that fall which "is retaled early in bed and later on life down through all christian minstrelsy." But on the last page of the *Wake*, a page or ending which turns to or simply is the beginning of the epic, Anna Livia Plurabelle, who at the very least is Dante's Beatrice reborn, declares that she is going back to "you," a you who is "my cold father," a return and a far return which is: "Coming, far! End here." This ending is the beginning of the epic, for it is an eternal beginning which is an eternal ending, an eternal return which is "Given!" The mature Joyce who believed so profoundly that there is nothing whatsoever which cannot be expressed, and expressed in language and writing, is the epic poet who gave us our ending, an ending which actually occurs and is spoken in this text. Now language in its totality is a fallen and wholly fallen language, a language which is the language of Satan. But precisely for that reason it is the language of all, and not in the sense that it is simply the language that we speak, but rather in the sense that it is the language that speaks us, and speaks us with a finality that we hear and know to be our own.

The very first pages of the *Wake* to be written, 380–382, eventually became the conclusion of Book II, chapter iii, which is both the central or axial chapter of the *Wake* and also the most difficult and complex section of this dream or night epic. Now the cosmic mass is a dream mass, but it is a Eucharist nontheless, and a Eucharistic feast, a feast culminating in the cosmic consumption of Earwicker or H.C.E., who is Bloom reborn into "The Eternal Great Humanity Divine." But the virtually literal center of the earliest writing in the *Wake* is a divine acceptance of eucharistic death — *I've a terrible errible lot todue todie todue tootorribleday* — a death which is not only the center of a historically cosmic Holy Week, but which is reenacted again and again throughout the course of the epic. If the universal humanity of the *Wake* is both a legendary Ireland and a contemporary Dublin pub, and "Here Comes Everybody" is both a local innkeeper and the most glorious divine and heroic king of our archaic past, then both the action and the speech of the *Wake* are divine and human simultaneously, a simultaneity which is also present in a mystery play or drama which is the universal history of humanity. While everything is the same in this eternal recurrence or return, it is the "seim anew" (215.23), and the "mystery repeats itself todate" (294.28).

A constantly repeated prayer in this epic is a prayer for sleep — "Grant sleep in hour's time, O Loud!" (259.4) — a sleep which is the deepest sleep in the "Ainsoph" or En Sof, the mystical Godhead of this Christian Kabbalah. Yet arising from the center of this sleeping Godhead is original sin or "original sun," a "felicitous culpability" or *felix culpa*, and a *felix culpa* which this epic poet derives from "*Hearsay in paradox lust*" (263). Nevertheless, original sin in the *Wake* evolves into full linguistic actuality, an actuality which is cosmic and historical and exterior and interior at once, and an actuality which is a Eucharistic sacrifice of the Godhead. Therein and thereby Godhead itself is guilty in the *Wake*, a guilt which is present and realized in the speech and acts of deity, acts and speech which are embodied in the creation of the world, and acts which are embodied and eternally repeated in all language and speech. Therefore the language of the *Wake* is not only human and divine at once, it is totally guilty and totally gracious at once, for our final epic language is a cosmic and historical Eucharist, a Eucharist centered in an apocalyptic and cosmic sacrifice of God. Now a primordial chaos and abyss is indistinguishable from Godhead, just as an original chaos has passed into the center of speech. But now this ultimate chaos is fully and finally present, and present in and as this apocalyptic and liturgical text.

While the language of *Finnegans Wake* initially appears to be far more narrow and constricted than is the language of *Ulysses*, this gradually but ever more fully becomes manifest as an illusion, and most particularly so insofar as this night language realizes itself within its reader as both a cosmic and an interior totality. So likewise all narrative structure and linguistic order seems to break down and dissolve in the *Wake*. But this, too, is an illusion, and an illusion because a resurrection or renewal here occurs which is the very opposite of a dark and empty abyss which is simply and only chaos. *Finnegans Wake* is every bit as much an epic as is the *Commedia*, and it is a Christian epic, an epic moving from Fall to Apocalypse, and evolving by way of a necessary and inevitable movement, even if that movement now occurs by way of the pure immediacy of a totally present and actual language and speech. Just as cosmos and chaos are now fully and wholly one and united, so chaos and cosmos are now ended as such, and ended in that final and apocalyptic "Given!" that is embodied in this text. True, that "Given!" can never be heard or envisioned as such, but that is because this is a final ending, and therefore every distinct or individual meaning or identity is no longer manifest or speakable.

However, this ending is a full resolution of the Christian epic tradition, one which has always been grounded in a full and actual opposition or dichotomy between light and darkness, or Fall and Apocalypse, or Satan and Christ. An epic tradition beginning with a new language envisioning and sounding pure darkness and pure light ends with a new night language resurrecting the primordial word of creation. And if Dante's epic language both begins and founds the Christian world as historial and imaginative word and world, Joyce's epic language both resolves and consumes its origin or source in a total linguistic world or cosmos that finally and apocalyptically ends both the Christian imagination and the Christian historical world. Yet nowhere does this occur more fully than in an apocalyptic and total union of Christ and Satan, a union resolving and fulfilling the dialectical but violent polarity of Satan and the Son of God in *Paradise Lost*, and the cosmic and apocalyptic but nevertheless mythical and visionary union of Christ and Satan in *Milton* and *Jerusalem*. Now that union passes into the pure immediacy of an actual and factual language and speech, a speech and language more brutally and factually precise than can be found in any other text or epic, as a primordial and Christian mythical and ritual *coincidentia oppositorum* now becomes all in all.

But even as in *Jerusalem* Christ and Satan become one through the ecstatic and apocalyptic union of the Creator and Jerusalem, so in *Ulysses* and *Finnegans Wake* this ultimate union begins with the inverse and only potential union of Bloom and Molly in bed, and ends with the silent and invisible resurrection of H.C.E. in the "All" and the "Given!" of the final voyage and ecstatic celebration of A.L.P. Not only is Dante's Beatrice present once again, and present in both Jerusalem and A.L.P., but so likewise the Catholic Mother of God now undergoes her ultimate epiphany, an epiphany or epiphanies ecclesiastically sanctioned by the proclamation of the dogma of the Immaculate Conception by Pius IX in 1854, and by the proclamation of the dogma of Mary's bodily assumption into heaven by Pius XII in 1950. Each of these papal bulls followed rather than preceded their epical source, for each reflects an act and enactment of the Christian imagination, an enactment wherein and whereby the Mother of God is the Mediatrix of all grace. While this enactment is fully present in the *Commedia*, here it is not yet fully incarnate historically and interiorly, an incarnation and embodiment which cannot occur until the end of Christendom, until the death of the Christian God. So it is that when the fullest epical and poetic presence of the Christian God occurs and is real in *Paradise Lost*, it is accompanied by the silence and invisibility of the Mother of God, a Mother who can only be absent in the presence of the Father, and who can be fully or totally present only in the total absence or death of the God who is God and God alone.

Just as Milton is the greatest purely theological thinker and visionary in the Christian epic tradition, a poet and thinker who seemingly ended for all time the presence and actuality of the Mother of God, so Joyce is the least theological thinker in that tradition, and precisely thereby renewed and resurrected the archaic and primordial Goddess. While this resurrection and renewal begins in Blake's epics, and thus begins with the first modern vision of the death of God, the goddesses of Blake's prophetic poetry commonly if not predominantly embody a destructive and demonic presence, a presence which is itself the primary source of repression and violence in the history of the world. Dante's actual vision of Beatrice as the source of all grace is not fully and comprehensively renewed until the advent of Molly Bloom, and the Molly who undergoes an apocalyptic apotheosis into Anna Livia Plurabelle is also the Molly who is the first female presence in the Christian imaginative tradition of an actual and living center of joy and grace. Nevertheless, Molly, even as Bloom, is neither mythical nor divine, for she, too, is a profane and prosaic center, and one who is inseparable from both an ordinary and a factual presence.

It is the profane and prosaic presence of *Ulysses* that is comprehensively present in the night language of the *Wake*. Even if that presence is now far more fully a ritual presence, and a ritual presence above all in the eternal repetition and return of a primordial and divine sacrifice, and a divine and primordial fall and guilt, that sacrifice and even that liturgical sacrifice is present only in the words of this text. It is in and by these words, and these words alone, that a primordial sacrifice and origin is now actual and real. But these words are the most prosaic words in ours or any language, just as they are the dirtiest and most pornographic words which have ever passed into a text, for not only is this night language a wholly worldly or fleshly language, it is also a language which at least by intention never strays from an actually spoken speech. Writing or scripture finally ends in *Finnegans Wake*, for this is a text in which a written or writable language has wholly disappeared as such, and disappeared to make way for or to awake that primal and immediate speech which is on the other side of writing or text, and on the infinitely other side of that writing which is Scripture or sacred text.

Nevertheless, Scripture is more fully and more universally present in *Finnegans Wake* than it is in any other text, and not only is this true of the Bible as a whole, but the Koran is likewise present even if to a far lesser degreee, and so also are the Eddas, the Bhagavad Gita, the Egyptian and Tibetan Books of the Dead, and even Confucian and Buddhist scriptures, to say nothing of the virtually continual presence of the *Commedia*. But always these texts are present only by way of their emptiness or absence as sacred or mythical texts, their original sacrality now invariably passes into ribaldry, banality, and blasphemy, as all the grace of an archaic and sacred Heaven is now present and actual only by way of what Scripture could only name as Satan and Hell. The scripture or writing which is most fully present in the *Wake* is the New Testament, and it is present almost wholly by way of quotations from or allusions to the four gospels, even if these are invariably inversions or reversals of the gospel texts. Even the four evangelists are present once again as witnesses and narrators, but not only are they now false witnesses, they are reverse witnesses or narrators, who become yet another source of dissonance and disorder. Yet this is just the chaos that makes possible an apocalyptic epiphany of total grace, a grace realizing and enacting itself by way of the revelatory and sacrificial presences of H.C.E. and A.L.P.

Even as Dante is fully present in the *Commedia*, and Blake is actually present in *Milton*, so Shem the Penman is present in the *Wake*, but he is so only by way of a continual and violent conflict with his opposing brother, Shaun, a conflict wherein and whereby the total violence of the primordial sacrifice passes into the very act of writing. Now writing itself becomes indistinguishable from the original act of creation, and therein it becomes far more violent and chaotic than it has ever been before, and so much so that even if *Finnegans Wake* is for the most part written in English, it is written in an English that can be read only by learning to read anew. Every new epic calls for and demands a new art and act of reading, and there is no greater distance between *Finnegans Wake* and *Jerusalem* than there is between *Jerusalem* and *Paradise Lost*. What is new or newer in the *Wake* is that reading even as text seems to be ending, and ending in a text that is wholly and purely antitext, a text reversing the beginning of imaginative reading in *The Iliad*. Thereby ritual fully passes into writing, and so writing ends as a writing which is only writing, and a writing is born which is inseparable and indistinguishable from that chaos and abyss which appeared to come to an end with the advent of writing and art.

Thus there is no narrative structure as such in the *Wake*. Or, rather, narrative structure and epic movement are indistinguishable from a cultic and sacrificial violence, a violence wherein and whereby the breaking and dismemberment of the Host and Victim passes into the very words of this text. From one point of view, *Finnegans Wake* is a historical reversal of the Latin liturgy, a reversal renewing and resurrecting a primordial sacrifice and rite which is itself a primal ground of the Christian liturgy. So likewise the language of the *Wake* embodies a historical reversal wherein the English language itself returns to its Teutonic origin, an origin which is here renewed not only by a rebirth of Viking sagas, but also by a recovery or intended recovery of that Viking Danish which is the mother of the English language, and Danish is the most frequently employed foreign language in this epic. The "night" language of the *Wake* in Danish is *nat* language, pronounced "not language," and the text informs us in Nietzschean language that this night language is our origin: "in the Nichtian glossery which purveys aprioric roots for aposteriorious tongues this is nat language at any sinse of the world . . ." (83.10). The Dublin "ostman" or Norseman, H. C. Earwicker, is both "Haar Faagher" and the ancient Celtic hero, Finn MacCool, but he is also Yggdrasil or the cosmic Tree, which in the Eddas symbolizes the universe, a universe which goes on trial as the "Festy King" in chapter 4.

The fall, condemnation, and crucifixion of H.C.E. is the dominant epic action in the *Wake*, and it is repeated again and again, even as the host is ever broken in the mass. And just as the liturgical acts and action of the mass culminate in communion, so fall and death culminate in a festival or orgiastic communion in this apocalyptic epic, a communion whose very blasphemy, and scatological blasphemy, undergoes a constant ritual repetition in the text. But lying at the center of the epic, even as the breaking of the Host lies at the center of the mass, is the execution or crucifixion of "Haar Faagher," an execution which becomes both most dramatic and most scatological in the television skit by the comics Butt and Taff of "How Buckley Shot the Russian General." This occurs in the axial chapter of the *Wake*, and it culminates in that tavern orgy which is a cosmic repetition of an Easter which is Good Friday, an Easter or Resurrection which is an ecstatic consumption of the crucified body of God. But this cosmic Easter is possible only as a consequence of the breaking of the Host:

> How Buccleuch shocked the rosing girnirilles. A ballet of Gasty Power. A hov and az ov and off like a gow! And don't live out the sad of tearfs, piddyawhick! Not offgot affsang is you, buthbach? Ath yetheredayth noth endeth, hay? Vaersegood! Buckle to! (346.20)

After the announcement of this primal event, H.C.E. is himself accused of the primal crime. He pleads guilty (363.20), and goes on to associate or link himself with the executioner:

> . . . I am, I like to think, by their sacreligion of daimond cap daimond, confessedly in my baron gentilhomme to the manhor bourne till ladiest day as panthoposopher, to have splet for groont a peer of bellows like Bacchulus shakes a rousing guttural at any old cerpaintime by peaching (allsole we are not amusical) the warry warst against myself in the defile as a lieberretter sebaiscopal of these mispeschyites of the first virginial water who, without an auction of biasement from my part, with gladyst tone ahquickyessed in it, overhowe and underwhere, the totty lolly poppy flossy conny dollymaukins! (365.3–12)

For the death of God is the self-sacrifice of God, and not only is the executed the executioner, but the condemned one is the eternal Judge, and nothing whatsoever distinguishes guilt and condemnation or crime and execution, because Victim and Judge and Host and Creator are one. While these primordial and apocalyptic motifs are only indirectly and ironically present in Christian Scripture, they are directly and immediately present in the Eucharistic liturgy, a liturgy revolving about the breaking of the Host and Victim who is God Himself. True, these primal motifs are dismembered and disguised in Christian mythology and theology, but they are present with an immediate power in the Eucharist or mass, which is surely a decisive source of the power and authority of the mass. But that authority and power can only be recovered and renewed by reversing and inverting the given or manifest form and language of both liturgy and catechism, of both Scripture and creed, an inversion and reversal which is present in the *Wake*. Now the awe and solemnity of the mass passes into a comic ribaldry, but a ribaldry and even a scatological ribaldry which is absolutely essential to the epic project of inverting and reversing the mass, a project which can realize itself only by a reversal and inversion of the language of the mass. The language of the Roman rite becomes the very opposite of itself in the language of *Finnegans Wake*, but nothing less could effect a resurrection of liturgy, or an awakening of the Christian God.

Fortunately, we possess evidence taking us into this center of Shem the Penman, and this occurs in a letter that H. G. Wells wrote Joyce in 1928, a letter recording his response to *Work in Progress*:

> . . . I want language (and statement) as simple and clear as possible. You began Catholic, that is to say you began with a system of values in stark opposition to reality. Your mental existence is obsessed by a monstrous system of contradictions. You really believe in chastity, purity and the personal God and that is why you are always breaking out into cries of . . . . shit and hell.

Less than two weeks later Joyce wrote Harriet Shaw Weaver that he could wholeheartedly subscribe to these remarks in Wells's letter. Surely this is one of the very few times when Joyce unveiled his "soul" to anyone other than Nora, just as this is perhaps our only direct evidence of the sacred ground of modern blasphemy, evidence all too surely indicating that a sacred or primordial presence can be actual and real in our world only by way of a violent and total inversion, the very inversion which is comprehensively incarnate in *Finnegans Wake*. And this inversion is not only universally present in the *Wake*, it is repeatedly reenacted, and that reenactment is the epic action of our final novel.

Book One of the *Wake* closes with the passage of A.L.P. into "Night now!" — an A.L.P. who is the "same anew," Anna was, Livia is, Plurabelle's to be — and an A.L.P. who is inseparable from *Hircus Civis Eblanensis!*, the goat citizen or scapegoat of Dublin and the world. This is the H.C.E. who throughout Book One has repeatedly fallen, been condemned and pursued, and perhaps been resurrected, a resurrection which may or may not be the subject of a "polyhedron of scripture" that is the document and letter presented in chapter 5. But this document is presented and revealed and interpreted in such a way as to make its decoding or decipherment an absolute impossibility. Significantly enough, the letter chapter opens with the Lady's Prayer:

> In the name of Annah the Allmaxiful, the Everliving, the Bringer of Plurabilities, haloed be her eve, her singtime sung, her ril be run, unhemmed as it is uneven! (104)

Whether or not a resurrection of H.C.E. occurs in Book One, his crucifixion certainly occurs at the end of Book Two, a crucifixion which is "Fenegans Wick."

> One hyde, sack, hic! Two stick holst, Lucky! Finnish Make Goal! First you were Nomad, next you were Namar, now you're Numah and it's soon you'll be Nomon. Hence counsels Ecclesiast. There's every resumption. (374.21–24)

Witnesses to this Finsbury Follies include Don Gouverneur Buckley sporting the insides of a "Rhutian Jhanaral," witnesses who witness this "kinn of all Fenns" pass into and be consumed as a "Fisht" (376.34). This is at the very moment of "easter greeding" when we hear the solemn tones of the Sanctus: "Angus! Angus! Angus!"

> Laying the cloth, to fore of them. And thanking the fish, in core of them. To pass the grace for Gard sake! Ahmohn. Mr. Justician Mathews and Mr. Justician Marks and Mr. Justician Luk de Luc and Mr. Justinian Johnston-Johnson. And the aaskart, see, behind! Help, help, hurray!

Allsup, allsop! Four ghools to nail! Cut it down mates, look slippy! They've got a dathe with a swimminpull. Dang! Ding! Dong! Dung! Dinnin. Isn't it great he is swaying above us for his good and ours. Fly your balloons, dannies, and dennises! He's doorknobs dead! And Annie Delap is free. Ones more. We could ate you, par Buccas, and imbabe through you, reassuranced in the wild lac of gotliness. One fledge, one brood till hulm culms evurdyburdy. Huh the throman! Huh the traidor. Huh the truh. (377.29–378.6)

Without any question, this crucifixion is simultaneously a Eucharistic feast, and even if it occurs after closing time in a Dublin pub, it also occurs in and for "evurdyburdy." Such a Eucharistic feast, which is Crucifixion and Creation at once, is homiletically and juridically reenacted in Book Three, which closes with H.C.E. and A.L.P. in a fatal sleep: "O, foetal sleep! Ah, fatal slip! the one loved, the other left, the bride of pride leased to the stranger!" (563.10). All too clearly this sleep is a reenactment of the conclusion of *Ulysses,* but now this *felix culpa* culminates in the final and cosmic Resurrection of Book Four of *Finnegans Wake.* Yet H.C.E. never openly or manifestly appears as H.C.E. in Book Four, for this is the time of the first and last "rittler-rattle of the anniverse" or riddle of the universe: "when is a nam nought a name whenas it is a" (607.11). This is that time, and that unique time, when darkness is light, and pure darkness is pure light:

It was a long, very long, a dark, very dark, an allburt unend, scarce endurable, and we could add mostly quite various and somewhat stumbletumbling night. Endee he sendee. Dieu! The has goning at gone, the is coming to come. Greets to ghastern, hie to morgning. Dormidy, destady. Doom is the faste. Well down, good other! Now day, slow day, from delicate to divine, divases. Padma, brighter and sweetster, this flower that bells, it is our hour or risings. Tickle, tickle. Lotus spray. Till herenext. Adya (598.6–14)

If this is that day when East and West meet in darkness (598.15), it is also and thereby "Adya" or today. For this is the Day of Resurrection, an Easter that is realized only as the consequence of a total and chaotic actualization of Crucifixion.

The Easter celebration of Book Four opens with that Sanctus which is the preface to the great prayer of consecration in the canon of the mass — "Sandhyas! Sandhyas! Sandhyas! — now chanted in Sanskrit inasmuch as West and East are now one. And an elusive leitmotif of the *Wake* now becomes decoded. This is the Augustinian phrase, "securus judicat orbis terrarum," which converted John Henry Newman, and which is the center and leitmotif of the *Apologia Pro Vita Sua*. This phrase, in various transpositions, appears again and again in the *Wake*, and not only is it testimony to Joyce's conviction that Newman is the greatest prose stylist in the English language, but it offers yet another Catholic theological ground of Joyce's vision, and one which itself was not fully or decisively articulated until the composition of this epic. For this is the theological ground which states both the nature and the identity of Catholic authority: the judgment of the whole world cannot be wrong. But not until *Finnegans Wake* does a Catholic work appear which realizes both the universal and the cosmic identity of the *orbis terrarum*. Now "securus judicat" becomes "securest jubilends" (593.13), as an external and exterior authority passes into a *missa jubilaea*, a cosmic and apocalyptic mass.

Only one Catholic thinker has given us a philosophical and theological exposition of the *missa jubilaea*, and that is D. G. Leahy, who does so in the third appendix of his *Novitas Mundi*. *Novitas Mundi* can be read as a Joycean and epic reenactment of the history of pure thinking in the West, although here epic poetry passes into systematic thinking, a pure thinking which is just as radically Catholic as are Joyce's epic works. And it is radically Catholic by being apocalyptically Catholic, celebrating a new thinking which *is* the unleavened bread of existence itself, as over against the essential finitude of past thought: "What happened before now in the Mass exclusively (*missa solemnis*) now happens in the Mass inclusively (*missa jubilaea*) (347). At the end, *in extremis*, and by a Hegelian irony of history, it became the fate of the Eucharist to be the substantial experience of the world at large.

What now occurs in thought for the first time in history (transcending in fact the end of the world in essence) is *the perception itself of the body*

— God in God in essence — the Temple of the New Jerusalem —
effected now in essence inclusively in the *missa jubilaea*, the center of
an essentially new consciousness in the conversion of the universe into
an entirely new stuff. (348)

The universe is converted into an entirely new stuff when the universal body of humanity finally appears and is real as the Lamb of God,
and therefore in and as that Eucharistic table wherein and whereby
the matter of the universe becomes the apocalyptic and sacrificial body
of God.

Nothing is more fundamental to this cosmic and apocalyptic
metamorphosis than a radically new integration of mind and matter,
of body and soul, as body or matter finally becomes indistinguishable
from both the center and the depths of mind and consciousness.
Accordingly, a real presence that once was real in the moment of consecration and thereafter now becomes real in a cosmic and universal
epiphany. That epiphany heralds the termination of history itself,
thereby inaugurating a new world, a world realizing the "eucharistic
essence of existence itself":

> In the celebration of the infinite passover the appearance of the
> eucharist, *qua* appearance, is now seen for the first time in history to
> be itself the eucharist in essence: to transcend appearance, to be
> appearance itself. No longer are the elements on the table seen to be
> other than what they are in essence, namely, the flesh and blood of
> God in the form of man. (345)

Thus the end of the world in essence is the beginning of the world
in the form of "man." Blake's Albion passes into an apocalyptic Luvah
as the primal elements of existence become manifest and real as the
body and the blood of the sacrificial Victim and Host.

> Now the Mass (*missa jubilaea*) proclaims what is in fact happening in
> essence. It becomes *essentially prophetic of the fact that now the appearance
> itself of faith in essence is effected in a transcendentally differentiated substance,*
> that is, without being other than itself in essence, in the appearance

itself of the eucharist. What is in fact happening in essence is the transcendental repetition of the creation itself. (350)

If an infinite passover is the transcendental repetition of the creation itself, then surely it is not amiss to understand *Finnegans Wake* as an infinite passover, and an infinite passover in which the primal elements of existence undergo a cosmic and interior epiphany as the universal Body of the Lamb. And if a universe is now coming into existence for the first time in history which "itself is to be in its perfection essentially the conception of creation itself wherein nothing is to be known of an essence distinguished substantially from existence itself" (353), then *Finnegans Wake* embodies this universe more fully and more decisively than does any other language and art that we have been given. Nor has any literary critic or scholar given us an interpretation of *Finnegans Wake* which unveils this apocalyptic epic so fully as does Leahy's understanding of the *missa jubilaea*:

> *The annulment of the ideal actuality (actuality thought in essence) is the perception of the fact itself: the perception of a new transcendental,* existere ipsum. *The essence of the new transcendental involves the conception in essence of everything, the absolute nullification of the possible. Everything now comes to exist actually in the form of the body itself.* (360)

Everything comes to exist in the form of the body itself when absolutely nothing is possible but what actually exists. Now everything is essential, and there is no idle word, for every word which is actually or fully spoken is the voice and embodiment of the depths of existence itself.

So it is that possibility and actuality are now wholly passing into each other, and inasmuch as this occurs nothing whatsoever stands outside the brute facticity of "matter" or existence itself. Now being itself is essentially historical or "for-itself," in Hegelian language, or it "begins" in every now, in Nietzschean language, or in Leahy's language: "What is now broken through in essence in thought itself is this world's dominion over its own fall" (362). But as opposed to

Hegel's and Nietzsche's thinking, and virtually the whole body of truly modern thinking, Leahy's is a Catholic thinking, and not only because of the centrality therein of the Eucharist, but also because in this thinking it is the Mother of God who is the one exception in essence to the evidence of creation's being an act of absolute freedom in which everything comes into existence without exception.

> In the virgin the appearance of the transcendental essence of existence came to be everything without exception for the first time in essence. She, in whose existence the essence of history is, *qua* essence, implicit, is the exception in essence. She, the virgin, is essentially implicated in the essential repetition of creation itself. For her nothing existed in essence but God himself. In her being, conceived before now in time without death in essence (extending even to the flesh), was perfectly prepared the way of the messiah. (362)

While there is no Mary, no Mother of God, apart from the Son, it is nevertheless the Mother of God who essentially transcends death, and does so in her very body and flesh. Indeed, the virgin birth itself now becomes the "proof" of the possibility of the transparency of the Eucharistic essence of existence itself, a transparency which is now universally and cosmically occurring for the first time in history.

But images and symbols of the virgin birth have long since ceased to be compelling presences in any form of Christian theology, and even Dante's images of Beatrice and the Mother of God are now only imaginatively and epically alive in Blake's Jerusalem and Joyce's Anna Livia Plurabelle. But therein those images and that presence are alive, and just as A.L.P. is the one presence in the *Wake* which essentially transcends death, it is that very exemption in the epic totality of the *Wake* which is the "proof" or sign of the Eucharistic essence of the language and action of the *Wake*. That language and action finally effect a resurrection in which all of the living pass into the realm of the dead, and do so in the final voyage of A.L.P., a voyage culminating in an apocalyptic death in which there is no longer a difference between the living and the dead. Thus it is that: "now for the first time in history, death is clearly perceived to be nothing in essence" (369).

There now exists the transcendental annulment of the substance of death. Death is now thought to be life itself; the transcendental identity of transcendental death is the resurrection (the absolute contradiction of self-transcendent death). Transcendental death is the death of self which is the flesh and blood of Jesus the Nazarene. Death is nothing in essence except it be the eucharist substance of the communion of saints, the absolute nullification of another individual in essence (the utter annihiliation of the self in essence), the unleavened bread of existence itself. Death is now conceived to be the manna upon which the body itself lives, the sweet fruit which has come down from heaven. (373f.)

Transcendental death is the blood shed of the Lamb of God, a shedding which is continually enacted and reenacted in the epic language and action of the *Wake*. But this repetition now becomes both a cosmic and a historical Eucharist, or a historical Eucharist which is a cosmic Eucharist or a *missa jubilaea*. The *missa jubilaea* is the infinite passover of God, a passover which is enacted in the text of the *Wake*, and Eucharistically enacted in the body of the text.

Before now the word was made flesh. Now the word is spoken in essence, that is, *Christ's imagination is now flesh*. . . . Now Christ suffers death in essence; now Christ is perceived to be embodied in God himself; now the world is seen to be the embodiment in essence of the transcendental passion of existence itself in essence. It is now the essentially transcendental perception of the body itself. (378)

The world, that is, is now the transcendental perception of the body of God. For the transcendental passion of existence is the transcendental death of the Lamb of God, a death wherein "God is bereft of God in essence" (374), and a death whose new and apocalyptic embodiment now clearly and decisively makes manifest that before now "the name of God was essentially misused" (379). Now there is essentially the infinite passover of the God who is absolutely Christ, and therefore: "God is in fact (being there) in the absolute nullification of God" (364). That nullification is the blood of the Lamb, and thus it is the resurrection or glorification of existence itself, a glorification which *is* the resurrection of the body.

Just as the *Paradiso* culminates in a visionary voyage into the depths of the "Infinite Goodness," depths wherein an interiorly resurrected Dante sees the scattered limbs or leaves of the universe bound by love "in one single volume" (XXXIII, 86), so *Finnegans Wake* culminates in Anna's final soliloquy with the cosmic dispersal of her body or leaves:

> So. Avelaval. My leaves have drifted from me. All. But one clings still. I'll bear it on me. To remind me of. Lff! So soft this morning, ours. Yes. (628.6–9)

But as opposed to the final "Yes" of *Ulysses*, this "Yes" is followed by a summons to the divine Father and Creator:

> Carry me along, taddy, like you done though the toy fair! If I seen him bearing down on me now under widespread wings like he'd come from Arkangels, I sink I'd die down over his feet, humbly dumbly, only to washup. Yes, tid. There's where. First. (628.9–13)

This Leda, even as Yeats's, absorbs the knowledge and power of the Godhead, but in this radical Catholic scripture or text, the "Infinite Goodness" finally passes into that *the* which Joyce believed is the weakest word in the English language:

> We pass through grass behush the bush to. Whish! A gull. Gulls. Far calls. Coming, far! End here. Us then. Finn, again! Take. Bussoftlhee, mememormee! Till thousendshee. Lps. The keys to. Given! A way a lone a last a loved a long the (628.12–17)

Now the Joyce who believed so deeply that the inexplicable does not exist did not choose this word lightly. Not only does this final *the* inaugurate once again the beginning of the epic, but its very sounding here reverses that word which Joyce believed is the strongest word in any language, *God*. *God* is the Creator, just as this *the* inaugurates the beginning of the cycle of eternal return: but precisely because this is a speakable and hearable beginning, this cycle is not and cannot be a meaningless round of chaos and disruption. On the contrary, the very speakability of beginning, even if it most decisively occurs in an apocalyptic ending, itself makes manifest and embodies a chaos and abyss which *is* language and word: "In the beginning was the word." Now the word *is* "God." But now it is so not simply in writing or text but rather in that "single volume" which is cosmos or world. And this apocalyptic cosmos is in full continuity with Dante's Catholic cosmos, and particularly so insofar as Dante's is an apocalyptic cosmos, a cosmos that even now is passing into a love which is all in all. Indeed, the "leaves" of Anna are even in continuity with Aquinas's conception of the perfection of God:

> Since therefore God is the first effective cause of things, the perfection of all things must pre-exist in God in a more eminent way. Dionysius implies the same line of argument by Saying of God (*Div. Nom. v*): *It is not that He is this and not that, but that He is all, as the cause of all.* Secondly, from what has already been proved, God is existence itself, of itself subsistent (I,3,4). Consequently, He must contain within Himself the whole perfection of being. (*Summa Theologica*, I,4,2, Singleton translation)

The *ipsum esse* or existence itself of Being or God is now fully passing into actual speech, and nowhere so fully as in *Finnegans Wake*, a passage or metamorphosis which resurrects the body as word or speech.

The "nullification" of God embodied in the Resurrection of Book Four of the *Wake* is thereby, and precisely thereby, a realization or self-realization of God wherein the whole perfection of being realizes itself in the pure actuality of *ipsum esse* or existence itself. But that actuality is here realized not simply through language and speech, but *in* and *as* word and speech, for now God is fully and finally *logos* or "word." That "word" is pure immediacy, an immediacy which is darkness and light, and pure darkness and pure light, a light which is the cosmic and apocalyptic sacrifice of God. If the epic action of the *Wake* proceeds out of the dark abyss of primordial sacrifice, a primordial sacrifice which *is* creation, that sacrifice culminates in the transcendental repetition of the creation itself, a transcendental repetition which is the apocalyptic repetition of "God said." But an apocalyptic repetition reverses primordial repetition, so that "Let there be light" becomes "Let there be darkness," an apocalyptic darkness reversing but nevertheless renewing the primordial abyss and night. For the night language or "not language" of the *Wake* embodies the brute and formless matter of the primordial "water." But now that "water" speaks, and it speaks with an immediacy that has never been sounded before, or not sounded since the original act of creation.

Nevertheless, *Finnegans Wake* does not stand alone, nor does it speak or sound in solitude. And it does not do so because we hear it, and we hear it even if we have not read it, for it speaks the night language of our world, a world in which the interior and individual speaker has come to an end. But that ending is the culmination of our epic tradition, a tradition beginning with Homer, a Homer who is the Adam of our world, for he is our first individual voice and speaker. In Virgil that epic speaker undergoes a historical metamorphosis recording and embodying the advent of universal empire, an empire which is possible and real only by way of the prior advent of an anonymous transcendence and consciousness. That anonymous consciousness and transcendence is reversed with the advent of Christianity, a reversal inaugurating the negative interiority of self-consciousness, an interiority which can realize itself only by crucifying or negating itself, in a Crucifixion which *is* Resurrection. The *Commedia* is a revolutionary transformation of Western poetry if only because for the first time the fullness and actuality of self-consciousness passes into poetic language itself, and thereby an epic is born which is the interiorization of the City of God, and an interiorization which is a secularization or cosmic and historical realization of transcendence itself.

That transcendence undergoes a dark and revolutionary transformation in *Paradise Lost*, a transformation heralding the advent of pure self-consciousness, a pure self-consciousness which is the revolutionary energy of modernity. But this energy is occasioned or released by the advent of an absolute polarization or opposition, an opposition embodied in *Paradise Lost* in the polar coinherence or unity of Satan and the Son. That unity breaks asunder in Blake, thus ending the organic order and structure of our epic poetry, as a new dissonance and chaos sounds in our epic language, even if it is precisely by this dissonance that our historical and interior ground undergoes a full reversal. Indeed, this is the revolutionary reversal which is consummated in *Ulysses* and *Finnegans Wake*. But that consummation is a full resolution of our epic tradition, and it is just because of the actual presence of Homer, Virgil, Dante, Milton and Blake in Joyce's epics that his epics embody a power and authority that is undeniable and inescapable. While it is true that Homer, Virgil, and Milton are only indirectly present in Joyce's epics, that presence is nevertheless an actual presence because of the very epic power and form of *Ulysses* and *Finnegans Wake*. For if Homer, Virgil, and Milton were epic founders of new historical eras, that founding passes into ending in Joyce. Yet this is an ending whose authority and power would be impossible and unreal apart from Joyce's epic predecessors, predecessors who created the very language which Joyce transformed.

So it is that *Ulysses* and *Finnegans Wake* do not simply end the Western epic tradition, they rather resolve and fulfill it, and fulfill it so that a real and actual beginning passes into an actual and real ending. Here, neither ending nor beginning are arbitrary or illusory points in a circle of eternal return. And they cannot be so if only because they actually speak and sound, and sound with an immediacy, and a prosaic and everyday immediacy, that has never been present in a mythical tradition, or not present in any mythical tradition which can be heard with a Western ear. Thus *Finnegans Wake* is no more grounded in a primordial myth of eternal return than is Nietzsche's *Zarathustra*. It is far rather that the ending of that Western consciousness and history which each effects evokes and echoes that very ground out of which the West was born. But only an echo of that ground sounds here, and not an embodiment, for such an embodiment is impossible in a reversal which actually and immediately speaks. The miracle of the Resurrection in *Finnegans Wake* is the miracle of the full presence of word and speech. Anna speaks as she disperses her leaves, and we hear her words as speech itself, as actual and immediate speech. Now the language of the resurrected Christ in the Gospel of John passes into real speech, a real speech which is a real presence, the actual and immediate presence of Resurrection, and thus a presence inverting and reversing the eternal presence of an eternal return: "Rise up now and aruse! Norvena's over" (619.28).

Thus Resurrection here is total and actual presence, the presence of the *missa jubilaea*, a *missa jubilaea* which is the cosmic, interior, and historical actualization of the *missa solemnis*. But the *missa jubilaea* can be actually and really present only by way of an inversion and reversal of the *missa solemnis*, a reversal making necessary not only a universal presence of blasphemy, ribaldry, and scatology, but also a reversal and inversion of the liturgical order of consecration. Bread and wine continue to pass into the real presence of the Crucified and Resurrected Christ, but transsubstantiation is reversed, and is so insofar as the "matter" of the bread and wine now becomes essential, and the "form" of Christ or Spirit now becomes accidental. Moreover, the bread and wine are now real in the actual words and language of the *Wake*, words whose very scatology, ribaldry, and blasphemy sacramentally embody the real presence of "Lff," and do so because that love and life is now brutally and immediately present. This immediate presence is the transcendental annulment of the substance of death, for death now becomes life itself. This is the new or resurrected life which appears and sounds to "soul" or Spirit to be the darkness of brute matter. That darkness sounds and speaks in the purely blasphemous and chaotic language of the *Wake*, but this is precisely the language that is most immediate and alive to us. For it is the only language that we both actually and immediately speak, just as it is the only language that can be spoken by a speaker whose identity has ended as an individual and interior speaker.

Soon we will be "Nomon," but only because we were first "Nomad," and nomads who strayed or fell from "prefall paradise peace" (30.15). This "felicitous culpability" is the "archetypt" of our destiny, a destiny which is fully and finally realized in a purely immediate speech. That speech is the real presence of resurrection, and its full enactment is the total presence of Apocalypse, a presence in which the dark and negative passion of God becomes immediately at hand. And it is immediately at hand insofar as it is actually spoken. Then the total silence and emptiness of an original abyss becomes an immediately present chaos, but a chaos which is cosmos when it resurrected in language and word. This cosmos is the resurrected Christ, but a resurrected Christ who is inseparable and indistinguishable from the crucified Christ, for now the Christ of glory *is* the Christ of passion. So it is that the body of this Christ can only be a dark and broken body, but it is a body which is present in all the immediacy of an unformed and primordial matter, as a totally fallen body now realizes itself in the pure immediacy of word. In that immediacy death is life, and "Lff" is all in all.

Index